Architecture Thinking across Boundaries

Architecture Thinking across Boundaries

Knowledge Transfers since the 1960s

edited by
RAJESH HEYNICKX, RICARDO COSTA
AGAREZ and ELKE COUCHEZ

BLOOMSBURY VISUAL ARTS
LONDON · NEW YORK · OXFORD · NEW DELHI · SYDNEY

BLOOMSBURY VISUAL ARTS
Bloomsbury Publishing Plc
50 Bedford Square, London, WC1B 3DP, UK
1385 Broadway, New York, NY 10018, USA
29 Earlsfort Terrace, Dublin 2, Ireland

BLOOMSBURY, BLOOMSBURY VISUAL ARTS and the Diana logo are trademarks of
Bloomsbury Publishing Plc

First published in Great Britain 2021
Paperback edition first published 2022

Selection and editorial matter copyright © Rajesh Heynickx, Ricardo Costa Agarez
and Elke Couchez, 2021
Individual chapters © their authors, 2021

Rajesh Heynickx, Ricardo Costa Agarez and Elke Couchez have asserted
their right under the Copyright, Designs and Patents Act, 1988, to be
identified as Editors of this work.

Cover design by Namkwan Cho
Cover: *Umbilly* (detail), 1976 by the Belgian artist Panamarenko (1940–2019).
Photo © Luc Scrobiltghen.

All rights reserved. No part of this publication may be reproduced or transmitted
in any form or by any means, electronic or mechanical, including photocopying, recording,
or any information storage or retrieval system, without prior permission in writing from
the publishers.

Bloomsbury Publishing Plc does not have any control over, or responsibility for, any
third-party websites referred to or in this book. All internet addresses given in
this book were correct at the time of going to press. The author and publisher regret
any inconvenience caused if addresses have changed or sites have ceased to exist,
but can accept no responsibility for any such changes.

A catalogue record for this book is available from the British Library.

A catalogue record for this book is available from the Library of Congress.

ISBN: HB: 978-1-3501-5317-2
PB: 978-1-3502-0213-9
ePDF: 978-1-3501-5318-9
eBook: 978-1-3501-5319-6

Typeset by RefineCatch Limited, Bungay, Suffolk

To find out more about our authors and books visit www.bloomsbury.com
and sign up for our newsletters.

CONTENTS

List of Illustrations vii
Notes on Contributors xi

Introduction: The Mobile Landscape of Post-war Architectural Thought   *Rajesh Heynickx, Ricardo Costa Agarez and Elke Couchez* 1

PART ONE Translations and Appropriations   13

1   Deconstruction and Architecture: Translation as a Matter of Speculative Theory   *Céline Bodart* 15

2   Gehry's Lou Ruvo Center in Las Vegas as a Housing Critique   *Yael Allweil* 29

3   'Boomerang Effect': The Repercussions of Critical Regionalism in 1980s Greece   *Stylianos Giamarelos* 43

4   The Autonomy of Theory: *Tendenzen – Neuere Architektur im Tessin*, ETH Zurich, 1975   *Irina Davidovici* 60

PART TWO Imprints and Undercurrents   81

5   Royston Landau and the Research Programmes of Architecture   *Jasper Cepl* 83

6   Theoretical A/gnosticisms: Paul Tillich, Colin Rowe and the Theology of Architecture   *Karla Cavarra Britton and Kyle Dugdale* 103

PART THREE Vehicles 117

7 Cedric Price's Chats: Orality and the Production of Architectural Theory   *Jim Njoo*   119

8 Alternative Facts: Towards a Theorization of Oral History in Architecture   *Janina Gosseye, Naomi Stead and Deborah van der Plaat*   136

9 Abandoning the Plan   *Michael Jasper*   149

10 Deltiology as History: Informal Communication as Praxis   *Nicholas Boyarsky*   162

11 Theorizing from the South: The Seminar of Latin American Architecture   *Catherine R. Ettinger*   180

Index 192

ILLUSTRATIONS

Chapter Two

2.1 Lou Ruvo Center, first floor plan and building section.   32
2.2 Lou Ruvo Renter 'duck' event space and 'shed' decor.   33
2.3 The Pruitt-Igoe explosion vis-à-vis Gehry's Lou Ruvo Center.   34

Chapter Three

3.1 The 'grid' pattern in the austere work of Aris Konstantinidis and his Archaeological Museum at Ioannina (1964), echoed in the Antonakakis's Archaeological Museum on Chios (1965).   46
3.2 Dimitris Antonakakis's interpretation of Pikionis's landscaping project around the Acropolis (1958) exemplifies the 'pathway' pattern that is echoed in the two Antonakakis's House at Spata (1973–4). The 'pathway' is used as a principle of design that organizes movement from the exterior to the interior as a series of intermediate meeting points with varying degrees of privacy and publicity.   47
3.3 Cover of the Pikionis–Antonakakis exhibition catalogue at the Greek Festival in Delft (27 October–1 December 1981).   50
3.4 Views of the Pikionis and Antonakakis exhibition sections at the Greek Festival in Delft. Suzana and Dimitris Antonakakis's first meeting with Aldo van Eyck, at the exhibition opening (27 October 1981), marked the start of a long friendship.   54

Chapter Four

4.1 ETH Zurich, gta Organisationsstelle für Ausstellungen der Architekturabteilung. Poster of the exhibition *Tendenzen – Neuere Architektur im Tessin*, 1975.   62

4.2 ETH Zurich, gta Organisationsstelle für Ausstellungen der Architekturabteilung. First of the five A4 inventory sheets showing the exhibition panels in reduced size. The original wall panels, 90cm × 120cm, and the landscape A4 catalogue pages shared the same graphic layout for all projects. 64

4.3 *A+U Architecture and Urbanism* 9 (1976). Cover: Bruno Reichlin and Fabio Reinhart, Casa Tonini, Toricella (1972–4). Featuring private houses from the exhibition, this monographic issue of *A+U*, edited by Toshio Nakamura, indicates how quickly Ticinese architecture gained an international currency through the agency of the exhibition. 65

4.4 Aurelio Galfetti, Casa Rotalinti, Bellinzona (1960–1), as shown on original exhibition panel (detail). 67

4.5 Martin Steinmann, *Die Tessiner*: provisional exhibition title and notes of meeting with Luigi Snozzi, 11 December 1973. The notes (attributed to Heinz Ronner) from this preparatory discussion reveal the historical self-understanding of Ticinese architects within a regional modernist genealogy. 68

4.6 Diener & Diener, St Albal-Tal, Basel (1981–6) – *répétition différente* in German-Swiss architecture. Different aspects of this residential complex respond to various found conditions on the site. The facades are a synthesis of interwar Basel modernism, Swiss Timber modernism and industrial vernacular. 76

Chapter Five

5.1 Portrait of Royston Landau (1988). Photographer: Valerie Bennett. 84

5.2 Cover of Landau's *New Directions in British Architecture* (1968). Jacket design by Toshihiro Katayama. 92

5.3 Group photo of faculty and participants in the 'History and Theory' programme at the AA, with Roy Landau on the left and Micha Bandini in the middle of the back row. 95

5.4 Cover of *UIA International Architect*, comprising the documentation of Landau's work on 'The Culture of Architecture: A Historiography of the Current Discourse' (1984). 97

Chapter Six

6.1 The *Systême figuré des connoissances* [sic] *humaines*, from the *Encyclopédie, ou dictionnaire raisonné des sciences, des arts et des métiers*, Vol. 1 (Paris, 1751). 104

6.2 *Système figuré des connoissances humaines*, detail. 106
6.3 Paul Tillich (1958) and Colin Rowe (1992). 107
6.4 *Système figuré des connoissances humaines*, detail. 113

Chapter Seven

7.1 Cedric Price, lecture notes c. 1994, Cedric Price Fonds. 121
7.2 Cedric Price, 'Starting Price' column, *Building Design*, 5 April 1985. 123
7.3 Cedric Price, 'The Exchange', *AA Prospectus 1980–81*. 126
7.4 Cedric Price, Task Force 'Contract', AA Diploma Unit 12a, 1994–5, Cedric Price Fonds. 128
7.5 Entertainer at Borough Music Hall, Southwark, London, 1859, Mander and Mitchenson Collection. 130
7.6 'Lecture Given At Drive-In Theatre', *Ann Arbor News*, 30 October 1968, Cedric Price Fonds. 131

Chapter Nine

9.1 Peter Eisenman, *House II*, Ground Floor Plan, 1969. Original drawing by the author after a drawing by Peter Eisenman. 154
9.2 John Hejduk, *Texas House 5*, 1960–2. Original drawing by the author after a drawing by John Hejduk. 156

Chapter Ten

10.1 Vintage postcard of the Facteur Cheval at his *Palais Idéal* near Hautrives. 163
10.2 Vintage postcard of 'Chatham Square showing Doubledeck Elevated', New York City. 164
10.3 'Circling the loop of the screeching overhead railways … and looking down at the tumultuous, active, mobile and everywhere dynamic centre of a vast distribution centre system, which consisted of broad gridded avenues, commuting railways and expanding electric streetcar networks, on to its re-ordered crust.' Layout spread from 'Chicago a la Carte' (Boyarsky 1970: 604–5). 166
10.4 Layout spread from 'Chicago a la Carte' (Boyarsky 1970: 640). 168
10.5 From *Advertisements for Architecture* (Tschumi 1978). 169
10.6 Arrived Safely. 'Nolli's Map of Rome (detail)'. Spread from Venturi, Scott Brown and Izenour (1972: 15). 171

10.7	Vintage postcard of Coney Island. 'In a laughing mirror-image of the seriousness with which the rest of the world is obsessed with Progress, Coney Island attacks the problem of Pleasure, often with the same technological means' (Koolhaas 1978: 47).	172
10.8	Vintage postcard cover from *Europa/America* (Raggi 1978).	173
10.9	International Institute of Design, postcard, 1971.	174
10.10	'London: Cities like London, Buenos Aires, Tokyo, New York, etc. contain sufficient slack to be used as laboratories and workshops. It is possible to co-opt space from recessed institutions, take over cheap pads from vacationing students and use the abundant resources of information, professional and interdisciplinary back up, co-ordinating agencies and local talent, ranging from those with below-the-surface 'alternative' interests, to the leading guns on the scene to further enrich the learning possibilities for many from all parts of the world.' International Institute of Design, postcard, 1971.	175
10.11	'Caught up in the Byzantine intrigues, labyrinthine curricula, procedures and objectives, as if from some former era. A workshop and a platform. Key Words. A market place and a forum. A well laid table and a banquet for free ranging souls as opposed to your local cafeteria's battery fare. Use the resources of London. Star turns. A cool look at the world scene.' International Institute of Design, postcard, 1971.	176
10.12	'The On-Going Line: Bring your own projects. Plug in to Faculty projects. Use London facilities. Consult Resident Panel. Workshop Line: Research Groups. Special Interests. Polemical Groups Oracular Circle Line. Seminars. Chance visitor contacts. Lectures. Cross Fertilisation and Interchange. Continental link up.' International Institute of Design, postcard, 1971.	176

Chapter Eleven

11.1	Humberto Eliash's caricature illustrates a central theme in the SAL, the search for an architecture of identity.	181
11.2	A photograph of the second SAL shows the informal character of the round-table discussion.	182
11.3	Salmona used traditional brick construction in the Torres del Parque complex in Bogotá.	184

CONTRIBUTORS

Ricardo Costa Agarez is Assistant Professor at Évora University (Portugal). He trained as an architect and architectural historian and specialized in the history and theory of nineteenth- and twentieth-century cities and buildings, national and regional identities, phenomena of knowledge dissemination and circulation of forms, ideas and techniques, housing and public architecture and the architectural culture in bureaucracy. He is the author of *Algarve Building: Modernism, Regionalism and Architecture in the South of Portugal, 1925–1965* (2016); coordinated the multidisciplinary research, exhibition and publication project 'Housing: 100 Years of Public Policies in Portugal, 1918–2018' (2017–2018), and is now the Principal Investigator of the European Research Council Starting Grant project 'Built Environment Knowledge for Resilient, Sustainable Communities: Understanding Everyday Modern Architecture and Urban Design in the Iberian Peninsula (1939–1985)' (2021–2026).

Yael Allweil BArch, PhD is Assistant Professor in the Faculty of Architecture at Technion, Israel, where she heads HousingLab: History and Future of Living. She completed her PhD in architecture history at UC Berkeley, exploring the history of Israel-Palestine as a history of the gain and loss of citizen housing. Her research was published in the monograph *Homeland: Zionism as Housing Regime 1860–2011* (2017) and several journal articles in *Urban Studies, Footprint, Architecture Beyond Europe, City, TDSR* and *IJIA*. Yael is co-chair of the research group 'Re-Theorizing Housing as Architecture' at the Institute for Advanced Studies (IIAS) in Jerusalem 2019–20.

Céline Bodart is an architect and post-master in 'Architecture and Philosophy' (ENSA Paris La Villette) and a graduate of the Experimental Program in Arts and Politics, Sciences Po Paris (dir. B. Latour and V. Pihet) in 2014. In 2018, she received a PhD in Architecture (University of Paris 8 and University of Liège, Belgium). Working at the interface between philosophy and architecture, her doctoral research focused on a specific episode of recent architectural history marked by the crossover of these two practices under the influence of Derridean deconstruction. She is currently associate professor at ENSA Paris La Villette (Gerphau-lab) and research assistant at the Faculty of Architecture at the University of Liège.

Nicholas Boyarsky PhD, AA Dipl., is an architect and teacher. He is a partner in the London based studio Boyarsky Murphy Architects and a Professor of

Architecture at RMIT University where he is involved with practice-based research PhD programmes in Europe and Asia; he is a fifth year Studio Lead at Oxford Brookes University. Nicholas is a founding member of the Asian-based Urban Flashes network. Current research interests include the medium of ephemera in architectural discourse, Bogdan Bogdanovic and the Partisans' Necropolis in Mostar, and exhibitions and publications related to the Alvin Boyarsky Archive.

Karla Cavarra Britton is Professor of Art History at Diné College on the Navajo Nation, and has written extensively about modern and contemporary sacred architecture. Her publications include *Auguste Perret* (2001); the edited volume *Constructing the Ineffable: Contemporary Sacred Architecture* (2010); and with Robert McCarter, *Architecture and the Lifeworld: Essays in Honor of Kenneth Frampton* (2020). She taught at the Yale School of Architecture (2003–18), the University of New Mexico's School of Architecture + Planning and the programme in Paris of Columbia University's Graduate School of Architecture, Planning and Preservation. Karla received her PhD in Architecture from Harvard University.

Jasper Cepl was born 1973 and is Professor of the Theory and History of Modern Architecture at Bauhaus University in Weimar, Germany. He studied architecture at RWTH Aachen and TU Berlin, where he graduated with a diploma in architecture in 2000. He received his doctorate in 2006 for a study of Oswald Mathias Ungers, published as *Oswald Mathias Ungers: Eine intellektuelle Biographie* in 2007. Jasper taught at TU Berlin (2003–13) and, as a professor for architecture theory, at Hochschule Anhalt, Dessau (2014–19) before being appointed as a professor at Bauhaus University in October 2019.

Elke Couchez's work explores the intersections between architecture, visual studies, intellectual history and pedagogy. She studied Fine Arts (Sint-Lucas Academy, Ghent) and Art History (KU Leuven) and defended her PhD 'Gestures make Arguments. Performing Architectural Theory in the Studio and the Classroom 196x-199x' in June 2018 at the KU Leuven Faculty of Architecture. In 2018, she worked as a post-doctoral fellow on the project 'Is Architecture Art?' at the University of Queensland's Centre for Architecture, Theory, Criticism and History in Australia. As of October 2019, she teaches art and architecture history at UHasselt (Belgium) and works on an intellectual history of the *International Laboratory for Architecture & Urban Design* (1976–2005). Elke's work has been published in the journals *Image & Narrative*, *Paedagogica Historica*, *History of Intellectual Culture*, *Architecture & Culture* and in several magazines of contemporary art.

Irina Davidovici is a Romanian-British architect and historian based in Zurich, where she lectures and coordinates the doctoral programme at the

GTA Institute for History and Theory of Architecture, ETH Zurich. Irina is the author of *Forms of Practice: German-Swiss Architecture 1980–2000* (2012, and 2nd expanded edition, 2018) and editor of *Colquhounery: Alan Colquhoun from Bricolage to Myth* (2015). Her articles have been published in *AA Files*, *ARCH+*, *Casabella*, *OASE*, *Joelho*, *Project Journal*, *Werk*, *Bauen + Wohnen* and *Archithese*. She has recently obtained her habilitation with the thesis 'Collective Grounds: Housing Estates in the European City, 1865–1934'.

Kyle Dugdale is an architect and historian. He teaches history, theory and design at the Yale School of Architecture and at Columbia Graduate School of Architecture, Planning and Preservation. Kyle holds a BA from Corpus Christi College, Oxford, an MArch from Harvard's Graduate School of Design and a PhD from Yale. His work has been published in journals including *Clog*, *Perspecta*, the *Journal of Architectural Education* and *Utopian Studies*. His first book, *Babel's Present*, was published in 2016. Kyle maintains an interest in architecture's claims to metaphysical significance, with a particular curiosity for architecture as a recurring figure in biblical narratives.

Catherine Ettinger is Professor-Researcher at the School of Architecture of the Universidad Michoacana de San Nicolás de Hidalgo in Mexico. She has lectured and published extensively on the intersection of modernity and tradition in Mexican architecture, including the book *La arquitectura mexicana desde afuera* (2017), and is particularly interested in questions of transnational phenomena such as the architectures of migration and the circulation of ideas between Mexico and the United States in the twentieth century. Catherine is the author of *Richard Neutra en América Latina* (2018).

Stylianos Giamarelos is an architect, historian and theorist of postmodern culture. He is a Senior Lecturer in Architectural History and Theory at the Bartlett School of Architecture UCL, and the Executive Editor of the *Journal of Architecture*. Among others, he has published in the *Journal of Architecture*, the *Journal of Architectural Education*, *Architectural Design*, *Architectural Histories*, *Footprint*, *OASE*, *FRAME*, *San Rocco* and *Metalocus*. In 2018, his article on the cross-cultural authorship of critical regionalism was a runner-up for the biannual EAHN Publication Award. Stylianos is currently writing a book that further explores the cross-cultural roots of critical regionalism before globalization.

Janina Gosseye is Associate Professor of Urban Architecture at the TUDelft Department of Architecture. Her research is situated at the nexus of 20th century architectural and urban history on the one hand, and social and political history on the other. Janina's work has been published in several leading academic journals, including the *Journal of Architecture* and the *Journal of Urban History and Planning Perspectives*. She has edited and authored several books, including *Shopping Towns Europe* (with Tom Avermaete, 2017) and *Speaking of Buildings: Oral History Methods in Architecture* (with Naomi Stead and Deborah van der Plaat, 2019).

Rajesh Heynickx is Professor of Architectural Theory and Intellectual History at the KU Leuven. He has published articles in *Modern Intellectual History*, *Modernist Cultures* and *Architectural Theory Review*, among many others. In 2018, together with Stéphane Symons, he acted as co-editor of *So What's New About Scholasticism? How Neo-Thomism Helped Shape the Twentieth Century*, and in 2020 he edited, together with Hilde Heynen and Sebastiaan Loosen, the volume *The Figure of Knowledge: Conditioning Architectural Theory, 1960s–1990s*. At the KU Leuven Department of Architecture, Rajesh is spokesman of the FWO-Scientific Research Network 'Texts = Buildings: Dissecting Transpositions in Architectural Knowledge (1880–1980)'.

Michael Jasper is Professor of Architecture at the University of Canberra where he directs the Master of Architecture course and teaches in the major projects studio and advanced architectural analysis streams. While a partner in the New York office of Cooper Robertson & Partners (2002–11) he directed many of the firm's institutional and urban scale projects. Jasper was recently Visiting Scholar at Columbia University Graduate School of Architecture Planning and Preservation and Visiting Scholar at the American Academy in Rome. He is the author of *Architectural Aesthetic Speculations*, *Deleuze on Art* and the forthcoming *Trajectories in Architecture* and *Architectural Possibilities in the Work of Eisenman*.

Jim Njoo is an architect, an Associate Professor at the École Nationale Supérieure d'Architecture de Paris-La Villette and a PhD candidate at Delft University of Technology, where he is currently preparing a thesis on the writings and lectures of Cedric Price. Jim is also a member of the Gerphau architecture research lab and teaches at the École des Ponts and Rice School of Architecture in Paris.

Naomi Stead is Professor of Architecture and Head of the Department of Architecture at Monash University (Australia). Her research interests lie in architecture's cultures of re/production, mediation and reception. She was the leader of the ARC Linkage project 'Equity and Diversity in the Australian Architecture Profession: Women, Work and Leadership,' which led to the co-founding (with Justine Clark and others) of Parlour, an Australian activist group advocating for greater gender equity in architecture. Naomi is a widely published architecture critic, having written more than fifty commissioned features and review articles in professional magazines over the past decade.

Deborah van der Plaat is an Honorary Senior Research Fellow at the Architecture Theory Criticism History Research Centre (ATCH) at the University of Queensland (Australia). Her research examines the architecture of nineteenth- and twentieth-century Australia and its intersection with theories of artistic agency, climate, place, migration and race. Writing histories of Queensland architecture is also a focus within her work. Recent publications include *Speaking of Buildings: Oral History Methods in Architecture* (edited with Janina Gosseye and Naomi Stead, 2019) and *Hot Modernism Queensland Architecture 1945–1975* (edited with John Macarthur, Janina Gosseye and Andrew Wilson, 2015).

Introduction:
The Mobile Landscape of Post-war Architectural Thought

Rajesh Heynickx, Ricardo Costa Agarez and Elke Couchez

Around 1908, the German sociologist Georg Simmel reflected on the significance of mobility infrastructures, such as paths and bridges. These divisions of space, he wrote, were more than physical facts. They resulted from a subjective understanding of space, namely the human will to link distinct elements. Boundaries, paths and bridges were creations of a human being, the 'connecting creature who must always separate and who cannot connect without separating'. Simmel called this double act of separation and connection, resulting in a dynamic intertwining of physical place and mental spaces, the 'miracle of the road' (Simmel [1909] in Leach 1997: 64–7).

By stating that spatial boundaries were formed and reproduced by social action, Simmel advanced a non-static configuration of space. He suggested, moreover, that spatiality and ways of thinking changed simultaneously – a claim that left an important legacy: Simmel had a profound influence on the so-called 'mobilities paradigm'. From the mid-1990s on, contributions from anthropology, cultural studies, geography, migration studies, science and technology studies, tourism and transport studies and sociology started to look at society as a complex flow of people, objects and information. Authors often referred to Simmel when highlighting the meanings, politics and social implications of mobility (Sheller and Urry 2006).

Yet, besides illuminating the interdependence between physical places and social realms, Simmel's concept of mobility can also be helpful in studying the circulation of knowledge in the world. In his 1903 'Metropolis' essay, he suggested that a new mental geography emerged in the modern city when old social and material boundaries became obliterated by the unseen tempo of modernity (Simmel [1903] in Spillman 2001). Or, as the historian John Randolph noted in his reflective article 'The Space of Intellect and the Intellect of Space', Simmel's 'miracle of the road' urges us to dissect ideas through the mobility of their constantly shifting rearrangement; when reflecting on path-building as a human achievement, Simmel demonstrated that the (mis)use of ideas and concepts turns us into travellers in 'a landscape of starts and stops, anchors and thoroughfares, limitations and freedoms' (Randolph in McMahon and Moyn 2014: 214).

This book argues that the post-war field of architectural thought was a mobile landscape, formed through a dialogical process between the physical and mental realms of practices, intentions and ways of knowing. The essays collected here all concentrate on specific connections and separations between the domains of practice and knowledge production in architecture. Their authors show how ideas and concepts about architecture transferred between coexisting and even contradictory paradigms, mutating as a consequence of the journey described, the route taken and the vehicles employed. Yet such mobility cannot simply be described as movement, as the transmission of something from one point to another, be it material/geographical or spiritual/ epistemological. As we will see, architectural theory in the period studied could be embodied movement or performative movement; on other occasions it was only potential movement. Sometimes it was free movement, at other moments severely restricted. The works in this volume will therefore not only describe where theory resided, but also how and by which means it constructed its own space and in which interactions it was enmeshed.

By looking at specific case studies, the essays brought together in this book point to the complex and unstable nature of architectural thinking. Many accounts of architectural theory seem to have lost that sense of movement, and neglected the non-linear processes that produced little-explored connections between disciplinary perspectives and contexts. The anthologies that have emerged since the 1990s, essential as they have been, focused mainly on theory in its published, edited form, ostensibly addressing non-specific audiences (e.g. Nesbitt 1996; Hays 2000; Mallgrave 2005; Crysler, Cairns and Heynen 2012; Sykes 2012). However, architectural knowledge is produced, disseminated and tested along the road and across various media. Architectural thought, we posit, is not only a high-speed game of racing cars on the highway focusing only on the destination, but also, as Simmel would have put it, of physical and mental movements and detours along bridges, boundaries and pathways.

But how can we realize Simmel's 'miracle of the road' when studying architectural theory? If theory is indeed mobile, and if its agendas, tools, paradigms and functions became increasingly diverse in the recent past, heading towards an open-ended diversity, how then does one historicize 'the discipline's intellections' (Jarzombek 1999: 201)? The authors gathered here addressed this challenge by offering answers to three essential sets of questions: one first set of questions might be framed as, what was theory's journey?

Where did it travel to and from, and which routes did it take? Secondly, how did it travel? In other words, what were the vehicles that theory used? And lastly, since there is no transfer without mutation, no transposition without transformation – how did theory transform while travelling?

Knowledge on the move

Raising questions about the travelling nature of theory in the post-war world entails an important challenge: to make fluid again what has been congealed by the spatial, temporal and medial boundaries installed by theoreticians and historians, often through the above-mentioned anthologies. During the last decade, attempts to cross these boundaries have been made; large parts of the humanities have, in effect, come under the spell of dissecting transfers between disciplines, cultures and historical periods. The acceptance that our knowledge depends on 'travelling concepts' or 'nomadic theories', and therefore demands a combination of multiple approaches, turned out to be a complex yet very rewarding endeavour (Weigel 2018).

In architectural theory and history, this increasing attention to how ideas and theories transformed when migrating from one culture to another has intersected with the field of postcolonial studies: readings of Edward Said's 1982 essay on travelling theory sparked considerable debate, and numerous publications ensued. Scholars like James Clifford, Vivek Dharsschwar and Paul Rabinow helped to advance the study of the itineraries of theories and practices. Their work turned out to be inspirational, even crucial, for those studying transnational processes of exchange in (post)colonial architecture. Invention and migrancy, import and acculturation: postcolonial theory gave the analysis of these processes a much-needed vocabulary (Frank 2009; Moyn and Sartori 2013: 5–17).

Although architectural studies from the 1990s on increasingly explored different ways of thinking about the broad production, dissemination and – often 'global' – circulation of ideas, the work collected in this volume contends that paying attention to specific discursive turns and decisive moments of (re)import and transfer remains essential. As Anna Kinder recently argued, these formative moments run the risk of being overshadowed by a superficial understanding of transfers (Kinder 2017); they were, occasionally or by nature, too delicate, subtle or difficult to record at the time, or to identify in hindsight. In the first section of this book, Kinder's concern is taken seriously, as four authors meticulously examine instances of theory's journey between geographic, disciplinary and reflection contexts or practice spheres. They do this by scrutinizing interactions and (mis) receptions, or 'Translations and Appropriations' as we have called them, shedding light on the tensions rising between the reality-on-the-field, theory-suggesting design instances, and a 'dreamed', aimed-at reality of theoretical ideal constructs.

Translations and appropriations

In the first chapter, 'Deconstruction and Architecture: Translation as a Matter of Speculative Theory', Céline Bodart examines the encounter between the French philosopher Jacques Derrida and a cohort of American architects in the mid-1980s. The impact Jacques Derrida had on architectural theory is well known. Yet while in the Anglo-American sphere the role played by Derrida in the *Gilded Age of Theory* has probably been overstressed, in France this narrative still elicits a kind of discomfort, and even silence, in the architectural debate. Where does this disparity stem from?

Bodart demonstrates that when two different narratives about one and the same encounter with architecture coexist, the speculative gap between both needs to be addressed. In this case, it is important to look into the translation of Derrida's ideas. Situated between extraction and appropriation, she argues, the mechanism of translation can be considered as the agent for unprecedented mobility. Through the discussion of the challenges encountered in translating Mark Wigley's 1993 book, *Derrida's Haunt*, into French, the exercise of translation is employed to a double end. Bodart begins by rereading the convoluted movements of deconstruction in architectural discourses, before exploring how the fortune of theoretical pursuits is conditioned by appropriation.

In our second chapter, 'Gehry's Lou Ruvo Center in Las Vegas as a Housing Critique' by Yael Allweil, a reading of Frank O. Gehry's building-based tectonic theory in Las Vegas – positioned as a response to postmodernist thought and architectural theory's reliance on text as medium – is the starting-point for a critique of the architect's own legacy. In her text, Allweil travels from the building(s) to the theory (both Gehry's and PoMo's) and back to the building(s). She reads Gehry's Las Vegas building as a tectonic reconstruction of the spectacular 1972 demolition of the Pruitt-Igoe housing schemes in the city of St Louis, Missouri, thereby revealing Gehry's self-critique of the desertion of housing as a core premise of modern architecture and of the current class system within his own discipline. In this sense, the chapter entails a journey between a tectonic reading of the building as a 'duck' and a 'decorated shed' constructing a frozen 'Pruitt-Igoe collapse', and a critique of a discipline that turned its back on housing as one of its foundation stones.

Bodart and Allweil both demonstrate that architectural theory is a field teeming with what Dana Cuff called the designers' 'espoused' theories: their chapters – to follow on with this concept – also suggest that theories employed by architects in their discourse are often inconsistent with their practices (Cuff 1992). Theories are used to pursue architects' own agendas and are therefore purposely selected as useful threads to weave narratives, enabling them to cope with a rapidly changing word. This is what Stylianos Giamarelos clearly demonstrates in 'Boomerang Effect: The Repercussions of Critical Regionalism in 1980s Greece', the third chapter in this book. He approaches theory as a situated historical artefact that acquires agency through the conditions of its production and dissemination in specific contexts. Giamarelos describes how, before becoming a novel 'international' discourse that could apply to diverse 'local' contexts in the hands of Kenneth Frampton (1983), critical regionalism was originally moulded by Alexander Tzonis and Liane Lefaivre (1981) around the work of the Greek architects Suzana and Dimitris Antonakakis. The subsequent deflected 'return' of critical regionalism as an 'international' discourse to its 'originary' locus thus exemplifies an unexamined 'boomerang effect' of the 'travelling' postwar theories. The historical ramifications of Frampton's discourse on Suzana and Dimitris Antonakakis's own practice and the broader architectural field of 1980s Greece practically short-circuited the original theoretical intentions. Critical regionalism, Giamarelos contends, served as an alibi for the inward-looking interests of conservative traditionalists and Greek modernists of the period.

Whereas critical regionalism started to cloud the reception of Suzana and Dimitris Antonakakis's work from the moment it turned into a broad-scope approach to architecture, the 'international' celebration of their 'peripheral' work reflexively endowed them with the aura of the 'internationally famous' architects in Greece. Effectively reinforcing a regional inferiority complex, this celebration estranged them from their peers and accelerated the dissolution of their twenty-year-old collaborative practice, Atelier 66, in 1986. This was an unintended yet lasting effect. Something not dissimilar happened with the exhibition *Tendenzen – Neuere Architektur im Tessin*, which opened at ETH Zurich in 1975. The sophisticated reading of Ticinese architecture by the curator Martin Steinmann created a universalizing narrative, transcending the original exhibit and the buildings it depicted to formulate an autonomous theoretical framework for other forms of practice. In the chapter entitled 'The Autonomy of Theory: *Tendenzen – Neuere Architektur im Tessin*, ETH Zurich, 1975', Irina Davidovici dissects how this exhibition brought Ticinese architecture to the keen attention of Swiss architects in other cantons, specifically in the German-speaking north. Unlike a conventional survey, the exhibit pursued the articulation of conceptual positions, subsuming the regional characteristics of Ticinese architecture under the headings of an ultimately transferable methodological approach. This reframing of a production in the dialectical terms of architectural realism formed a crucial contribution to the profound shift that affected the self-understanding and the historiography of Swiss architecture in the 1980s and 1990s.

Imprints and undercurrents

The chapters by Irina Davidovici and Stylianos Giamarelos both suggest that the awareness of a specific production can reside in a process of interpretation and rearticulation of the built work, either through the medium of the exhibition or through a handful of texts. This type of reconfiguration, rooted in a densely woven net of relationships and places, is often traceable at 'the surface' of cultural processes. One can easily disclose what was at stake in the 1975 catalogue of the *Tendenzen* exhibition or in the programmatic, often cited, articles on critical regionalism: these were approaches countering the perceived placelessness and lack of identity of Modern Movement architecture, while also rejecting the whimsical individualism and ornamentation of postmodern architecture. It seems more difficult, in turn, to discover the imprint that philosophical or ideological currents left on texts or exhibitions while operating underneath the direct readable surface. It certainly triggers numerous questions: which sediments of old thought frames are detectable in new ideas? Which concepts were quickly digested or slowly metabolized, thereby eventually becoming the ferment of theoretical frameworks?

Such questions, among others, emerge in the chapters forming the second section of this book. In 'Royston Landau and the Research Programmes of Architecture', Jasper Cepl examines the theory of the intellectual and educator Royston Landau (1927–2001), head of the Graduate School at the Architectural Association (AA) in London from 1974 until 1993. In his writings, Landau contributed both to update the agendas of contemporary practice and critically reflect on the structures of the architectural culture in which he was immersed. Through an early exchange with the MIT-based architectural historian Stanford Anderson, a former student of the philosopher of science Paul Feyerabend, Landau became aware of recent developments in the theory and sociology of scientific knowledge. He became one of the most fervent promoters of the theories of thinkers such as Karl Popper, Thomas Kuhn and Imre Lakatos, all working on the ways through which scientists put forward their theories.

Cepl focuses on how Landau adopted Lakatos's 'methodology of scientific research programmes' and, in what the former called 'positional analysis', turned this concept into a method that allowed him to clarify how architects set up their agendas. This appropriation of developments in the philosophy of science in the 1960s – namely, the Lakatosian idea that research is mostly conducted on the basis of 'first principles' (the 'hard core') which are shared by those involved in the research programme – structured architects' decision-making processes at the AA. This case, configuring an outspoken implementation, shows how theory travels between fields of knowledge and how ideas and methods morph when sojourning in new intellectual and educational contexts.

Whereas Cepl offers a strong evidence-based illustration of how philosophical connections became established and unfolded, Karla Britton and Kyle Dugdale reveal in 'Theoretical A/gnosticisms' – the sixth chapter of this volume – that well-known intellectual claims governing architectural knowledge, like the one Landau made, are not the only possible claims.

Besides the history of architecture, often held to be the primary material of architectural knowledge, and its theory, deemed amenable to more esoteric speculations, it also makes sense to consider the theology of architecture. In Britton and Dugdale's chapter, this argument is bracketed by an analysis of two talks. The first, an address given at the Museum of Modern Art in 1964 by the theologian Paul Tillich, suggests how the sacred may be found in building types (beyond ecclesiastical architectures) as an extension of theological language itself. The second, a lecture delivered in London in 1979 by Colin Rowe on the occasion of the publication of *Collage City*, adopts the language of theology to articulate a critique of modern architecture. The chapter discusses how both Tillich and Rowe claimed, albeit using different registers, that modernity's architectural knowledge cannot be contained within familiar demarcations but must be pursued through categories that transcend predictable boundaries between architecture's material and immaterial concerns.

Vehicles

In the third section of this book, the circulation and manipulation of knowledge as such leaves centre stage, and this is given to the networks of informal communication between architects and the platforms or tools which were crucial for the reconceptualization of the role of architecture in the post-war period. More precisely, four authors focus on the relays and instruments that theory and theorists employed, knowingly or not, in the transmission of their (shifting) knowledge. They do this by looking beyond the common text-based understanding of theory and by exploring other possible vehicles for the production and transmission of knowledge. The notion of 'vehicle' is therefore interpreted here in two possible senses. On the one hand, vehicles are discussed as the 'intended means' employed in the original iteration, production or dissemination of a theoretical construct, with contributions re-examining more common instances of such 'means': a seminar (in Buenos Aires) and the plan of a house (in Texas). On the other hand, vehicles may be understood as the 'non-intended' means, employed a posteriori in order to reinforce, extend or reconfigure ideas. This line, we will see, requires new 'mining' processes and new methodologies both from those who pursue the exercise first-hand, and from those who study it in hindsight. Postcards and oral testimonies will offer concrete entries to illuminate this understanding of the concept of 'vehicle'.

Against the background of the post-war period, at a moment that disciplinary discourse and popular culture became more and more entangled, the chapters presented in this section contribute to expand the traditional loci of architecture theory's discursive practices. Still, even when 'vehicles' help to disclose how and by which means architects and theorists disseminated and conveyed knowledge, tracking ideas on the move remains notoriously difficult. As the cultural theorist Sibylle Baumbach remarked, even just by observing the movement of knowledge one risks destroying that movement. The trajectories scholars enthusiastically reconstruct, she argues, are often nothing more than linear templates, keeping important detours or anomalies from view. Moreover, multiple media or various types of knowledge are so deeply intertwined that the beginning and end of a theoretical discourse often simply cannot be determined (Baumbach, Michaelis and Nünning 2012).

This idea clearly resonates in the chapter 'Cedric Price's Chats: Orality and the Production of Architectural Theory', by Jim Njoo. The author argues that even though printed text has been the privileged medium of architectural theory, speech and writing continue to be deeply interdependent, even in a society increasingly dominated by non-literacy. He reveals how the public lectures of the British architect Cedric Price, although spoken, were often mediated through writing, whereas his personal letters, though written, were spoken-like in many respects. Price also referred to his writings and lectures as 'chats': casual, open-ended conversations that encouraged the participation of his audience. Price thus actively enacted architectural theory, not only in what he wrote or said but also through the proximity and interaction he developed with his interlocutors.

If 'talk' remains fundamental to human experience and communication, Njoo asks, how might one take into better account architectural theory's orality as a dialogical phenomenon? And how might its consideration reframe architectural theory's critical autonomy? Cedric Price is definitely not the only one whose complex interactions of orality link with a wider field of performance-related practices at the crossroads of art, entertainment, education and science. In 'Alternative Facts: Towards a Theorization of Oral History in Architecture', the eighth chapter of this volume, Janina Gosseye, Naomi Stead and Deborah van der Plaat advance the theorization of oral history as a method in architectural research by examining both its direct nature and the complexities of its use. The biggest hurdle in using oral history to study architecture from the past, they contend, resides in the fact that architecture remains a strongly authorized practice. The 'authority' to speak about buildings is still attached to author figures: consequently, speaking with architects about their own work risks perpetuating the valorization of architects' intentions above all other narratives and modes of knowledge. Furthermore, architects (generally, white men) are often at pains to shape and protect their legacy, to dictate how their work and persona will be written into history. The catalogue of 'great masters' in the architectural canon, the ideology of genius, the foregrounding of the lone author – these metanarratives could turn out to be *reinforced* by an unreflective use of oral history methods. Drawing upon the theory of oral history in architecture and other disciplines, Gosseye, Stead and van der Plaat reflect on the complexities attending the use of this particular method, and its particular conventions and conceptual frames, within the discipline of architecture.

If the use of oral history by architectural historians can be problematic, the interpretation of one of the most basic sources for architectural history – the plan – can equally generate problems. The reason? The plan may form a symptom of, and even a mask for, underlying conceptual assumptions. In 'Abandoning the Plan', Michael Jasper argues that certain problems characterizing architectural thought are specifically conveyed by the plan as a conceptual device and a locus of knowledge. Through a comparative formal analysis of Peter Eisenman's House II (1969) and John Hejduk's Texas House 5 (1962), Jasper comes to the conclusion that a plan can offer evidence not of theory in the making – as a formative force – but of theory in deformation and dissipation. Jasper discusses a little-cited text from 1969 in which Peter Eisenman laments that the importance of the plan as conceptual device has been dwindling. In the same years, John Hejduk discerns the apparent loss of certain modernist spatial sensibilities. Which shifts did Eisenman and Hejduk sense at the time, in architecture's trajectory? Are they right, and did knowledge swerve from the plan to reside elsewhere? By attempting to answer these questions, Jasper reveals a unique episode in twentieth-century architectural thought and tests an analytic approach that addresses the methodological challenges confronting architects and historians in their engagement with the changing shapes of architectural discourse.

In the tenth chapter of this volume, 'Deltiology as History: Informal Communication as Praxis', this same kind of versatility stands central. Here, Nicholas Boyarsky focuses on how the use of ephemera, and in particular the vintage postcard, became, for a brief moment in the early 1970s, a predominant tool in enabling and representing critical discourse on architecture and urbanism. Boyarsky traces how the surreal and the everyday life are adapted and mingled by five protagonists – Alvin Boyarsky, Robert Venturi, Denise Scott Brown, Bernard Tschumi and Rem Koolhaas – and how these strands mutate and cross-contaminate to surface in key publications of the period (*Chicago a la Carte*, 1970; *Learning from Las Vegas*, 1972; *Advertisements for Architecture*, 1976–7; and *Delirious New York*, 1978). He highlights how these publications established a platform for discussions of architecture beyond the narrow parameters of academic modernism to engage with the political, the banal, eroticism and transgression, and the mythic. Alvin Boyarsky adopted deltiology, the collecting of postcards, as a structuring device for radical education at the AA's International Institute of Design Summer Sessions (1970–2); employed as a means of informal communication between the avant-garde, it became an emblem of the confrontation between European and American protagonists at the 1976 Venice Biennale before lapsing into obscurity.

The plans and postcards discussed by Jasper and Boyarsky are prime indicators of how architects are able to devise their own codes of meaning, projecting their visions independent from mainstream discourses or media. The postcard is ephemeral by nature, following an unpredictable trajectory as it is stamped, addressed, sent, received, read and discarded, forgotten or remembered. The plan is hermetical, possibly congealing intersecting discourses. Being volatile or being arcane and even obscuring vibrant types of thought, in both cases architectural knowledge exposes its ability to operate beyond known categories or to be composed out of multiple hidden layers. This flexibility makes it difficult to pinpoint the inception of ideas and obviously complicates the understanding of any formative context. Contexts, as it turns out, are never stable, univocal entities. They seem to possess a constantly shifting nature and are, as the intellectual historian Ed Baring rightly indicated, clearly elusive: 'Like texts, contexts travel because even at their purported point of origin, they are already slipping away' (Baring 2016: 586).

Nonetheless, it is possible to get hold, to some extent, of the formative contexts of architectural knowledge. In 'Theorizing from the South: The Seminar of Latin American Architecture (SAL)', Catherine Ettinger discusses how a context-related slight had significant impact in empowering peripheral cultures of architecture. In 1985, at the first Biennial of Architecture organized in Buenos Aires, European and North American architects presented their work in the morning sessions downtown at the Teatro San Martin; Latin American architects were relegated to afternoon and evening sessions at the University of Buenos Aires. This slight led to an impromptu meeting of architects from the region who signed a manifesto constituting the informal founding of the Seminar of Latin American Architecture (SAL / Seminario de Arquitectura Latinoamericana).

The SAL proposed the development of a Latin American architecture theory and, through informal round-table discussions, the group encouraged the collective construction of central notions, such as 'arquitectura apropiada' (meaning, in Spanish, both appropriated and appropriate architecture). Dialogue among the participants was an important vehicle for reflection and for the consolidation of a shared framework that questioned metropolitan constructs such as the idea of 'critical regionalism'. The SAL gave visibility to individual voices and cohesion to ideas present in the region both before and after the meetings. They were instrumental in the consolidation of a network of Latin American architecture magazines and the establishment of a documentation centre (CEDODAL), both of which played a relevant role in creating awareness of shared problems and perspectives of the discipline in the region. In this final chapter, the seminar allowed designers and theorists to claim the identity of practice and thought in a part of the world that, in a postcolonial time, still felt the weight of 'Western' cultural hegemony and its trappings: theory, fluid and alive, shall not be co-opted or straightjacketed by European and North American academy, the proponents of SAL seemed to say.

Whereas most recent writing on architectural theory has been concerned with the 'what' – what has been said and written, and by whom – this book is concerned with the 'how': how theory has been developed and transmitted. It attempts to decentre the architectural object and the traditional figure of the architect as synthesizer and creative visionary and focuses on reciprocal relations and situated networks. Translation; interdisciplinary exchanges (philosophy, theology science); transfers from practice to theory, and back again; the international circulation of ideas, with the resulting transformations and resistances – these are some of the main stops in the journey we propose here.

Architecture Thinking across Boundaries: Knowledge Transfers since the 1960s offers a rich understanding of the landscape of architectural thought as it formed over the last six decades. The authors of this book go well beyond the narratives, agents, contexts and production modes that have primarily been considered the highlights of this landscape: they do so by thoroughly and critically enquiring the interstices – geographical, temporal and epistemological – that lie between and behind such focal points, showing how unstable, vital and eminently mobile the processes of thinking about architecture have been. The prerogative of architectural theory is, after all, much more widely shared than the discipline itself is often willing to admit.

*   *   *

Architecture Thinking across Boundaries: Knowledge Transfers since the 1960s *includes the extended versions of a selection of papers presented at the international conference 'Theory's History, 196X–199X: Challenges in the Historiography of Architectural Knowledge', convened in Brussels from 6 to 8 February 2017. The conference was organized by this volume's editors together with Yves Schoonjans, Hilde Heynen, Sebastiaan Loosen and Maarten Delbeke. The editors thank their fellow conference organizers, the speakers and authors, the reviewers and the publisher, whose combined efforts made this volume possible.*

References

Baring, E. (2016), 'Ideas on the Move: Context in Transnational Intellectual History', *Journal of the History of Ideas* 77, no. 4: 567–87.
Baumbach, S., B. Michaelis and A. Nünning (2012), 'Introducing Travelling Concepts and the Metaphor of Travelling: Risks and Promises of Conceptual Transfers in Literary and Cultural Studies', in S. Baumbach, B. Michaelis and A. Nünning (eds), *Travelling Concepts, Metaphors, and Narratives: Literary and Cultural Studies in an Age of Interdisciplinary Research*, 1–24, Trier: WVT Wissenschaftlicher Verlag Trier.
Crysler, C. G., S. Cairns and H. Heynen, (eds) (2012), *The SAGE Handbook of Architectural Theory*, London: SAGE Publications.
Cuff, D. (1992), *Architecture: The Story of Practice*, Cambridge, MA: MIT Press.
Frank, M. C. (2009), 'Imaginative Geography as a Travelling Concept: Foucault, Said and the spatial turn', *European Journal of English Studies* 13, no. 1: 61–77.

Hays, M. K. (ed.) (1998), *Architecture Theory since 1968*, Cambridge, MA: MIT Press.
Jarzombek, M. (1999), 'A Prolegomena to Critical Historiography', *Journal of Architectural Education* 52, no. 4: 197–206.
Kinder, A. (2017), 'Narratives of Theory Transfer', *New German Critique* 44, no. 3: 221–37.
Leach, N. (ed.) (1997), *Rethinking Architecture: A Reader in Cultural Theory*, London: Routledge.
Mallgrave, H. F. and D. J. Goodman (2011), *An Introduction to Architectural Theory, 1968 to the Present*, Oxford: Wiley-Blackwell.
McMahon, D. M. and S. Moyn (eds) (2014), *Rethinking Modern European Intellectual History*, Oxford: Oxford University Press.
Moyn, S. and A. Sartori (eds) (2013), *Global Intellectual History*, New York: Columbia University Press.
Nesbitt, K. (ed.) (1996), *Theorizing a New Agenda for Architecture: An Anthology of Architectural Theory 1965–1995*, New York: Princeton Architectural Press.
Sheller, M. and J. Urry (2006), 'The New Mobilities Paradigm', *Environment and Planning A* 38, no. 2: 207–26.
Sykes, A. K. (2012), *Constructing a New Agenda: Architectural Theory 1993–2009*, New York: Princeton Architectural Press.
Weigel, S. (2018), 'Wandering, Thinking in Transition, and Boundary cases: Knowledge set in Motion by Warburg, Benjamin and other authors of Kulturwissenschaft', unpublished lecture, https://vimeo.com/267827042.

PART ONE
Translations and Appropriations

CHAPTER ONE

Deconstruction and Architecture: Translation as a Matter of Speculative Theory

Céline Bodart

In the mid-1980s a French philosopher was *thrown into architecture* by some American architects. These are the words used by Jacques Derrida to describe his encounter with architecture. He told that he was *thrown into it* when Bernard Tschumi, who had just won the commission to design the Parc de La Villette in Paris, called and invited him to collaborate with the architect Peter Eisenman on a public gardens project (Michaud, Maso and Popovici-Toma 2015). The prelude to this encounter between Jacques Derrida and architecture is a well-known story, but I would tend to argue that ways of telling and transmitting what has been (for the recent history of architectural theory) one of the most influential cross-disciplinary experiments are quite different from one cultural context to another.

In the Anglo-American sphere, the vast body of literature produced by and on these so-called Derridean years of architecture argues that their encounter played a major role in the implementation of 'the gilded age of theory' (Mallgrave and Goodman 2011). With regard to anthologies of architectural theory published in the late 1990s, this particular moment of history appears as a sort of benchmark, from which each of their editors situates his/her version of the history: for example, in *Theorizing a New Agenda for Architecture* (1996), Kate Nesbitt dedicates an entire chapter to essays written by architects who have worked in close contact with Derridean philosophy, while K. Michael Hays (1998) directly includes Derrida's texts about architecture among the main theoretical writings dating from the same period. And in a slightly different manner, when the editors of *The SAGE Handbook of Architectural Theory* (2012) introduce their volume by 'revisiting Parc de La Villette', they insist on how this project 'encapsulated' and 'embodied' the theoretical effervescence of the 1980s – even though they do so only in order to distance their editorial proposal from it.

And yet, in France, that same story still causes a kind of discomfort in the architectural debate, often marked by a strange editorial silence about that specific episode of its own theory's history. While the influence of Jacques Derrida is largely debated among English language works on the theory of architecture, French architectural literature is much less prolific on that subject. Aside from the three texts about architecture written (originally in French) by the philosopher and published in *Psyché* in 1987, Derrida's main public interventions on architecture (lectures, letters, interviews, articles and so on) were not translated into French before 2015 and were still presented as 'unpublished' some thirty years after he had been *thrown into architecture*. Even though his lack of translation could be seen to have scant significance in that English is recognized as architectural theory's dominant language (Crysler, Cairns and Heynen 2012), this linguistic (and institutional) hegemony affects not only the construction of the history, but also its legacy. What the Derridean deconstruction has left in the Anglo-American architectural debate today has no equivalent in France, forasmuch as its fragmented reception poses the problem of its legacy. On the one hand, the narrative of this cross-disciplinary encounter is told as an active agent of a long and oscillating history; on the other hand, it appears as if immobilized in a silent past, frozen in its own (but limited) archives, preserved as witness of an event that took place but rarely called to account for the effect it has had on actual architectural discourses. In other words: going from one linguistic milieu to another, the same historical episode creates different theoretical narratives and pursuits.

This point needs to be further developed, and this could be done by drawing on specific modes of investigation such as those employed by the sociology of knowledge. Based on the number of publications, references or cultural events (more or less) directly addressed to this specific historical episode, a comparative study could be carried out in order to quantitatively assess its presence in recent architectural discourses through different linguistic contexts (Lamont 1987). Nevertheless, even if such an analysis would certainly provide a valuable contribution to this study of the ongoing effects of the Derridean years of architecture, it is not through these particular modes of analysis that this question will be pursued here. Instead of a sociological approach, the present chapter proposes to approach the question of the effects – both on Anglo-American and French architectural discourses – of this cross-disciplinary encounter by *the matter of translation*. More precisely, it is the question of accounting for the speculative gap between the overlapped French and Anglo-American narratives of deconstruction in architecture by reflecting on a particular case: the French translation of Mark Wigley's 1993 essay, titled *The Architecture of Deconstruction: Derrida's Haunt*.

In what follows, I will start by clarifying how the concept of deconstruction produced multiple narratives by travelling from one cultural context to the other; I will then discuss why the act of translation is chosen as a privileged way of (re-)questioning what deconstruction has produced in architectural discourses; and why Wigley's essay has been chosen as a case suited to this task. Lastly, I will focus on some of the challenges encountered in translating *Derrida's Haunt* into French, in order to see how the exercise of translation can be set out as a pretext for rereading convoluted movements of deconstruction in architectural discourses and to explore how appropriation conditions the fortune of theoretical pursuits.

Deconstruction as a concept in motion

The matter of translation underpins the entire debate on deconstruction.[1] Since its invention as a philosophical concept in the 1960s (Derrida 1967; translated into English in 1976), and until the question of its inheritance in current architectural discourses arose, the term of deconstruction went through several successive forms of translation, moving from one language to another, but also and in particular from one intellectual and institutional milieu to many others. To outline that point, I distinguish three sequential movements of translation.[2]

The first movement is related to the massive and concurrent importation of a large number of French intellectuals' works into the United States throughout the 1970s; a movement that produced what is today known under the label of 'French Theory'. Barthes, Deleuze, Foucault, Kristeva, Lacan and others were translated and imported into the Anglo-American intellectual and institutional milieu, 'presented as a package ... despite sometimes weak substantive similarities in their works and, at times, decidedly divergent aspects of their overall positions' (Lamont 1987: 613). Within this wide and loose movement of importation, Derrida's trajectory seems to trace a distinctive pattern, fitting particularly well with the 'climate of the times' (McLaughlin 1998: 218). In her study about the process of legitimation of interpretative theories in two cultural and institutional contexts as different as France and the United States, Michèle Lamont points out that the American importation of Derrida's work 'was made possible by its adaptation to [an] existing intellectual agenda', especially given its ability to fit with the disciplinary crisis of literary criticism. Literature departments provided an 'exceptionally strong and concentrated academic support' to Derrida's American position, but also reframed his philosophical discourses 'so that they become understandable and relevant for new audiences'. As Lamont argues to conclude her study, 'the adaptability of Derrida's work ... is one of the most important conditions of its success' (Lamont 1987: 612–16; Schrift 2004; Breckman 2010; Currie 2013). From French to English, and (in the same gesture) from philosophy to literary criticism, Derrida's major concept of deconstruction is both translated and transformed into some theoretical method newly applicable to every kind of text: 'A study of the reception of deconstruction would trace how the political implications of this keyword of postmodern theory have been continually reinvented – transformed via reception – by the cultural, intellectual and disciplinary contexts in which it has been used' (Thomas 2006: 3).

The second movement of translation is initiated from this strong anchor point of deconstruction in American Literature departments. But through this specific movement, the translation is no longer seen as a mere passage between languages, but between different disciplinary boundaries traced within the same cultural, institutional and intellectual milieu. Throughout the 1980s, 'a number of books and articles treating deconstruction in relation to Marxism, Feminism, psychoanalysis and so forth' concurrently disseminated Derrida's work across a wide range of fields (Lamont 1987: 610) and, in the United States, the cultural and institutional field of architecture has to be seen as one of those. Infiltrating academic circles through a large number of essays, journals, exhibitions and conferences, the new theoretical apparatus constructed by the literary criticism of Derridean philosophy widely contaminated the architectural debate.[3] A new *'theoretical practice* of architecture took shape' in the wake of French Theory: 'Theory was more than just a tool – it came to represent a veritable architectural outlook' (Cusset 2008: 244). Architects – both theoreticians *and* practitioners – affirmed a new sort of 'engagement with a particular kind of theory', deploying and experimenting with various forms of encounters 'with this extra- and interdisciplinary body of work' (Crysler, Cairns and Heynen 2012: 8).

My point here is to state that Mark Wigley's essay, *Derrida's Haunt*, has to be considered as one of these products of French Theory in Architecture. It participated and still belongs to the expansion of 'architectural outlook' under the influence of the Anglo-American invention of a new sort of 'theory'. And, reciprocally, it has to be seen as one of these operations that fully participated in the large movement of translation, restructuring and reappropriation of French philosophy by the Anglo-American intellectual milieu. I will develop this point further later on.

The third movement – with which the present reflection attempts to engage – is related to the translation into French of all those discourses produced in different Anglo-American fields of study by French Theory. In an article published in 2012 in the French journal *Esprit*, the philosopher Guillaume Le Blanc argues that, considering the history of contemporary thought, there is a sort of *mésentente* provoked by 'an impossible translation'. He argues that two expressions appear today as *untranslatable*, which are (in brief) 'French Theory' and '*American Philo*': a pair of labels that attempt to 'anchor ways of thinking to geographical areas' (2012: 75). However, the two epithets are not foreign to each other: if 'French Theory' might be used to designate the American reinvention of French philosophers' work, '*American Philo*' would be its contemporary 'flipside' – a French invention, whose name tends to bind together all writings and other theoretical works marked by the influence of French Theory in the United States. According to Le Blanc, '*American Philo* is an experimental prototype currently being launched in France'; it is 'a translation of what is coming back from that first translation which was French Theory'.

French Theory is coming to France,[4] presenting itself as a new task of translation dedicated to a bunch of texts shaped by multiple forms of translation. In other words, what the mechanisms of translation of French philosophy have produced in the United States in the 1980s is now calling for new *forms* of translation. So how can the architectural field respond to such a call? What does the translation today into French of what French Theory has produced in architectural discourses over the past decades now mean for the French architectural milieu? This chapter focuses precisely on those questions. For various study fields, as for the architectural one, this new task of translation raises lots of questions, which I would like to attempt to introduce through a personal translation into French of Wigley's essay, *Derrida's Haunt* (1993).

Translation as a way of investigation

Before discussing the task of translating *Derrida's Haunt* into French, it seems necessary to develop further what I mean here when I say that I see translation as a way of investigation. In his commentary on Benjamin's essay 'The Task of the Translator' (1923), Antoine Berman insists that translation is not *essential* for the original but is *required* by it. He writes that a work calls with all its strength for the act of translation, but also that the original work only regards the results of translation with an ironic indifference (Berman 2008: 68). Such a description of the relationship between the original and translation appears to make a distinction between the *act* of translation and the *result* of translation. In the present case of a French translation of *Derrida's Haunt*, drawing a distinction between the *result* and the *act* of translation is a crucial point. It is to be understood that the real concern about translating Wigley's essay is not tied to the validity or legitimacy of its *result*, but to the study of what is activated by the *act* of translation; what this specific process can produce, besides its own object. Following Berman's argument about the act of translation and its ability to revive what became immobilized, recent comments on translation studies insist on how the linguistic migration forced by the act of translation initiates a mutation process of the original text, producing movements and agitations of knowledge (Ettlin and Pillet 2012). It is through such a dynamic – both created and regenerated by the translation process – that an original French version of *Derrida's Haunt* needs to be explored and discussed.

In other words, refusing to *use* the translation-object here doesn't mean that the translation-process is *useless*. Still, saying that the act of translation is not *useless* is not the same as saying that it is *useful*. Is it useful to translate *Derrida's Haunt* into French today? And if so, to what end or for whom is it useful? According to Berman, the purpose of translation can be reduced to a simple question: how useful is the translation when one can read the original? He claims that, even when one can read the original, the translation will still be required in as much as it enriches our knowledge of the original: 'Because the translation is firstly made for people who can read the original, our relation to the foreign work is fully achieved by going back and forth between original and translation(s)' (Berman 2008: 53). When no longer considered as a mere (and unidirectional) *passage* between languages and cultures, the *act* of translation reconfigures knowledge communities around the original work. It opens up a space to discuss a specific textual object and to enable a rethink of its original context. In these terms, the challenge when translating Wigley's text is to see how it could transform our relation to its initial context, how it could reassess the *effects* of Derridean philosophy on the field of architecture and its discourses, practices and institutions.

As the philosopher Barbara Cassin argues about her vast project entitled *Dictionary of Untranslatables* (2004), to translate is to 'understand that different languages produce different worlds of which they are both causes and effects', but it is also to *make* these worlds communicate by having one language question the other. Such a *'making'* dimension of translation is precisely my concern here, following Cassin's conviction according to which translation can serve as a model of know-how with differences for our ways of doing philosophy or theory (2016: 242–66).

Derrida's Haunt as a symptomatic case of investigation and translation

Mark Wigley published *The Architecture of Deconstruction: Derrida's Haunt* in 1993,[5] as an essay, reworking the research pursued for his doctoral thesis, entitled 'Jacques Derrida and Architecture: The Deconstructive Possibilities of Architectural Discourse' (University of Auckland, 1986). Wigley's main hypothesis is that there is an architectural sense embedded in the overall deconstruction discourses and that such an embedding of architecture in deconstruction precedes their institutional encounters as separate disciplines in the 1980s. In that sense, his entire research is to track down the multiple traces of this 'architecture' always and already present in Derrida's work from the start – to put it somewhat briefly. But instead of going deeper into the contents of this essay, I will emphasize here one of the main features which makes it a relevant case to be translated into French, namely that Wigley presents his work as an unprecedented translation of deconstruction in architecture.

According to Wigley, deconstruction has been too easily imported into architectural discourses: 'Not a translation, just a metaphoric transfer, a straightforward application of theory from outside of architecture to the practical domain of the architectural object ... just a literal application, a transliteration ... the last layer, just an addition, no translation' (Wigley 1993: 1–2). Yet, this task of translation is required and Wigley commits himself to it, presenting his essay as an 'architectural translation of deconstruction', a translation that doesn't 'simply transform the condition of the material architectural object' nor make itself 'the source of a particular kind of architecture', but one that questions 'the ongoing discursive role of architecture' (Wigley 1993: 30). However, if this task of translation has not yet been carried out, there is 'a logic of translation already in operation' between architecture and deconstruction. On the basis of 'Des Tours de Babel' (1987) – Derrida's commentary on Benjamin's essay 'The Task of the Translator' – Wigley argues that a form of translation is already occurring between them, because architecture and philosophy are bound together in a sort of 'ancient contract ... that is inscribed within the structure of both discourses', and 'to think of such a contract here will not only be to think of architecture as the possibility of deconstruction, but likewise to think of deconstruction as the possibility of architecture' (Wigley 1993: 6). Architecture, translation, and deconstruction – these notions were always closely related to each other. Hence, an architectural translation of deconstruction is a sort of ongoing event, occurring far beyond the task that Wigley sets himself in *Derrida's Haunt*.

In *Derrida's Haunt*, Wigley describes a sort of *meta*-relation between architecture and deconstruction, but to do so the author chooses to keep such a relation (artificially) out of its cultural and institutional context. The author refuses to use for his investigation every source bound to the contemporary introduction of Derrida into the architectural milieu, and specifically writings where the French philosopher directly addresses the architectural question (Derrida 1987). But if this methodological frame is a strong point of Wigley's argument, it also appears as *untranslatable* into French insofar as deconstruction has not produced a similar intellectual and institutional passion in that context. However, it is precisely the 'untranslatable' dimension of *Derrida's Haunt* that makes it a significant text to translate today. The act of translation is meant to address the distance separating us ('us' meaning here the French-speaking community in the architectural debate) from the original context of the textual object – that specific context that Wigley wants to keep out of his argument, but whose powerful presence is at the same time and paradoxically reaffirmed.

The point here is to consider translation not as a way of communication but as a matter of transformation: the transformation of our relation to the original context and the reinterrogation of the actual conditions of the inheritance of deconstruction in architectural discourses. How to think afresh the *spacing* between the original and the translation – both historical and cultural – as a speculative matter? In that sense, the task of translating *Derrida's Haunt* is not presented here as a detailed study of the contents of the translated text, but from the perspective of the theoretical potential of the text's own (un)translatability.

Derrida's Haunt as an experiment of (un-)translation

Between extraction, restructuring and appropriation, mechanisms of translation are considered as active agents of the history of Derridean concepts and their unprecedented mobility. But traces of those cross-cultural movements call today for a new mode of investigation for their French translation. If the act of translation is to be considered a movement of transplantation of a specific work into a *linguistic otherworldliness* (Berman 2008: 82), the French cultural and institutional milieu is not just *any* otherworldliness for the work of deconstruction. I would like to discuss that point through my experience as a translator of *Derrida's Haunt* into French, insisting on its challenges: how and why does the text resist its translation into French? It is essential here to see how those resistances of the text bring out the stakes of its cultural context.

First, I want to refer to a particular part of the translation experience concerning quotes in the text, and more specifically the large number of Derrida's quotes that draw on English versions of the philosopher's work. The 'logical' operation would be not to translate the English quotes into French, but rather to search back for original quotes in the French editions of Derrida's texts. Such an operation seems completely obvious and difficult to question, and yet this very operation is certainly the greatest 'betrayal' of the text.

Replacing translated quotes (in English) with their originals (in French), and doing so *as if* this was 'logical' or 'natural', at once covertly erases a major part of the history that makes this textual object significant. The most seemingly faithful reproduction of the sense of a quote would cause the dissolution – or even the loss – of what is here at stake, that is to say the mobility of philosophical concepts and their ability to diversely produce new theoretical frameworks from one cultural context to another. Such a statement needs to be developed in relation to the enquiry led by François Cusset in his book about the American invention of the so-called French Theory (Cusset 2008).

Through his investigation, Cusset describes how a particular non-coherent group of French authors – mostly philosophers whose texts are quite demanding – were enrolled into the cultural and intellectual life of the United States in the 1970s. On the one hand, Cusset details a large set of *operations* conducted firstly by departments of literature, in order to 'decontextualize' and 'reappropriate' French philosophy. On the other hand, he depicts various *operators* ('overlooked mediators', 'anonymous purveyors', 'illicit campus purveyors and translators') involved not only in importing French philosophy across the Atlantic, but also in developing an importation ingenuity (between translating, extracting and restructuring these texts) that allowed the freshly 'recomposed theories' to find a renewed (or even just new) political force on American soil. His main argument is that French philosophy texts have been transformed by the American academic machine, making them operative, resetting their concepts as usable and useful, and artificially gathering them together under the label 'French Theory'. In this sense, the historian tracks down the invention of French Theory through several overlapping factors: the recent transformation of the American academic model, characterized by its university enclave, pursuit of excellence, competition between universities and departments and so on; the emergence of alternative journals, diffusing the first flawed translations of French authors beyond official academic programmes, invading this new body of texts as a field for graphical and theoretical experiments; the '*literalization*' of French philosophy, operated by diverse institutional strategies; the implementation of multiple lexical techniques (linked to edition and translation) that succeeded in establishing a new community of knowledge; and many others. Yet, among the extensive operations orchestrated by the American literary sector, Derrida is a case that must be considered differently.

According to Cusset, 'there is a Derrida mystery'. He argues that such a mystery is based not only on an unprecedented interest in philosophical thinking that it is as 'opaque', 'demanding' and 'difficult to categorize and to transmit' as Derrida's, but also on the very scope of this interest, which goes beyond academic borders to become a sort of cultural phenomenon (Cusset 2008: 107–21). Without detailing here the enigmatic track through which the Derridean deconstruction discourse was transformed into a real theoretical opportunity for some American scholars – and in order (also) to directly jump to the 'conclusion' proposed by Cusset – one could say that Derrida's philosophy has been reinvented to respond to the directives of the American academic system. With great editorial and institutional effort, deconstruction has been rebuilt to become *useful* for knowledge production. Through his inquiry into the American invention of French Theory, Cusset insists that translation has to be fully understood as one of these production modes and maybe the most powerful of them all: 'The translator always encounters the experience of a limit – and a primary negativity – of language. The ruse that he must carry out is also a way of replacing the impossible neutrality of a mere semantic transmission by the more voluntary, more affirmative gesture of an appropriation. In short, he must *speak*, instead of simply reporting' (Cusset 2008: 91). It is in this sense that *Derrida's Haunt* must be read today. I consider indeed that Wigley's essay has participated in an overall process of translation, from Derrida's philosophy to the invention of new forms of theories. It is one of those gestures that recomposes the original philosophical discourse through the invention of its theoretical narrative.

Returning to the issue of quotes in translating *Derrida's Haunt,* first from the French to English (translation), then from the English to French (transfer), the latter movement of quotes acts like a migrant forced to return to her or his homeland: the journey has transformed the migrant into a foreigner to their original soil. Grafting the original French extracts onto Wigley's argument entails losing the history of their American importation and setting aside the question of their reinvention. Yet this context is precisely the original scene of the mid-1980s, in which the encounter between Derridean philosophy and architectural discourse was played. Beyond any of its conceptual narratives, this encounter was built from within the American academic machine (conferences, roundtables, publications, translations, exhibitions and so on) and is deeply marked by these institutional operations. It seems important to consider *Derrida's Haunt* as a theoretical object strongly linked to these *multi*-operations of French philosophy's reinvention.

To take this speculative matter further, we can also rethink the translation of the very word 'deconstruction'. As a form of cultural and institutional translation, Wigley's essay has participated in the American transformation of the French philosophy of deconstruction into what one could recognize from the nickname '*decon*' (note that Wigley's book cover is illustrated by a mousetrap on which the word 'd.con' can be read), but '*decon*' cannot be translated into French as 'la déconstruction': the two terms are not branded by the same history.

When he defines the task of translation, Walter Benjamin points out that 'even words with fixed meaning can undergo a maturing process' and that the act of translation is disturbed by such changes insofar as it must prevent itself from denying the 'powerful' and 'fruitful' dimensions of that historical process (Benjamin 2002/1923). In the same way, the philosopher Paul Ricœur argues that the translation of philosophical works cannot escape the problems brought about by cultural features of meaning. He writes that the translator has to face a very particular difficulty, since the carving out of semantic fields cannot be exactly overlaid from one language onto the other. This is a difficulty that is reinforced in the translation of concept-words ('les maîtres-mots'), because they are a sort of 'condensed textuality' in which entire contexts are reflected (Ricœur 2004). So, to translate today what deconstruction has been in architecture is to re-form its historical and cultural process; to give a new form to its affairs of textuality and its '*decon*-construction'.

And, as a conclusion

So, in the end, how does one translate a form of translation anew? What form can such a translation take, now, in its turn? If the question of the form appears here as truly central, it also comes as no surprise. In 'The Task of the Translator', Walter Benjamin states that the translation is a form, or it reclaims its own specific form, and that form must not imitate the sense of the original, but must rather incorporate it. The translation is not a mere reflection of the original, in as much as the original work still ripens through its translation. To translate a work is to give a form to what is alive in it, to account for the historical evolution of its subjectivities and to take part in the survival of the original. Benjamin states that the relationship between the translation and the original is based on a 'survival mode' that transforms both languages and engages the translator's creativity. In that sense, the chosen task of translating *Derrida's Haunt* is seen here as a way to explore theoretical stakes inscribed in the *invention* of such a form – a form that enables the representation of how this particular encounter with philosophy evolves in architectural discourses diversely and conditions different theoretical pursuits (Bodart 2018).

To that point, I would add two other considerations about the task of translation. On a 'meta' level, I would say that, if *Derrida's Haunt* can be considered as a form of translation, the form of its own translation into French cannot come full circle. It cannot be presented as a sort of 'retour aux sources', nor as an effort of undoing the work of the first translation. It cannot aim to backtrack, seeking in its American and theoretical invention some pure and authentic philosophical origins. Instead, such a version should attempt to *intensify the effects* of this invention. No nostalgic gestures are embedded in the translation of *Derrida's Haunt*, but rather a way to scale up the entangled traces of deconstruction's effect on architectural discourses. This is not a movement circling back, but instead, in the words of Kierkegaard, a way to 'recollect forwards' (Kierkegaard 1946/1843).

And then, on a more 'practical' level (so to speak), it needs to be clear that *more than one* form of translation has to be experienced. *More than one* act of translation has to be discussed. That French Theory as produced into architectural discourses is taken as available for all because it is firstly written in English, but as Antoine Berman argues, 'our relation with a foreign work can only be fully achieved through a back and forth movement between an original and its translation(s)' (Berman 2008: 53). Consequently, the fact that Wigley's essay has never been translated into French (nor into other languages) doesn't suggest a gap to be filled nor an opportunity to be seized. Rather, it is a symptomatic *absence* to be rearticulated: the absence of translations to discuss, question and reassess the effects of deconstruction philosophy (and, in general, the effects of French Theory) on the field of architecture and its discourses, practices and institutions: *plus d'une langue*.

Notes

1   On the one hand, it needs to be recalled that Derrida himself describes the work of deconstruction in terms of translation (Crepon 2008); on the other

hand, Derrida's work provides some theoretical perspectives in the field of translation studies (Davis 2001).

2   It would be more accurate to speak about *four* movements of translation, considering that Derrida developed his concept of 'deconstruction' as a sort of translation of the German terms *Destruktion* and *Abbau*, from his reading of Heidegger's *Time and Being*. This very first movement of translation is not followed here, insofar as it requires further elaboration of the philosophical dimensions of the term, which goes beyond the scope of this chapter. Regarding the reception of German philosophy in France and the emergence of structuralism, led by thinkers such as Derrida, Foucault, Deleuze and Lacan, see F. Dosse (2012/1991), *Histoire du structuralisme, Vol. 1: Le champ du signe, 1945–1966*, Paris: La Découverte.

3   To mention only a few: along with his *Chora L Works* project with Eisenman (1985–8), Derrida was invited to lecture in different scientific events in the architectural field, first in Europe (Paris, 1985; Trento, 1986) and then in America (New York, 1987, 1991; Irvine, 1989); he also participated in the ANY conferences in Los Angeles (1991) and Yufuin (1992). In the United Kingdom, Papadakis organized a symposium entitled 'Deconstruction at the Tate Gallery' in March 1988 (see Papadakis, Cooke and Benjamin (eds) (1989), *Deconstruction, Omnibus Volume*, London: Academy Editions); and the *AD* journal dedicated three special issues to deconstruction: 2, no. 3–4 (1988); 3, no. 1–2 (1989); and *AD Profiles* 87 (1990). The exhibition *Deconstructivist Architecture* (Johnson and Wigley, Metropolitan Museum of Art, New York, June 1988) must also be mentioned, although Derrida's name appears nowhere as a reference.

4   For example, the field of 'études littéraires' recently discovered Gayatri Spivak's work, only translated into French in 2006; within institutional fields attached to the new 'études du genre', Judith Butler was translated in 2005; and, for the so-called 'études culturelles', Stuart Hall was translated into French after 2007. These ongoing translations of French Theory produce new movements of thought in the French intellectual and institutional milieu.

5   Also, this text has been partly published in different professional journals: M. Wigley (1987), 'Postmortem Architecture: The Taste of Derrida', *Perspecta* 23: 156–72; M. Wigley (1989), 'The Translation of Architecture: The Production of Babel', *Assemblage* 8: 7–22; M. Wigley (1994), 'The Domestication of the House: Deconstruction After Architecture', in P. Brunette and D. Wills (eds), *Deconstruction and the Visual Arts: Art, Media, Architecture*, 203–27, Cambridge: Cambridge University Press.

References

Benjamin, W. (2002/1923), 'The Task of the Translator', in M. Bullock and M. W. Jennings (eds), *Selected Writings, Volume 1: 1913–1926*, 5th edition, Cambridge, MA: Belknap Press of Harvard University Press.

Berman, A. (1984), *L'épreuve de l'étranger*, Paris: Gallimard.

Berman, A. (2008), *L'âge de la traduction: 'La tâche du traducteur' de Walter Benjamin, un commentaire*, Paris: Presses Universitaires de Vincennes, coll. 'Intempestives'.
Bodart, C. (2018), Architecture et déconstruction, remises en jeu d'une rencontre: raconter, traduire, hériter, Ph.D. diss., Paris8 University – ULiège.
Breckman, W. (2010), 'Times of Theory: On Writing the History of French Theory', *Journal of the History of Ideas* 71, no. 3: 339–59.
Cassin, B. (2016), 'Translation as a Paradigm for Human Sciences', *Journal of Speculative Philosophy* 30, no. 3: 242–66.
Crépon, M. (2008), 'Déconstruction et traduction: le passage de la philosophie', in M. Crépon and F. Worms (eds), *Derrida, la tradition de la philosophie*, 27–44, Paris: Ed. Galilée.
Crysler, C. G., S. Cairns and H. Heynen (eds) (2012), *The SAGE Handbook of Architectural Theory*, London: SAGE.
Culler, J. (1994), 'Introduction: What's the Point of Theory', in M. Bal and I. E. Inge (eds), *The Point of Theory: Practices of Cultural Analysis*, Amsterdam: Amsterdam University Press.
Currie, M. (2013), *The Invention of Deconstruction*, London: Palgrave Macmillan.
Cusset, F. (2008), *French Theory: Foucault, Derrida, Deleuze & Cie et les mutations de la vie intellectuelle aux États-Unis*, 2nd edition, Paris: Ed. La Découverte.
Davis, K. (2001), 'Deconstruction and Translation', in A. Pym (ed.), *Translation Theories Explained*, Vol. 8, Manchester: St. Jerome Publishing.
Derrida, J. (1987), 'Point de folie – maintenant l'architecture' (1986); 'Pourquoi Peter Eisenman écrit de si bons livres' (1987); 'Cinquante-deux aphorismes pour un avant-propos' (1987), in *Psyché – Inventions de l'autre*, Vol. 2, Paris: Ed. Galilée.
Ettlin, A. and F. Pillet (eds) (2012), *Les mouvements de la traduction: Réceptions, réalisations, créations*, Geneva: Métis Press.
Hays, M. K. (ed.) (1998), *Architecture Theory since 1968*, Cambridge, MA: MIT Press.
Kierkegaard, S. (1946/1843), *Repetition: An Essay in Experimental Psychology*, trans. W. Lowrie, Princeton, NJ: Princeton University Press.
Lamont, M. (1987), 'How to Become a Dominant French Philosopher: The Case of Jacques Derrida', *Journal of Sociology* 93, no. 3: 584–622.
Le Blanc, G. (2012), 'De la *French theory* à l'*American philo*', *Revue Esprit* 3 (March–April): 62–75.
Leach, N. (ed.) (1997), *Rethinking Architecture: A Reader in Cultural Theory*, London: Routledge.
Mallgrave, H. F. and D. Goodman (2011), *Introduction to Architectural Theory: 1968 to the Present*, Malden, MA: Wiley-Blackwell.
McLaughlin, N. (1998), 'How to Become a Forgotten Intellectual: Intellectual Movements and the Rise and Fall of Erich Fromm', *Sociological Forum* 13, no. 2: 215–46.
Michaud, G., J. Maso and C. Popovici-Toma (eds) (2015), *Jacques Derrida, Les arts de l'espace: Écrits et interventions sur l'architecture*, Paris: La Différence.
Nesbitt, K. (ed.) (1996), *Theorizing a New Agenda for Architecture: An Anthology of Architectural Theory, 1965–1995*, New York: Princeton Architectural Press.
Ricoeur, P. (2004), *Sur la traduction*, Paris: Bayard.
Schrift, A. (2004), 'Is There Such a Thing as "French Philosophy"? Or Why Do We Read the French So Badly?', in J. Bourg (ed.), *After the Deluge: New*

Perspectives on Postwar French Intellectual and Cultural History, 21–47, Lantham, MD: Lexington Books.

Thomas, M. (2006), *The Reception of Derrida: Translation and Transformation*, London: Palgrave Macmillan.

Wigley, M. (1993), *The Architecture of Deconstruction: Derrida's Haunt*, Cambridge, MA: MIT Press.

CHAPTER TWO

Gehry's Lou Ruvo Center in Las Vegas as a Housing Critique

Yael Allweil

This chapter examines the routes of architectural knowledge, migrating between text and built form as they create and challenge architectural theory and the foundational goals and premises of our discipline. I point to contemporary built *starchitecture* as a neglected vehicle of architectural theory, by looking into the 'routes of knowledge' communicated by built form in conversation with textual architectural history search for disciplinary autonomy in the 1960s–1990s period, which has arguably shaped it.

As a housing historian, my work has largely focused on the everyday 'architecture of bread and butter' as a key disciplinary premise (Agarez and Mota 2015). Moreover, my historical and geographical context is Israel–Palestine, where no discussion of architecture and urbanism can avoid the social theory of the political and ideological role assigned to it (Allweil 2017).

Nonetheless, here I do not look at a housing project per se, but rather at a fascinating, provocative and greatly surprising reconsideration of housing as a basic premise by *starchitecture* in an attempt to theorize and critique the present moment. I look at a case study – Frank Gehry's 2010 Lou Ruvo Brain Health Center in Las Vegas – as a theoretical piece responding to key theoretical texts revolving around the year 1972 that have transformed architectural knowledge: Venturi and Scott Brown's *Learning from Las Vegas*, the spectacle demolition of Pruitt-Igoe upon which Charles Jencks established his *Language of Post-Modern Architecture*, *Five Architects* and (since 1973) the publication of the *Oppositions* journal (Venturi et al. 1972; Jencks 1984; Rowe 1972; Eisenman et al. 1973). This chapter transitions from a reading of the building's tectonics as direct engagement with the history of architectural theory, to a re-examination of the historiography of housing theory in the 1960s–1990s period. Subsequently, it points to Gehry's building as a theoretical provocation contemplating a post-capitalist architecture.

Theory in built form?

Gehry has declared that his ambition was to 'build a piece of serious architecture in Las Vegas', relating to the city's significance for architectural history and theory, which had a direct impact on his own work. Gehry had refused a number of large-scale projects in Las Vegas before this one (Goldberger 2015: 403; Al 2017). I therefore read this building as a conscious attempt on Gehry's part to produce a 'serious' statement about architecture.

Clearly invoking Venturi and Scott Brown's study of architectural elements as signs (Venturi et al. 1972), as well as the deep engagement of Las Vegas architecture with signs and their communications, Gehry's building is a small complex composed quite explicitly of a 'duck' and a 'decorated shed'. Using the duck and decorated shed in-situ in Las Vegas clearly converses with – and re-examines – the main polemic within architectural theory of the 1960s–1990s, revolving around the communicative quality of architecture, defined by McLeod as 'the single objective [which] aligns both postmodernists and deconstructivists ... the search for architectural communication ... seeking ideological justification in meaning – a problem never solved by the Modern Movement'. Postmodernity has embraced a broader formal language whose strength 'no longer lay in its redemptive social power but rather in its communicative power as a cultural object', spurred by semiology and communication theories, to which deconstructivism posed 'an explicit position regarding the dissolution of meaning, therefore questioning Postmodernism's attempt at communicative architecture' (McLeod 1989: 23–4). This discourse of meaning and communication, which has largely dominated the textual theory of architecture from the 1960s to the 1990s, generated an internal discussion within the discipline, revolving around its communicative capacities, articulating an architectural theory whose primary object was architecture itself (Ockman 1993; Colomina and Ockman 1988). This project was posited on the discourse and objective of safeguarding architecture's disciplinary autonomy (Hays 2000; Crysler et al. 2012).

Surprisingly, little discussion addresses the obvious question: safeguarding the discipline *from what?* I find surprising answers to this question in Gehry's Las Vegas Lou Ruvo Center by looking into what its duck and decorated shed communicate: if the original duck was a poultry shop and the decorated shed sold doughnuts, what is communicated by the Lou Ruvo Center?

The 'shed' part of the building is a regular office building, 'decorated' with a collapsing metallic shell peeling off of its facade. The 'duck' part of the Center employs Gehry's well-recognized, self-referential, formal language producing a 'deconstructed' building in the form of a deconstructed building. Its formal function is as an event space, leaving it mostly empty of function except for its 'duckness' – a representation of the incommunicability of the experience of Alzheimer's and Parkinson's diseases, which the donor wanted to express via the building, having lost his father to Alzheimer's (Goldberger 2015). Alzheimer's disease involves memory loss and therefore also identity loss for people suffering from the disease, while Parkinson's involves loss of one's capacity to control the movement of one's limbs. The collapsing facade of the 'shed' office building and deconstructed 'duck' event space convey two stages – two conditions – of lost identity and control of one's own body. Gehry's official historian, Paul Goldberger, describes the building in these terms:

> Multiple curving surfaces of stain-less steel are set one against the other, as if they had *crushed* together; the composition forms both the walls and the ceiling of the space, and all of the stainless steel sections are punctuated with windows. The combination of *conventional punched windows* and Frank's *unusual clashing shapes* [creates the] effect, from a distance, of a *building in the midst of an explosion.*
>
> GOLDBERGER 2015: 403, emphasis added

The rhythm and size of the building's 'conventional punched windows', as Goldberger defines them, quite clearly communicate this 'building in the midst of an explosion' as a housing building type (see Figs 2.1 and 2.2). For reference, while many of Gehry's buildings include 'unusual clashing shapes', few of them include window-like openings conveying any relationship to the architecture of dwellings. The building's mass and proportions, window-like openings and two-tier structure produce a facade composed of a front mass 'collapsing' onto itself surrounded by white 'dust', and a taller back mass, about to collapse, its facade peeling and sliding off onto the ground. While Gehry has not explicitly linked the two, I propose that the 'explosion' communicated by the main facade resembles an image whose communication was among the most powerful in post-war architecture, its imprint inescapable: the image of the Pruitt-Igoe housing estate explosion, broadcast live on national television and rehashed again and again in mainstream and professional media. Charles Jencks famously declared this 'the day modern architecture died', proposing postmodernism as a new theory and formal language for a new architecture culture (Jencks 1984) (see Fig. 2.3).

This 1972 image of failure and devastation communicated a number of messages to the public and the architectural profession: first, the failure of state-funded social projects; second, the failure of modern architecture (and

FIG. 2.1 *Lou Ruvo Center, first floor plan and building section. Source:* Gehry Partners LLP

the Modern Movement at large) to affect and better society; and third, the failure of housing as an arena for formal and theoretical experimentation in architecture (Bristol 1991; McLeod 1989).

In response to the question 'safeguarding the discipline from what?', I therefore suggest that the 1960s–1990s obsession with disciplinary autonomy attempted to guard the discipline from its own limitations when designing housing. Contemporary high architecture, whose routes of knowledge extend to this theoretical project, has thus been deeply invested in rejecting housing in order to keep the discipline alive.

FIG. 2.2 *Lou Ruvo Renter 'duck' event space and 'shed' decor. Photography: Iwan Baan, 2011.*

FIG. 2.3 *The Pruitt-Igoe explosion vis-à-vis Gehry's Lou Ruvo Center. Source: State Historical Society of Missouri. Photography: Leonard Cottrell.*

A discipline in crisis

Contemporary architecture is often discussed as a discipline in crisis. This crisis involves a global housing crisis affecting cities of the global North on top of those of the global South, coupled with contempt for *starchitecture*'s outrageous costs, proclaimed disinterest in social consequences and production of a 'new monumentality' to global capitalism. One notorious example is the public and scholarly outrage over Zaha Hadid's statement that it was not her 'duty as an architect' to make sure that construction workers survive the construction of her buildings (Hadid in Quirk 2014).

More disturbing to me still is *starchitecture*'s proclaimed statement that design theory is the privilege of a fraction of the built environment worthy of the title of 'architecture', explicitly voicing what we have been experiencing for a few decades now as a solidified class system within our discipline. Gehry himself articulated this class system most clearly in response to a provocation that his designs were 'mere spectacle': 'In this world we are living in, ninety-eight percent of everything that is built and designed today is pure shit ... Once in a while, however, a group of people do something special ... God, leave us alone' (Gehry in Winston 2014). Stardom itself is not the core issue at play here, but rather the culture of high architecture as a 2 per cent milieu of an elite, privileged, late capitalist profession, serving the very rich or producing 'public' white elephants. Despite his notorious statement (over which he later apologized), I suggest here that Gehry's Lou Ruvo Center is a theoretical piece that contemplates a possible *fin* to *starchitecture*'s uncritical service of money-as-power and disregard for social needs and consequences. This tectonic theory interestingly involves *reinvoking housing*.

By the year 2000, Gehry's career had brought him to a prominent position that enabled him to choose his design projects (Goldberger 2015). His choice of projects can therefore indicate his design considerations and agenda. Examining Gehry's oeuvre, we can see that during the decade 2000–9 he had designed twenty-two major projects worldwide, none of which were for residential purpose. However, following the Lou Ruvo Center in 2010, in the years between 2010 and 2017 Gehry engaged with four residential complexes out of thirteen projects, namely 30 per cent of his creative production in the past seven years. These include a seventy-six-storey residential tower in Manhattan (2011); a twelve-storey residential block in Hong Kong (2011); a duplex residence in New Orleans for Make It Right Foundation (2012); and Frank Gehry's new residence in Santa Monica (2017). These housing projects, while hardly affordable, nonetheless examine the application of high architecture to the challenge of dwelling. Moreover, throughout this decade Gehry has been designing his new residence (initially in Venice, CA, and eventually in another location in Santa Monica), closing a circle with his first Santa Monica home, which was his first important building (Barragan 2016).

While not a housing project per se, I propose that Gehry's reconstruction of a frozen-collapse invoking the Pruitt-Igoe spectacle is a 'weather balloon' conversing with the post-structuralist argument that architectural communicability is impossible, by asking what it might mean for the city of Las Vegas and for architecture as a discipline: will it be read? Will it communicate? Or will *starchitecture* maintain its practice of incommunicability with the general public and continue conversing only with itself? Does this discussion of the building demonstrate the communicability of Gehry's theorization of a possible 'death of late capitalist architecture'?

Housing as architecture

Gehry is not the only *starchitect* referring to housing in recent times, the latest example being Patrick Schumacher's notorious keynote at the Berlin Architecture Festival in November 2016, titled 'Housing as architecture' (Frearson 2016). Schumacher argued for the reintroduction of high architecture for housing, while calling for revocation of any social policy involved in housing, thereby demonstrating an embarrassing misunderstanding of the concept. In response to Schumacher's keynote address, a small but very effective demonstration in front of the Zaha Hadid Architects' office in London claimed that the office was a 'crime scene', comparing Schumacher with Albert Speer and declaring the 'parasitic architect Patrick Schumacher [an] enemy of the working class' (Frearson 2016). In addition, numerous responses in the professional architectural press – primarily in online magazines and blogs – voiced outrage over Schumacher's statements (Woodman 2016).

Professional and popular resentment of Schumacher's 'housing as architecture' point to a perceived friction between 'housing' and 'architecture', apparently at the expense of one another. The term 'housing' has been framed in the Euro-American context of the post-Second World War period within the discipline of urban planning, where it was defined as the social problem of ensuring that all members of society had access to dwelling. Defined as such, 'housing' engages key social issues such as who counts as a 'member of society' and who is to ensure housing provision, focusing on policy and resource management. As housing has become the domain of planning, so, within architecture the matter of dwellings has experienced a gradual decline as a central category of innovative knowledge in the discipline (McLeod 1989; Engel 1999):

> Since the beginning of the [twentieth] century all the major interventions of European architects in the field of housing dealt with the aspect of collectivity which is intrinsically linked with mass housing. During the past two decades the conditions for such interventions have gradually disappeared ... leaving the profession in a more or less dramatic state of distress and depriving it of one of the essential factors for its status in society.
>
> ENGEL 1999: 34; SMITHSON 1974

Indeed, popular, policy and scholarly conceptions that architectural design was at fault in failed projects of mass housing, known as the 'Pruitt-Igoe myth', arguably marginalized architecture from its housing processes (Bristol 1991; Heathcott 2012). Schumacher seems to have hit a nerve here.

Following the 'death' of modern architecture, which was shaped by experiments in mass dwellings and habitats, the discipline's focus on housing as a key disciplinary premise experienced a setback, characterizing postmodernism primarily in the US and the UK.[1] As McLeod sums up, 'In the 1980s most schools stopped offering regular housing studios; gentlemen's clubs, resort hotels, art museums, and vacation homes became the standard programs. Design awards and professional magazine coverage have embodied similar priorities. Advocacy architecture and *pro bono* work are almost dead' (McLeod 1989: 38). This decline was most significant in the US, making the American sphere so important for my argument.[2] Nonetheless, as Van Gerrewey and Schrijver have shown, even the Netherlands experienced this decline of housing as an architectural problem (Schrijver 2015; Van Gerrewey 2017).

The 1972 'New York Five' exhibition at the Museum of Modern Art well reflected this disciplinary turn away from housing. 'The Five was never an official group, and its members had as much dividing them as joining them' wrote Goldberger of Richard Meier, Peter Eisenman, Charles Gwathmey, Michael Graves and John Hejduk. 'All they really had in common ... was a commitment to the idea that pure architectural form took precedent over social concerns, technology or the solving of functional problems ... determined to proclaim their work High Art ... was enough to set them apart in the early 1970s, when architecture was still ... a mix of corporate banality and heavy-handed brutalism' (Goldberger 1996: 38). In architectural pedagogy, John Hejduk's leadership role at the Cooper Union produced the well-disseminated 'nine-square grid design exercise', marking a distinct message regarding the core skills and values of the profession. I therefore suggest that the postmodern discipline – as practice and theory – was greatly shaped by its limitations when designing housing, and by its view of 'housing *or* architecture'.

Theoretical terrains of knowledge

Going deeper than the obvious tectonic references to Jencks and Venturi Scott-Brown, I locate Gehry's contemporary self-critique within the theoretical terrain that framed his work, whose extreme points were formulated in Europe, yet whose central discussion was framed in America through the journal *Oppositions*. Gehry has repeatedly stated the influence of *Oppositions* on his work and his wish that the journal still existed (Freeman 2014). The 1960s–1990s project of architectural theory as text, explored by a number of Italian, French and German journals, was nonetheless arguably canonized by *Oppositions*, which, more than any other journal of that period, produced a 'neither academic nor professional' search to save the discipline (Colomina and Buckley 2010; Ockman 1988). The *Oppositions* project has been theorized and historicized via Michael Hays' editorial selection for the widely disseminated *Oppositions Reader* of 1998. Hays' reader framed *Oppositions*' overt goal of disciplinary autonomy in conversation with the works of Manfredo Tafuri on the one hand and Colin Rowe on the other (Hays 1998). Hays, a distinguished scholar entrusted by Peter Eisenman himself with the task of curating the 'essence' of *Oppositions*, had an immense impact on historians' and theoreticians' perspectives of *Oppositions*' intellectual project. This project is little discussed in the context of housing, arguably since none of the key references to housing within its pages were included in Hays' *Reader*.

Specifically, Hays omitted two texts that appeared in *Oppositions* 1 and 4 out of the work of Alison and Peter Smithson: an essay by Peter Eisenman titled 'From Golden Lane to Robin Hood Gardens' (*Oppositions* 1, 1973) and a contribution by the Smithsons themselves on 'The Space Between' (*Oppositions* 4, 1974).

In his piece for the inaugural issue of *Oppositions*, Eisenman frames the architectural discipline in 1973 as extending 'from Golden Lane to Robin Hood Gardens', namely within the premise of housing:

> It is the dogged determination to stick with, develop and *build these ideas* in the face of those who would ebb and flow with the fickle tastes of the current avant-garde which establishes a *model of integrity* which forces each of us to question our own daily activity. The Smithsons represent an intellectual and ideological position, confirmed in a weight of writing, polemic, and criticism which is unparalleled since World War II. They possess a sensibility and an understanding of architecture as a history of social and cultural change; but above all, they have a total commitment to *architecture as a way of life*.
>
> EISENMAN 1973; emphasis added

Eisenman points here to the Smithsons' ethics of buildings as theory as one of *Oppositions*' significant starting-points. This statement indicates that the Smithsons and their housing-based project were far from ridiculed by *Oppositions*. Moreover, while it was not included in the *Oppositions Reader*, Eisenman did not disown this paper but rather included it in *Eisenman Inside Out: Selected Writings 1963–1988* (Eisenman 2004).

In their paper for *Oppositions* 4 of 1974, appearing under the category 'Theory', Alison and Peter Smithson propose 'the space between' as a void that is a space for appropriation. Max Risselada shows that 'the space between' refers to an Anglo-Saxon, and specifically to an American, concept of 'space', providing the opportunity for speculation and appropriation, hence for a new architecture (Risselada 1999; Smithson and Smithson 1974). Van den Heuvel observes that 'the space between is of special importance in the housing projects by the Smithsons' (van den Heuvel 1999: 4). While Robin Hood Gardens was their only mass housing project completed, Alison and Peter Smithson 'had identified both themselves and the destiny of modern architecture' with the welfare state and its 'system of distribution of housing' (Engel 1999: 34).

Reconsidering the Smithsons, I remap the theoretical terrain of *Oppositions*. As an alternative to the mapping proposed by Hays, I propose an intellectual terrain marked by Tafuri and the Smithsons as the two European critiques of CIAM, outlining two contrasting positions on the relationship between the history of architecture and theory in built form. Tafuri's widely-discussed influence on *Oppositions* included his position that any built architecture is already complicit with power, proposing text as the only relevant medium for rearticulating and reforming the discipline. His work served Eisenman and his colleagues as a justification for *Oppositions*' 'text as meaningful architecture' (Ockman 1988; Hays 2000). Vis-à-vis Tafuri's overt critique, the Smithsons were the direct successors of the Modern Movement (along with fellow members of Team X). First to search for saviours for the discipline within itself by turning to Geddes' survey methodology, they offered New Brutalism as a new ethic for architecture located in the built project, famously declaring, 'their aim is not to theorize but to build, for only through construction can a Utopia of the present be realized' (Smithson 1962; Volker 2003). The disciplinary discourse outlined by *Oppositions* extending between Tafuri and the Smithsons involves a debate over the arena for articulating architectural theory: built form versus text.

The Smithsons' 'utopia of the present' in built form was articulated primarily via the problem of habitat and design of housing estates. This project became increasingly fragile as state commissions ceased, to be replaced by capitalist commissions. Furthermore, Tafuri's textual architecture was deserted when the economic boom of the 1980s gave architects the opportunity to build, since 'it is not self-evident that architecture's relation to politics has any major impact on power relations', and architecture is political since 'anything is political' (McLeod 1989: 25). Stretching between the two, the *Oppositions* project came to a close in 1984.

Tafuri's warning to architects has in a sense materialized in criticisms of *starchitecture* as architecture serving capitalism and power which provide it the space-time for experimentation in the autonomous realm of material, form, scale and so forth. Delineating the retreat to traditional boundaries is paradoxically related to architecture's visibility in popular culture, rendering 'at least a few architects the celebrity status that earns them *Time* magazine covers' (McLeod 1989: 27). Late capitalism has since the mid-1980s produced an accelerating distinction between 'high architecture' and 'buildings', materializing a deepening class system within the discipline.

This class gulf parallels a theoretical gulf discussed by Crysler et al. between design theory and social theory – what many architects call 'politics' (Zaera-Polo 2008) – between architecture, the subject matter of design theory, and buildings, the subject matter of social theory, much of it outside architecture. This disciplinary and pedagogical gulf pits scholars and designers against each other within many architectural departments and questions the basic premises of the discipline. This gulf can be traced to two formulations of architectural theory offered by Hays and Leach that closed the period of textual theory in architecture. Hays pointed to critical theory as located within the autonomous discipline, while Leach located theory's critical capacity outside architecture, in other disciplines rethinking architecture outside its specificities of form, construction, materiality and so on (Hays 2000; Leach 1997).

Conclusion: housing as premise

Gehry's Lou Ruvo Center offers a third option: it critiques its lineage in architecture's theory of autonomy not by accepting Leach's outsider perspective, but rather, as I show here, by proposing to rethink architecture's contemporary crisis by turning an eye back to housing. Gehry's open question is reflected in the return of creative experimentations in housing to architecture with the Pritzker prize awarded to Alejandro Aravena and Balkrishna Doshi for housing projects; attempts to reinvent massconstruction technologies like 3D printing; and the use of high architecture for branding housing developments (Majerowitz and Allweil, 2019). In other words, I identify a surprising return of the architects who view design as privilege – 2 per cent – to the problem of housing, asking as Schumacher does, '[W]hat has happened to consideration of this building type as architecture?'

Of course, scholarly studies of housing since Pruitt-Igoe have exposed the idea that 'failed' housing architecture involved social, political, urban and financial issues, namely an important array of 'outsider' issues (Bristol 1991; Heathcott 2012; Smithson 1974). Nonetheless, since shelter is a core premise for architecture – rather than an outsider topic such as class or power – theorizing housing in text or built form is arguably within architecture's disciplinary premise.

Against the 1960s–1990s obsession with disciplinary autonomy, I propose the idea of disciplinary premise, reflecting a different kind of search from that characterizing the textual theory of the 1960s–1990s. The possible 'death' of contemporary high architecture communicated by Gehry's building involves a re-emerging return to housing as a core premise for architecture. What might this mean for design theory, for the class system within our discipline and for architecture's relevance beyond the 2 per cent?

I suggest that Gehry uses the communicative impact of this strong sign to articulate a surprising, even shocking, critique of contemporary high architecture by directly conversing with the textual constructions of postmodernism as sign architecture, in-situ in Las Vegas, deconstructed to produce an image contemplating the possible 'death' of contemporary high architectural theory. What might be the nature of this change? As architecture has been a leading discipline in shaping a number of grand movements in modern theory – modernism, postmodernism, deconstructivism – it may well be incubating a new process of post-neoliberalism. We can think of this in the Marxist terms of 'recuperation of the Elite and the people' towards reforming our discipline.

Notes

1   While in some countries, most significantly the Netherlands, housing continues to be significant in architectural practice and education, and while the construction of dwelling units continues to account for much of the construction and real estate industries, in the last quarter-century significantly less scholarly attention has been addressed at developing innovative dwelling architecture. See, for example, Engel 1999. This process occurred even in architectural cultures explicitly premised on housing, as in Israel (Allweil 2017).
2   In addition, see the Smithsons' discussion of 'space' as an American concept, relevant for their concept of 'the space between', appearing in *Oppositions* 4 (1974).

References

Agarez, R. and N. Mota (2015), 'Architecture of the Everyday', *FOOTPRINT* 15: 1–8.
Al, S. (2017), *The Strip: Las Vegas and the Architecture of the American Dream*, Cambridge, MA: MIT Press.
Allweil, Y. (2017), *Homeland: Zionism as Housing Regime, 1860–2011: Planning, History and Environment*, London: Routledge.
Barragan, B. (2016), 'Is Frank Gehry Finally Building his Dream Home?', *Curbed*, 26 July.
Bristol, K. G. (1991), 'The Pruitt-Igoe Myth', *Journal of Architectural Education* 44: 163–71.
Colomina, B. (2010), *Clip, Stamp, Fold: The Radical Architecture of Little Magazines, 196x to 197x*, New York: ACTAR Publishers.
Colomina, B. and J. Ockman (1988), *Architecture Production*, Vol. 2, New York: Princeton Architectural Press.
Crysler, C. G., S. Cairns and H. Heynen (eds) (2012), *The SAGE Handbook of Architectural Theory*, London: SAGE.
Eisenman, P. (1973), 'From Golden Lane to Robin Hood Gardens; or If You Follow the Yellow Brick Road, It May Not Lead to Golden Green', *Oppositions* 1: 27–56.
Eisenman, P. (2004), *Eisenman Inside Out: Selected Writings, 1963–1988*, New Haven, CT: Yale University Press.
Eisenman, P., K. Frampton, M. Gandelsonas and A. Vidler (1973), 'Editorial Statement', *Oppositions* 1: 1.
Engel, H. (1999), 'The Collective in Housing', *OASE* 51: 34–45.
Frearson, A. (2016), 'Patrik Schumacher Calls for Social Housing and Public Space to Be Scrapped', *Dezeen*, 18 November, https://www.dezeen.com/2016/11/18/patrik-schumacher-social-housing-public-space-scrapped-london-world-architecture-festival-2016/.
Goldberger, P. (1996), 'A Little Book That Led Five Men to Fame', *New York Times*, 11 February, 38.
Goldberger, P. (2015), *Building Art: The Life and Work of Frank Gehry*, New York: Knopf.

Hays, K. M. (1998), *Oppositions Reader: Selected Readings from a Journal for Ideas and Criticism in Architecture, 1973–1984*, New York: Princeton Architectural Press.
Hays, K. M. (2000), *Architecture Theory since 1968*, Cambridge, MA: MIT Press.
Heathcott, J. (2012), 'Planning Note: Pruitt-Igoe and the Critique of Public Housing', *Journal of the American Planning Association* 78: 450–1.
Jencks, C. (1984), *The Language of Post-Modern Architecture*, New York: Rizzoli.
Leach, N. (1997), *Rethinking Architecture: A Reader in Cultural Theory*, London: Psychology Press.
Majerowitz, M. and Allweil, Y. (2019), 'Housing in the Neoliberal City: Large Urban Developments and the Role of Architecture', Urban Planning Vol. 4 no. 4: 43–61.
McLeod, M. (1989), 'Architecture and Politics in the Reagan Era: From Postmodernism to Deconstructivism', *Assemblage* 8: 23–59.
Ockman, J. (1988), 'Resurrecting the Avant-Garde: The History and Program of Oppositions', in B. Colomina and J. Ockman (eds), *Architecture Production*, 180–99, New York: Princeton Architectural Press.
Ockman, J. (ed.) (1993), *Architecture Culture, 1943–1968: A Documentary Anthology*, New York: Columbia Books of Architecture/Rizzoli.
Quirk, V. (2014), 'Zaha Hadid on Worker Deaths in Qatar: "It's Not My Duty as an Architect",' *Archdaily*, 16 February, https://www.archdaily.com/480990/zaha-hadid-on-worker-deaths-in-qatar-it-s-not-my-duty-as-an-architect.
Risselada, M. (1999), 'The Space Between', *OASE* 51: 46–53.
Rowe, C. (1972), *Introduction to Five Architects: Eisenman, Graves, Gwathmey, Hejduk, Meier*, New York: Wittenborn.
Schrijver, L. (2015), 'Stubborn Modernity: IJ-Plein Amsterdam. Oma. The First Decade', *OASE* 94: 109–12.
Smithson, A. (1962), *Team 10 Primer*, Vol. 268, Cambridge, MA: MIT Press.
Smithson, A. (1974), 'The Violent Consumer, or Waiting for the Goodies', *Architectural Design* 44: 274–8.
Smithson, A. and P. Smithson (1974), 'The Space Between', *Oppositions* 4: 105–24.
Van den Heuvel, D. (1999), 'Editorial', *OASE* 51: 1–13.
Van Gerrewey, C. (2017), '1989: The Year Architecture Broke? Oma and the Theory of the IJplein', unpublished ms.
Venturi, R., D. Scott Brown and S. Izenour (1977), *Learning from Las Vegas: The Forgotten Symbolism of Architectural Form*, Cambridge, MA: MIT Press.
Welter, V. M. (2003), 'Post-war CIAM, Team X, and the Influence of Patrick Geddes', in *Team 10: Between Modernity and the Everyday*, 88–110, Proceedings of the conference, Delft University of Technology, 5–6 June 2003.
Winston, A. (2014), '"98% of What Gets Built Today Is Shit" Says Frank Gehry', *Dezeen*, 24 October, https://www.dezeen.com/2014/10/24/98-percent-of-architecture-is-bad-says-frank-gehry-middle-finger/.
Woodman, E. (2016), 'Architecture Needs a Spokesperson; Don't Let it be Patrik Schumacher', *Architects' Journal*, 30 November, https://www.architectsjournal.co.uk/10015236.article?search=https%3a%2f%2fwww.architectsjournal.co.uk%2fsearcharticles%3fparametrics%3d%26keywords%3dschumacher%26PageSize%3d10%26cmd%3dGoToPage%26val%3d5%26SortOrder%3d1.
Zaera-Polo, A. (2008), 'The Politics of the Envelope', *Log* 13–14: 193–207.

CHAPTER THREE

'Boomerang Effect': The Repercussions of Critical Regionalism in 1980s Greece

Stylianos Giamarelos

Introduction

This chapter studies a mobile architectural theory of the post-war years as a situated historical artefact. Focusing on the repercussions of critical regionalism in Greece in the 1980s, it shows how this border-crossing theory acquired historical agency through the conditions of its production and dissemination in a specific context. From the outset, critical regionalism enjoyed a special relationship with Greece. It was originally moulded around the work of Greek architects who in turn played their own subtle role in steering the theorists' initial accounts. More significantly, this chapter highlights the unexamined 'boomerang effects' of the refracted 'return' of critical regionalism as an 'international' theoretical construct to its 'originating' locus. In so doing, it shares Keith Eggener's concerns about the latent colonialism and the mythologizations implicit in critical regionalism (Eggener, 2002). Based on original archival evidence, the chapter goes beyond these debates to explore the historical consequences and implications of critical regionalism for the local architectural milieu in more detail. This in turn advances a different, historically grounded, critique of critical regionalism.

The chapter not only illuminates how a post-war 'international' theoretical construct appropriated a 'regional' design practice to run its own global course, but also shows how this historical course affected the design practice it originated from, and the broader field of architecture in Greece, in unforeseen ways. Owing to the competing – regional and international – agendas that were historically invested in it, Greek architects used critical regionalism both as an unreflective modernist haven from the international sirens of postmodernism, and as a plea for a national traditionalism that went against modernism. What had theoretically been devised to expand the international reach of Greek architecture had the opposite effect of turning the regional architectural culture inwards. These inward-looking ramifications of critical regionalism in 1980s Greece practically short-circuited the original theoretical intentions of its authors.

The origins of critical regionalism in 1980s Greece

The first occurrence of the term 'critical regionalism' is to be found in the 'obscure' annual review, *Architecture in Greece*, in 1981 (Canizaro 2007: 11; Tzonis and Lefaivre 1981). A year earlier, its publisher, Orestis Doumanis (1929–2013), had commissioned Alexander Tzonis (b. 1937) and Liane Lefaivre (b. 1949) to write an article on the work of Suzana Antonakaki (1935–2020) and Dimitris Antonakakis (b. 1933). The publication was meant to support Dimitris Antonakakis's candidacy for a chair of architectural design at the National Technical University of Athens (Antonakakis 2013). Tzonis had first met the architectural couple during his student years at the same School in the late 1950s. Although he moved to the United States to pursue his graduate studies at Yale University and a subsequent academic career abroad immediately after graduating, the three of them maintained an occasional correspondence. This is why Tzonis rose to the occasion when Doumanis prompted him to write a comprehensive article on the architects' work two decades later. The Greek publisher's request enabled Tzonis and Lefaivre to further explore 'The Question of Regionalism', an article they were then co-authoring with Anthony Alofsin (b. 1949).

Alofsin was one of Tzonis's graduate students at Harvard University at the time. He had worked on Lewis Mumford's (1895–1990) theories to extrapolate a 'constructive' conception of regionalism (Alofsin 2007). Aspects of this work were incorporated in the three authors' joint article that traced the development of regionalism in Western architectural history (Tzonis, Lefaivre and Alofsin 1981). In so doing, their article intended to renew a bottom-up tradition of social movements that could resist the anonymity of a technocratic built environment. Siding with Mumford, the authors' aspired regionalism went against 'the empty forms' of 'international style' modernism. Rather crucially, this regionalism also retained a cosmopolitan attitude devoid of nationalistic or racist undertones (Tzonis, Lefaivre and Alofsin 1981: 125–6). Although the term 'critical regionalism' was not used throughout the authors' first text on the subject, its main theoretical contours were already visible.

Despite its far-reaching aspirations, 'The Question of Regionalism' was mainly based on an abstract overview of Western European and North American historical movements from the eighteenth century onwards. By contrast, the architecture of Suzana and Dimitris Antonakakis provided Tzonis and Lefaivre with a concrete case study for a specific region they were already familiar with. This enabled them to illustrate and integrate their formerly abstract analysis within the socio-political and economic developments in modern Greece from the nineteenth century to the present. In addition, the work of the Antonakakis offered the authors an opportunity to explore the actual possibilities for a specific architectural expression of their aspired regionalism. This concrete architectural dimension had been left largely unexplored in their earlier article on the subject.

Tzonis and Lefaivre identified two major design patterns that characterized the work of the Antonakakis: the 'grid' – defined as 'the discipline which is imposed on every space element' – and the 'pathway' – defined as 'the location of place elements in relation to a movement' (Tzonis and Lefaivre 1981: 164). These two 'major patterns' were in turn contextualized within the socio-political history of modern Greece. They corresponded to two different phases of Greek regionalism, exemplified in the work of Aris Konstantinidis (1913–93) and Dimitris Pikionis (1887–1968). In their projects, Suzana and Dimitris Antonakakis combined the rationalist 'grids' of Konstantinidis with the topographical sensibility of Pikionis's 'pathways' (see Figs 3.1 and 3.2). In so doing, the Antonakakis also transgressed their forebears. In the eyes of Tzonis and Lefaivre, both Konstantinidis's and Pikionis's patterns were main escapist. Konstantinidis's 'grid' expressed a utopian push forward, and Pikionis's 'pathway' a nostalgic pull backwards. When the Antonakakis employed these patterns as organizing principles of their architectural designs, Tzonis and Lefaivre argued, they emancipated them from these escapist projections. This critical embeddedness of their design principles within the specific historical and social context rendered their work uniquely significant for the development of a 'critical' regionalism in Greece. Focusing on the rooted experience of the place, their architecture was a realistic intervention in the socio-political condition at the moment of its production.[1]

In short, 'The Grid and the Pathway' enabled Tzonis and Lefaivre to associate socio-political struggles with architectural production in modern Greece. Despite the shortcomings of a necessarily simplified account of long historical developments in broad strokes, their main points were significant for the Western European and North American debates of the period. The concluding lines of 'The Grid and the Pathway' rendered critical regionalism as the 'bridge over which any humanistic architecture of the future must pass'. In addition, the authors acknowledged the 'unique significance' of the Antonakakis's work 'not only to Greek architecture but also to contemporary architecture in general' (Tzonis and Lefaivre 1981: 178).

Rather crucially, their ideas were aligned with the optimism of Kenneth Frampton's own developing regionalist discourse at the time (Frampton

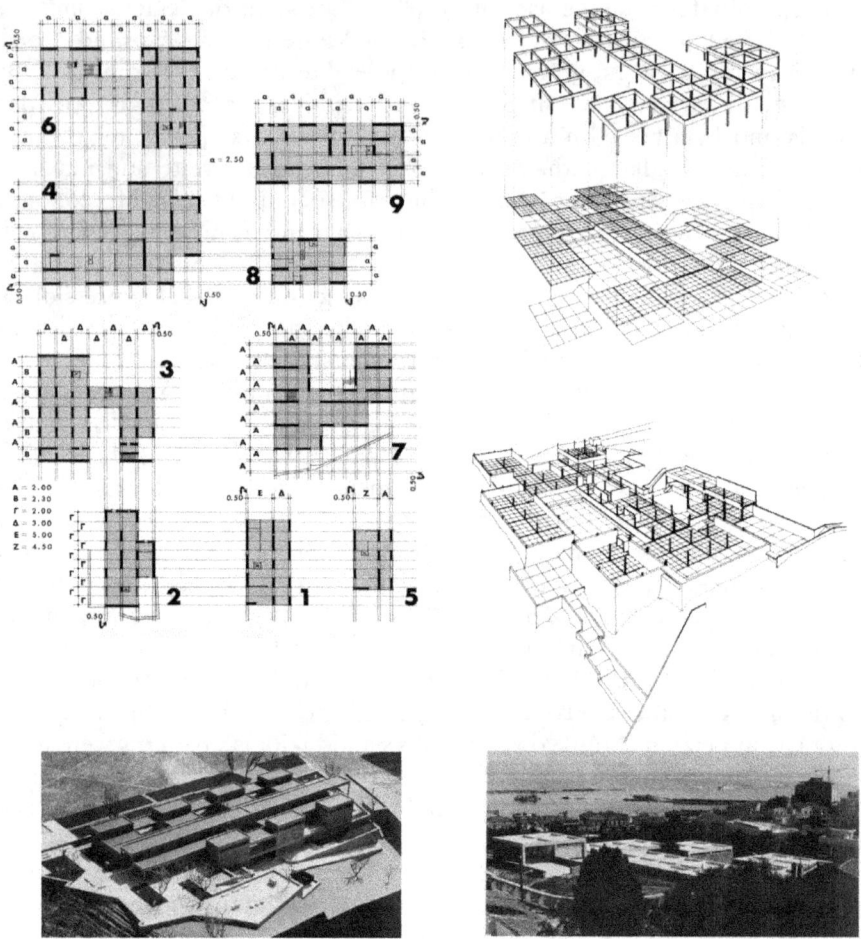

FIG. 3.1 *The 'grid' pattern in the austere work of Aris Konstantinidis and his Archaeological Museum at Ioannina (1964) (left), echoed in the Antonakakis's Archaeological Museum on Chios (1965) (right). Source: Aris Konstantinidis's and Suzana and Dimitris Antonakakis's private archive.*

1983a, 1983b).[2] In the eyes of Tzonis, Lefaivre and Frampton, the unfinished project of modernity could be saved by the unfulfilled pledge of a regionalism emancipated from its nationalistic connotations. This was their viable alternative to the superficial historicist eclecticism intensively promoted after the first Venice Biennale of Architecture in 1980.[3] In 'The Grid and the Pathway', Frampton found a theoretical analysis that combined his own critical and aesthetic concerns (Giamarelos 2016). He borrowed the term

'BOOMERANG EFFECT' 47

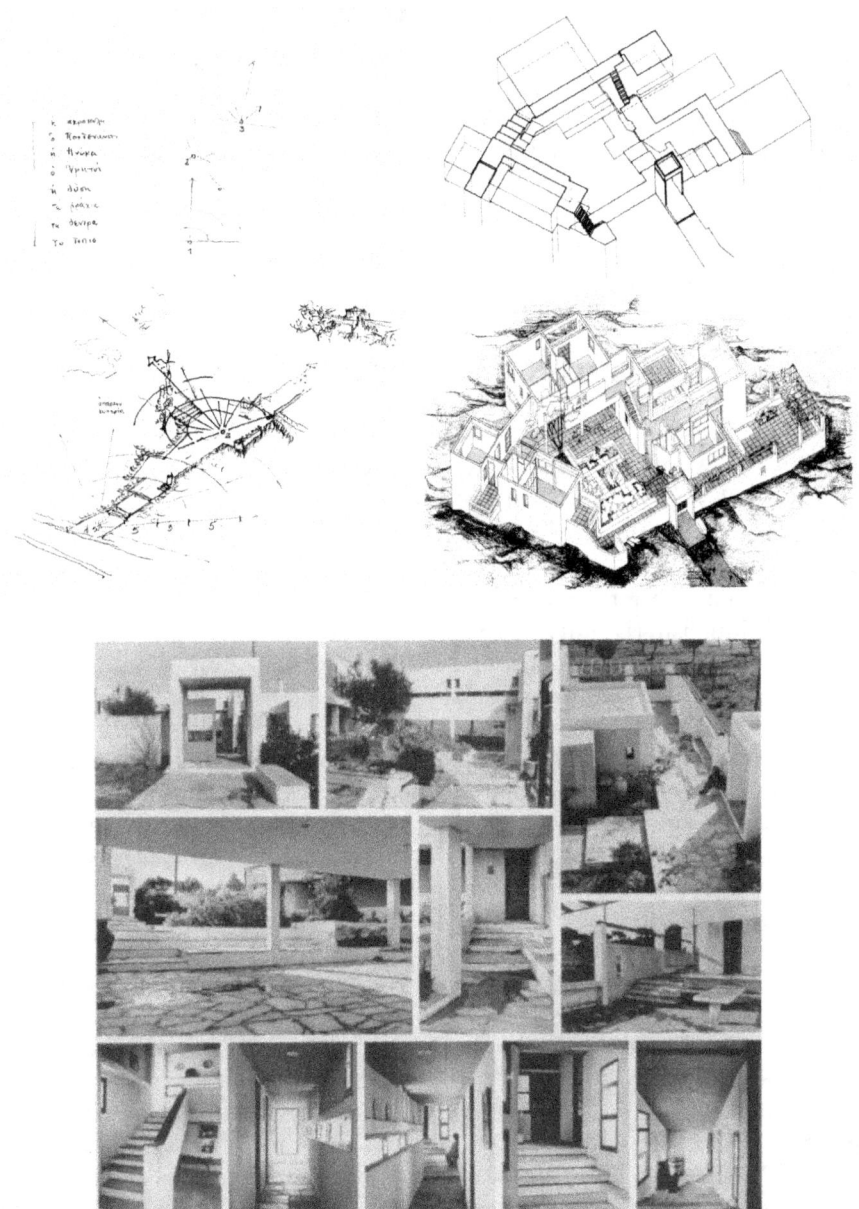

FIG. 3.2 *Dimitris Antonakakis's interpretation of Pikionis's landscaping project around the Acropolis (1958) (top left) exemplifies the 'pathway' pattern that is echoed in the two Antonakakis's House at Spata (1973–4) (top right). The 'pathway' is used as a principle of design that organizes movement from the exterior to the interior as a series of intermediate meeting points with varying degrees of privacy and publicity (bottom). Source: Suzana and Dimitris Antonakakis's private archive.*

'critical regionalism' from Tzonis and Lefaivre, and added Suzana and Dimitris Antonakakis to his international anthology of regionalist architects, with manifold repercussions in the architectural milieu of 1980s Greece.

In addition to the international attention generated by Frampton's recuperation of Tzonis and Lefaivre's article, there were also important regional reasons for the celebrated reception of critical regionalism in Greece. It is this simultaneous convergence of international and regional interest that explicates the long-standing impact of 'The Grid and the Pathway' in Greek architectural circles.

Inward-looking repercussions

Although not immediately perceptible by an external observer, 'The Grid and the Pathway' was a significant intervention in the Greek architectural milieu of the early 1980s. It offered a way to reconcile the Pikionis–Konstantinidis argument that haunted the local architectural field since the 1960s. Established by Doumanis in 1964, this either/or opposition was the defining dilemma for the future of architecture in Greece between modernism and traditionalism (Doumanis 1964). The normative message of Doumanis's analysis was that a 'Greek school' of national architecture should abandon Pikionis in favour of Konstantinidis. Before the publication of 'The Grid and the Pathway', Konstantinidis was associated with the assimilation of architectural qualities of the regional vernacular in his consistently modernist designs. Owing to the versatile references, replications, mixes and matches of regional architectural forms, Pikionis's work was easily associated with traditionalist approaches. Approximately two decades later, 'The Grid and the Pathway' presented this binary opposition as a false dilemma. After its publication, one no longer had to take sides. The influence of Pikionis and Konstantinidis could be successfully combined and transgressed in the work of a younger architectural generation. Focusing their analysis on the work of Pikionis, Konstantinidis and the two Antonakakis, Tzonis and Lefaivre offered a novel reading of the Greek architectural milieu. As a result, the discourse of critical regionalism corroborated the co-equal institutionalization of Konstantinidis and Pikionis as 'the two most important figures in the generation of contemporary Greek architecture' (Tournikiotis 2000: 55). In the 1980s, Greek architects increasingly understood themselves as guardians of this regional variant of modernism in the lineage of Konstantinidis and Pikionis: this was now the defining genealogy of modern architecture in Greece.

In this context, 'The Grid and the Pathway' effectively offered a reappraisal of Pikionis's work. Although his celebrated status in the local architectural field is undisputed today, Pikionis's regional reception was not positive from the outset. His now internationally renowned landscaping project around the Acropolis (1954–7) was originally denounced as a 'forgery' and an 'assault' on the archaeological sites in Greek journals of the period (Salmas 1958). From Doumanis's original article in 1964 to the publication of 'The Grid and the Pathway' in 1981, the Pikionis–Konstantinidis opposition was only further intensified. In the decade following Pikionis's death in 1968, esteem for his work was steadily on the decline. This was due to the emergence of a circle of high-class traditionalists, unofficially led by Angeliki Hadjimichali (1895–1965).[4] As self-proclaimed Pikionists, they posited they were the rightful heirs to his legacy. In his history of architecture in Greece, Anthony C. Antoniades marked 1976 as the year that this 'irreverence' for the work of Pikionis reached its highest point: this was the moment when Pikionis's work was derided as 'ruinology' (Antoniades 1979: 49). Konstantinidis himself encouraged this derogatory approach through his critical allusions to the 'scenographic' work of Pikionis and its negative association with postmodernism in his later writings (Konstantinidis 1992: 241–7). In this light, 'The Grid and the Pathway' was also an attempt to save Pikionis's work from its association with nostalgic 'ruinology' and conservative traditionalism. In contrast to Salmas and Konstantinidis, Tzonis and Lefaivre described the 'pathway' around the Acropolis as 'a catalyst of social life . . . the reenactment of a ritual, the confirmation of the human community and a criticism of the alienating effects of contemporary life' (Tzonis and Lefaivre 1981: 178). In so doing, they foregrounded the collective socio-cultural and critical aspects of Pikionis's work that were attuned with the pursuits of a younger generation of modern Greek architects of the period.

'The Grid and the Pathway' was also published at the most intense moment of the Western European and North American postmodern debate, in 1981. In this context, Frampton's recuperation of Tzonis and Lefaivre's article for his articulation of critical regionalism further endowed Pikionis with unexpected posthumous relevance. The Greek architect's ambivalent relation to modernism reinforced the pertinence of his work. Hence, in the course of the 1980s Pikionis was brought into the international spotlight. Within a decade, the international exposure of his work ranged from the exhibition of Greek Architecture in Delft (1981) (see Fig. 3.3) to the monographic exhibitions at the Architectural Association in London (1989) and the fifth Biennale of Architecture in Venice (1991).[5] This turn of events rendered Tzonis and Lefaivre's 'grid and pathway' interpretation indispensable to the international reception of his work. Forty years later, their account still holds: recent books on Pikionis's work, such as Alberto Ferlenga's *Le Strade di Pikionis* (2014), concentrate exclusively on his use of the pathway, considered in isolation from other prominent characteristics of his oeuvre.

After 'The Grid and the Pathway' was recuperated by Frampton, Tzonis and Lefaivre rightfully argued that 'Greek architecture [was] slowly finding its place in the international scene' (Tzonis and Lefaivre 1984: 23). But the wider postmodern context was essentially absent from the Greek

FIG. 3.3 *Cover of the Pikionis–Antonakakis exhibition catalogue at the Greek Festival in Delft (27 October–1 December 1981). Source: Suzana and Dimitris Antonakakis's private archive.*

understanding of critical regionalism of the period. Historically serving as a discursive haven, critical regionalism maintained Frampton's and the Greek architects' progressive distance from the reactive historicism of the Venetian 'postmodern eclecticists'. According to the rhetoric of critical regionalism, it was because these works were rooted to their specific region that they acquired their international significance. However, this also served as a motive for an inward-looking turn of the Greek architectural field. The rationale was simple: if the region could produce work of international significance on its own, then it should remain focused on its existing resources. It should continue following its own trajectory, ideally without any distorting contact with international architectural developments. The local architectural scene had already found the answer to the crisis of 'international style' modernism on its own. Hence, it was the rest of the world that should be paying attention to Greece, and not the other way around.

This inward-looking interpretation served the Greek modernists who wanted to resist postmodernism. In the preface to the second edition of his critical history of modern architecture, Frampton explicitly referred to critical regionalism as a 'revisionist' variant of modernism (Frampton 1985a: 7). Greek modernists used critical regionalism as an opportunity to revive the revered project of the generation of the 1960s that had been abruptly brought to a halt by the imposition of the military junta in 1967. They still sought to relate modernism to the Greek architectural tradition. At the same time, critical regionalism also served the traditionalists who wanted to oppose the modernists. Both of these architectural audiences succumbed to another round of introversion after the seven years of the military junta (1967–74). The obfuscated message of critical regionalism provided the alibi for both parties to push their respective progressive and conservative agendas forward. These undesired consequences of the otherwise empowering effects of the regionalist discourse were already visible in 1984. In their survey of post-war architectural developments in Greece at the time, Tzonis and Lefaivre regretted this reinforcement of traditional borders (Tzonis and Lefaivre 1984: 22–3). By then, the inward-looking, and eventually self-referential, reading of critical regionalism had reversed the focal intentions of 'The Grid and the Pathway'. Their discourse had inadvertently reinforced a cultural insularity. In the mid-1980s, critical regionalism was used as an excuse to look inward and backward, rather than outward and forward, as its authors originally intended.[6]

The boomerang effect

This inward-looking turn was also reflected in the accounts of Suzana and Dimitris Antonakakis's work after the publication of 'The Grid and the Pathway'. The couple's first steps in the architectural profession coincided with the appearance of the first historical surveys of architecture in modern Greece, and their work found its place in all of them. From the mid-1960s onwards, Suzana and Dimitris Antonakakis were consistently portrayed as outward-looking practitioners, following the lead of Mies van der Rohe and Le Corbusier (Doumanis 1964: 10; Loyer 1966: 913, 1193; Fatouros 1967: 33; Antoniades 1979: 122–7). Following the positive reception of Tzonis and Lefaivre's account in Greece and abroad, however, the interpretation of their work became increasingly inward-looking. Focusing on their rhetoric, for instance, Dimitris Philippidis (b. 1938) highlighted the Antonakakis's work in relation to Konstantinidis's agenda. In his canonical history of architecture in modern Greece, he portrayed the couple as the 'major successors of Konstantinidis's message' (Philippidis 1984: 374, 376–n566). Successive accounts of their work by Greek and international scholars from Jean-Louis Cohen to Costandis Kizis have not seriously challenged this regional genealogy of Pikionis and Konstantinidis (Cohen 2007; Kizis 2015). This is further testament to the impact that Tzonis and Lefaivre's account still has on the imagination of architectural historians. Four decades later, they have not escaped from the interpretative grip of 'The Grid and the Pathway'.[7] However, this account is not historically accurate. It distorts the actual formation of the Antonakakis's architectural outlook in late-1950s Greece.

In historical terms, the Antonakakis's contact with Konstantinidis was rather slight. They had first met him during their student years in the late 1950s. At the start of their career in the early 1960s, Konstantinidis had also agreed to advise them on their winning competition entry for the Archaeological Museum on Chios in 1965 (Antonakakis 2013). In addition, he had appreciated the work of the young architectural couple on the furniture design of the Theotokos Foundation and had asked for their permission to publish it abroad (Konstantinidis 1967). However, their correspondence waned over the years, especially after the publication of 'The Grid and the Pathway'. For Suzana and Dimitris Antonakakis, Konstantinidis's influence thus remained almost as distant as that of Mies van der Rohe. Even if they did study his built work, his influence in the formation of their architectural outlook was not as important as posited by Tzonis and Lefaivre. It was not built upon the deeper ties of a personal biographical connection, as in the case of Pikionis. Suzana Antonakaki references Konstantinidis only four times in the 107 articles she wrote for her monthly column on architecture in the popular daily newspaper, *Ta Nea* (1998–2009). By contrast, her substantial references to Pikionis number more than fifteen. In the short memorandum booklet for his academic candidacy at the National Technical University of Athens in 1978, three years before the publication of 'The Grid and the Pathway', Dimitris Antonakakis does not even mention Konstantinidis as an indirect influence (Antonakakis 1978: 7, 66–7). The couple's architectural outlook was shaped by an altogether different set of influences that harked back to their student years at the School of Athens in the late 1950s (Giamarelos 2018a). It was especially their lessons from Panayotis Michelis (1903–69), Nikos Hadjikyriakos-Ghika (1906–94), Dimitris Pikionis and A. James Speyer (1913–86) that conditioned the two architects' understanding of tradition through modernism, and thus their critical regionalism (Antonakakis 1989; Antonakaki 1997; Antonakaki 2018: 17–18).

Thus, Tzonis and Lefaivre's 'grid-and-pathway' interpretation could only present itself as an open question to Suzana and Dimitris Antonakakis. The theorists' words challenged the architects to rethink the role of the major influences in the development of their work. However, the architects' insider perspective on their personal formation also meant they did not remain passive recipients of others' accounts. In the decades that followed, they both rebelled against the 'grid-and-pathway' interpretation to promote their specific architectural concerns, and tried to reinterpret their work in that light. To counter a strictly inward-looking interpretation of their work, they consistently underscored its 'international' sides in global and regional fora from the mid-1980s onwards (Antonakaki 1988: 132). In the late 1990s, Dimitris Antonakakis went as far as devoting a masters seminar series to the systematic study of the work of Pikionis and Konstantinidis. As he characteristically noted in his preparatory notes for the seminar, retrieved from the architects' private archive, Tzonis and Lefaivre had used these two architects 'intuitively rather than analytically ... in order to set up the scene of "critical regionalism" in Greece' (Antonakakis 2000). He voiced his frustration with critical regionalism with regard to its actual meaning and the work of Pikionis and Konstantinidis.

However, the ramifications of 'The Grid and the Pathway' were not confined to the discursive plane of architectural history: critical regionalism also affected the architects' personal relationships with their peers. Unlike Pikionis, Konstantinidis was still alive when 'The Grid and the Pathway' was published in Greece. Recently retired, he devoted the last years of his life to constructing the legacy of his work, from the systematic organization of his archive to the recording of his thinking in written form. Dissatisfied with the presentation of his work in 'The Grid and the Pathway', he reportedly contacted Tzonis to inform him that the coupling of his life's work with that of young architects was inappropriate (Antonakakis 2013).[8] For the same reasons, Konstantinidis refused to take part in the exhibition of Greek architecture in Delft (1981). The exhibition was based on the 'grid-and-pathway' interpretation of architecture in Greece. It was therefore set to focus on Konstantinidis's work, alongside the architecture of Dimitris Pikionis and Suzana and Dimitris Antonakakis (see Fig. 3.4). After this episode, the couple lost contact with Konstantinidis. As the Antonakakis put it in a recent interview, the publication of 'The Grid and the Pathway' and its eventual recuperation by Frampton also generated hostility around them (Antonakakis 2013). Their personal relation with Konstantinidis was one of the undesired costs of the critical regionalist story.

FIG. 3.4 *Views of the Pikionis (top) and Antonakakis (bottom) exhibition sections at the Greek Festival in Delft. Suzana and Dimitris Antonakakis's first meeting with Aldo van Eyck, at the exhibition opening (27 October 1981), marked the start of a long friendship (middle). Source: Suzana and Dimitris Antonakakis's private archive.*

The discourse of critical regionalism also unsettled the non-hierarchical equilibrium in their collaborative architectural practice, Atelier 66 (Giamarelos 2018b). When Suzana and Dimitris Antonakakis's work was individually acclaimed at an international level by Frampton, the couple needed to alter their relations with their partners. The 'international' celebration of their 'peripheral' work reflexively endowed the Antonakakis with the aura of the renowned architect in Greece. They could no longer perpetuate the pretence of co-equality between the different group members: they had to become the clear leaders, as in Suzana and Dimitris Antonakakis and Associates. In this sense, critical regionalism ended up reproducing the effects of the star system, which it was originally supposed to resist, on the regional level. It accelerated the dissolution of 'the cultivated sense of collectivity' that characterized the stable architectural group of Atelier 66, one of the distinctive features of the Antonakakis's critical regionalism (Frampton 1985b: 5). Frampton's dissemination of critical regionalism from his own structural position at the 'centre' of Western European and North American theory production resulted in this boomerang effect of critical regionalism on the local architectural practices he had selected to foreground. Three decades later, Dimitris Antonakakis wrote in a disappointed tone:

> We underestimate architecture in Greece and revere only whatever is presented in the international scene, because we cannot, or do not want to, see it from a distance and evaluate it in the global context . . . [W]e regard this [international] work as something alien and inaccessible. Owing to the great technological and economic factors involved, it bears no relation to the everyday reality of Greek architectural production . . . The French, the British, the German . . . believe that their architecture is not only naturally situated in the global context, but it also shapes it . . . [Consequently,] if a Greek work happens to transgress the borders of our country . . . to be discussed in the supranational global context, the Greek architectural community regards it as an 'exaggeration'. Instead of instigating a renewal and a reevaluation of the Greek architects' endeavours, such an occurrence produces a short-lived turmoil that is followed by a constant 'conspiracy of silence' that attempts to reduce, to annul the significance and the contribution of this work to any relevant developments.
>
> ANTONAKAKIS 2011: 16–17

The international recognition of Suzana and Dimitris Antonakakis's work had not historically fulfilled its potential for the Greek architectural field. On the contrary, it had practically reinforced a regional inferiority complex. This also seemed to be at the source of the hostility towards the Antonakakis generated by critical regionalism. By this point, the original intentions of Tzonis, Lefaivre and Frampton had been historically short-circuited by this refracted 'return' of the 'international' discourse of critical regionalism to its 'originating' context. The same was the case for other loci across the world, where the theoretical construct of critical regionalism had comparable effects in architectural practice. Their study in detail as situated historical artefacts will further elucidate similar unexamined 'boomerang effects' of knowledge transfers and border-crossing architectural theories in the late twentieth century.[9]

Acknowledgements

This research was conducted under a three-year scholarship from the Greek State Scholarships Foundation ('Lifelong Learning' Programme, European Social Fund, NSRF 2007–13). I would like to thank Ricardo Agarez, Iain Borden, Elke Couchez, Murray Fraser, Rajesh Heynickx, Marina Lathouri, Peg Rawes and the anonymous reviewers for offering their insightful comments on successive versions of my manuscript. I am also indebted to Suzana and Dimitris Antonakakis for agreeing to be interviewed at length on several occasions, and for granting me access to their private archive.

Notes

1   'Realism' was a focal term in architectural debates from the late 1950s onwards. The various discourses that developed around it attempted to move away from the individual project to the collective aspects of architecture. More relevant to the critical regionalist discourse of the period were the debates around the Ticino School in the late 1970s. For a historical account of these interregional discussions, see Irina Davidovici's contribution in this volume.

2   In their seminal texts of 1981, Tzonis and Lefaivre (and Alofsin) did not reference Frampton's work; neither did Frampton mention Tzonis and Lefaivre until he came across 'The Grid and the Pathway' in early 1982. See Giamarelos (2016).

3   For a comprehensive history of this exhibition, see Szacka (2016).

4   Angeliki Hadjimichali was more interested in the study and preservation of Greek folk culture. Beginning in the 1920s, her work ranged from studies on the folk art of Skyros, and Greek ornament and garment, to the nomadic population of the Sarakatsani in the 1950s. For the comprehensive posthumous publications of her work, see Hadjimichali (1983; 2010).

5   For an account of the Pikionis–Antonakakis exhibition in Delft, see the special feature in the Dutch review *Wonen-TA/BK* 20–21 (1981), and Simeoforidis (1981). For the Pikionis exhibition in London, see Crompton (1989).

6   It took more than a decade to draw the theoretical connection between the critical regionalist discourse and the postmodern debate, as in Constantopoulos (1994: 18).

7   For the international architects and critics, this was to be expected. They trusted the opinion of Tzonis as an insider in the Greek architectural field.

8   A closer inspection of the relevant lines in the version of 'The Grid and the Pathway' that was republished in Frampton's 1985 monograph on the work of Suzana and Dimitris Antonakakis confirms this. The reworked version provides ample evidence of slight modifications that reappraised the work of Konstantinidis, in response to his dissatisfied pleas. The authors emphasized the superiority of the 'lucid, tectonic, functionalist intention' of Kontantinidis's 'austere, rough, uncompromising structures' over the Greek National Gallery project (1966–75) by Mylonas and Fatouros (and Antonakakis). The reappraisal culminated in acknowledging Konstantinidis as 'the doyen of contemporary Greek architecture' (Lefaivre and Tzonis 1985: 17–18).

9   To cite just one recent example, see Agarez (2016).

References

Agarez, R. (2016), *Algarve Building: Modernism, Regionalism and Architecture in the South of Portugal, 1925–1965*, New York: Routledge.
Alofsin, A. (2007), 'Constructive Regionalism', in V. Canizaro (ed.), *Architectural Regionalism: Collected Writings on Place, Identity, Modernity, and Tradition*, 369–373, New York: Princeton Architectural Press.
Antonakaki, S. (1988), 'Outdoor "Houses" and Indoor Streets', in M. Labadie and B. Tjhie (eds), *INDESEM '87: International Design Seminar*, 132–49, Delft: Delft University Press.
Antonakaki, S. (1997), 'Teacher and Friend', in J. Vinci (ed.), *A. James Speyer: Architect, Curator, Exhibition Designer*, 72–6, Chicago: University of Chicago Press.
Antonakaki, S. (2018), 'Αρχιτεκτονική: Επάγγελμα. Επαγγέλομαι = Υπόσχομαι', in D. Polychronopoulos (ed.), *Ίχνη αρχιτεκτονικής διαδρομής: Σουζάνα Αντωνακάκη και Δημήτρης Αντωνακάκης*, Vol. 1, 15–19, Athens: futura.
Antonakakis, D. (1978), 'Βιογραφικό Υπόμνημα', memorandum for the National Technical University of Athens School of Architecture, Suzana and Dimitris Antonakakis's private archive.
Antonakakis, D. (1989), 'Dimitris Pikionis: Elaboration and Improvisation', in D. Crompton (ed.), *Mega XI, Dimitris Pikionis, Architect 1887–1968: A Sentimental Topography*, 10–15, London: Architectural Association.
Antonakakis, D. (2000), 'Πικιώνης / Κωνσταντινίδης: Ασύμπτωτοι', National Technical University of Athens School of Architecture Graduate Seminar Notes, 15 February, Suzana and Dimitris Antonakakis's private archive.
Antonakakis, D. (2011), 'Αρχιτεκτονική εκπαίδευση και πράξη: Μία αμφίδρομη εκπαιδευτική διαδικασία', in L. Kalaitzi (ed.), *Τάσος Μπίρης – Δημήτρης Μπίρης. Το αμφίδρομο πέρασμα ανάμεσα στην αρχιτεκτονική και τη διδασκαλία*, 13–19, Athens: Papasotiriou/Benaki Museum.
Antonakakis, S. and D. (2013), Personal interview by Stylianos Giamarelos, 23 June.
Antoniades, A. C. (1979), *Σύγχρονη ελληνική αρχιτεκτονική*, Athens: Karangounis.
Canizaro V. (ed.) (2007), *Architectural Regionalism: Collected Writings on Place, Identity, Modernity, and Tradition*. New York: Princeton Architectural Press.

Cohen, J.-L. (2007), 'The Mediterranean Brutalism of Dimitris and Suzana Antonakakis', in P. Tournikiotis (ed.), *Atelier 66: The Architecture of Dimitris and Suzana Antonakakis*, 32–45, Athens: Futura.
Constantopoulos, E. (1994), 'On the architecture of Dimitris and Suzana Antonakakis', *Design + Art in Greece* 25: 18–25.
Crompton, D. (ed.) (1989), *Mega XI, Dimitris Pikionis, Architect 1887–1968: A Sentimental Topography*, London: Architectural Association.
Doumanis, O. (1964), 'Εισαγωγή στην ελληνική μεταπολεμική αρχιτεκτονική', *Αρχιτεκτονική* 48: 1–11.
Eggener, K. L. (2002), 'Placing Resistance: A Critique of Critical Regionalism', *Journal of Architectural Education* 55, no. 4: 228–37.
Fatouros, D. (1967), 'Greek Art and Architecture 1945–1967: A Brief Survey', *Balkan Studies* 8, no. 2: 421–35.
Ferlenga, A. (2014), *Le Strade di Pikionis*, Syracuse: Lettera Ventidue.
Frampton, K. (1983a), 'Prospects for a Critical Regionalism', *Perspecta* 20: 147–62.
Frampton, K. (1983b), 'Towards a Critical Regionalism: Six Points for an Architecture of Resistance', in H. Foster (ed.), *The Anti-Aesthetic: Essays on Postmodern Culture*, 16–30, Port Townsend, WA: Bay Press.
Frampton, K. (1985a), *Modern Architecture: A Critical History*, 2nd edition, London: Thames & Hudson.
Frampton, K. (ed.) (1985b), *Atelier 66: The Architecture of Dimitris and Suzana Antonakakis*, New York: Rizzoli.
Giamarelos, S. (2016), 'Intersecting Itineraries Beyond the Strada Novissima: The Converging Authorship of Critical Regionalism', *Architectural Histories* 4, no. 1: 11, 1–18.
Giamarelos, S. (2018a), 'The Formative Years of Suzana and Dimitris Antonakakis: A Transcultural Genealogy of Critical Regionalism', in A. Tostões and N. Koselj (eds), *Metamorphosis: The Continuity of Change*, 232–40, Lisbon and Ljubljana: Docomomo International.
Giamarelos, S. (2018b), 'The Anti-hierarchical Atelier that Could not Last', *San Rocco* 14: 122–32.
Hadjimichali, A. (1983), *Η ελληνική λαϊκή φορεσιά*, 2 vols, Athens: Melissa.
Hadjimichali, A. (2010), *Σαρακατσάνοι*, 2 vols, Athens: Angeliki Hadjimichali Foundation.
Kizis, C. (2015), 'Modern Greek Myths: National Stereotypes and Modernity in Postwar Greece' doctoral dissertation, Open University, http://ethos.bl.uk/OrderDetails.do?uin=uk.bl.ethos.700469.
Konstantinidis, A. (1967), 'Schulmöbel für zurückgebliebene Kinder', *Moebel Interior Design* 6: 72–74.
Konstantinidis, A. (1992), *Άρης Κωνσταντινίδης, Εμπειρίες και περιστατικά: Μια αυτοβιογραφική διήγηση*, Vol. 3, Athens: Estia.
Lefaivre, L. and A. Tzonis (1985), 'The Grid and the Pathway: An Introduction to the Work of Dimitris and Suzana Antonakakis in the Context of Greek Architectural Culture', in K. Frampton (ed.), *Atelier 66: The Architecture of Dimitris and Suzana Antonakakis*, 14–25, New York: Rizzoli.
Loyer, F. (1966), 'L'Architecture de la Grèce Contemporaine' doctoral dissertation, Université de Paris, Paris.

Philippidis, D. (1984), *Νεοελληνική αρχιτεκτονική: Αρχιτεκτονική θεωρία και πράξη (1830–1980) σαν αντανάκλαση των ιδεολογικών επιλογών της νεοελληνικής κουλτούρας*, Athens: Melissa.

Salmas, A. (1958), 'Παραποίηση και προσβολή του αρχιτεκτονικού χώρου'. *Αρχιτεκτονική* 9: 7–9.

Simeoforidis, Y. (1981), 'Σύγχρονη ελληνική αρχιτεκτονική στην Ολλανδία', *Journal of the Association of Greek Architects* 9: 24–6.

Szacka, L. (2016), *Exhibiting the Postmodern: The 1980 Venice Architecture Biennale*, Venice: Marsilio.

Tournikiotis, P. (2000), 'The Rationale of the Modern and Locus: A View of Greek Architecture from the Seventies to the Nineties', in S. Condaratos and W. Wang (eds), *20th Century Architecture: Greece*, 53–62, Munich: Prestel.

Tzonis, A. and L. Lefaivre (1981), 'The Grid and the Pathway: An Introduction to the Work of Dimitris and Suzana Antonakakis, with Prolegomena to a History of the Culture of Modern Greek Architecture', *Architecture in Greece* 15: 164–78.

Tzonis, A. and L. Lefaivre (1984), 'A Critical Introduction to Greek Architecture since the Second World War', in O. Doumanis (ed.), *Post-War Architecture in Greece, 1945–1983*, 16–23, Athens: Architecture in Greece Press.

Tzonis, A., L. Lefaivre and A. Alofsin (1981), 'Die Frage des Regionalismus', in M. Andritsky, L. Burckhardt and O. Hoffmann (eds), *Für eine Andere Architektur: Bauen mil der Natur und in der Region*, 121–34, Frankfurt: Fischer.

CHAPTER FOUR

The Autonomy of Theory:
Tendenzen – Neuere Architektur im Tessin, ETH Zurich, 1975

Irina Davidovici

'New Directions in Swiss architecture? One is tempted to say, there are none' (von Moos 1969: 11). In the post-1968 climate, these words combined the provocative and expectant mood of a new generation with the tradition of critical self-reflection long established among Swiss intellectuals (Davidovici 2012: 21–39). As painted by von Moos, Switzerland at the end of the 1960s was a pragmatic but uninspiring 'backyard of history', too wound up in its prosperous-democracy narrative to foster genuine artistic debates. Its best hopes for a substantial architecture lay in its unique status as 'Europe's meeting place', both in terms of a historical orientation towards neighbouring cultures and current possibilities of productive international exchanges (von Moos 1969: 13).

Sure enough, such a 'new direction in Swiss architecture' was taking shape at the time in Ticino. The Italian-speaking canton's southern cultural orientation allowed the early import of the design methods and ideologies circulating at the time in northern Italy, which later also captured the imagination of German Swiss architects. One of the most significant vehicles of this intellectual encounter was the exhibition *Tendenzen – Neuere Architektur im Tessin*, which took place at ETH Zurich in 1975. Providing an original and timely reading of architectural realism, the *Tendenzen* exhibition framed the architecture produced in the peripheral Ticino as the site of professional knowledge transfers between northern Italy and Switzerland. Arguably, this event's most conspicuous legacy was its contributions to the design methodology that permeated Swiss architecture in the following decades, involving the close analysis of urban environments, the integration of historical and contextual references, and a certain gravitas in the formal and material articulation of architectural objects. In the course of the exhibition, however, the migration of ideas and methods from the south to the north of the Alps was enabled through the sublimation of their historicity (Hays 1998: 506). The interpretation of buildings featured in the exhibition was detached from the actual historical conditions in which they were produced, glossing over their inner contradictions to advance instead a frame of interpretation that projected them directly into the realm of theory. I will argue that this strategy laid bare the double bind of architectural autonomy. On the one hand, it acknowledged architecture's obligation to react 'to the ruling powers and to the prevailing ideologies' (Steinmann 1976a: 155, AT).[1] On the other hand, it declared the primacy of formal and typological operations in the production of meaning. The exhibition entailed a process of interpretation of the Ticinese built production that transposed the dilemma of autonomy from the realm of buildings to that of theory. Through its emancipation from the very buildings it sought to justify, the exhibition's theoretical argument acquired an operative autonomy of its own.

Between built architecture and its representation

The *Tendenzen* exhibition ran between 20 November and 12 December 1975 at the Globus Provisorium on Bahnhofbrücke, used at the time by ETH as a temporary studio space (see Fig. 4.1). Organized by the architectural exhibitions programme under the direction of Professor Heinz Ronner, the show was curated by Martin Steinmann, a trained architect who worked at the time as researcher at the gta Institute for the History and Theory of Architecture.[2] This group exhibition provided a platform for younger architects including Mario Botta, Mario Campi, Aurelio Galfetti, Flora Ruchat-Roncati, Luigi Snozzi, Livio Vacchini, Bruno Reichlin and Fabio Reinhart, alongside the more mature figures of Peppo Brivio, Dolf Schnebli and Tita Carloni. Although no images are known to have survived, the original exhibit comprised sixty-six panels featuring forty-eight projects from the 1960s and early 1970s, including private houses, schools and kindergartens and a small number of public buildings. Graphically spare, most of the black-and-white display panels were given to the conventional architectural representations of buildings in orthogonal projection and photography. Apart from stating the projects' authors, dates and locations, there was minimal textual input, leaving the graphic representation of architecture to speak for itself. All panels, in a landscape format determined by a common grid, were reduced to A4 scale for inclusion in the accompanying catalogue (Boga and Steinmann 1975).[3] The importance of this publication

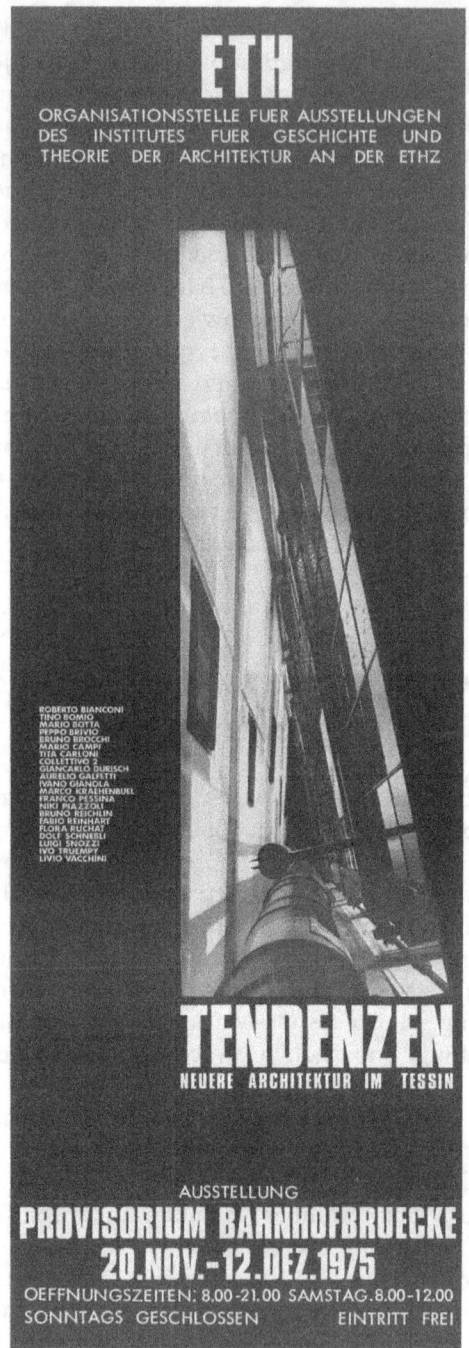

FIG. 4.1 ETH Zurich, gta Organisationsstelle für Ausstellungen der Architekturabteilung. Poster of the exhibition Tendenzen – Neuere Architektur im Tessin, 1975. Source: Courtesy of gta Archiv, Zurich.

cannot be overestimated. Republished in an expanded format in 1976, 1977 and 2010, it was widely circulated and remains the clearest documentation of the original display. The decision to reproduce all panels at a smaller scale rendered the exhibition essentially portable, thus securing its lasting impact (see Fig. 4.2). More important, however, was the fact that the catalogue offered a theoretical justification for the selection of works. It included a 'primary literature' section, in which Ticinese architects explained their designs, as well as two introductory essays offering the critical perspectives of their ETH hosts.

This content suggests that, from the outset, the *Tendenzen* exhibition was intended to provide more than a regional survey of new buildings from Switzerland's cultural periphery. Occurring one year after Aldo Rossi's departure from ETH, where he had taught as visiting professor between 1972 and 1974, the show was calibrated to assist architects and students in processing the momentous methodological discourse on typology, history and city that he had left behind (Hofengärtner and Moravánszky 2011).[4] To this end, the curators disregarded Ticino's modernist establishment, as represented at ETH by Alberto Camenzind, to focus on new voices indicative of a generational shift, both formally and ideologically. As suggested in its title, the exhibition sought to demonstrate affinities between the Ticinese work and the Italian *Tendenza* discourse south of the border. At the same time, it sought to establish a kind of regional identity, whose internal heterogeneity was made apparent in the plural form of the German title.

Notwithstanding the high currency of contemporaneous Italian connections, the exhibited projects were meant to convince on their own. Later described as 'one of the most influential exhibitions for the generation of [Swiss] architects born around 1950' (Hanish and Spier 2009: 659), and internationally as 'an important contribution to the discourse on realism' (Hays 1998: 246), the show enjoyed a swift and remarkable success. After a prompt remounting at EPFL Lausanne in January 1976 and Bellinzona later in the same year, for almost a decade it travelled to academic and professional venues in Basel, Munich, Karlsruhe, Innsbruck, Vienna, Salzburg and Barcelona.

International publications on Ticinese architecture followed suit. In the summer of 1976, *A+U* editor Toshio Nakamura organized a thematic issue on Ticino private houses, featuring texts and projects directly transposed from the exhibition (Nakamura 1976) (see Fig. 4.3). A year later, a selection of projects was republished in the *Formalisme – Realisme* issue of *L'architecture d'aujourd'hui* edited by Bernard Huet, under the heading 'La "tendenza" dans le Tessin' (Huet 1977). Notably, Huet disregarded the plural of the exhibition title, simplifying to the point of identification the more nuanced relation between the southern Swiss production and its Italian undercurrents. He was not alone in doing so. Kenneth Frampton cemented the hypothesis of a comprehensive Ticinese built production, with a unitary theoretical and ideological basis (Frampton 1978). Through such

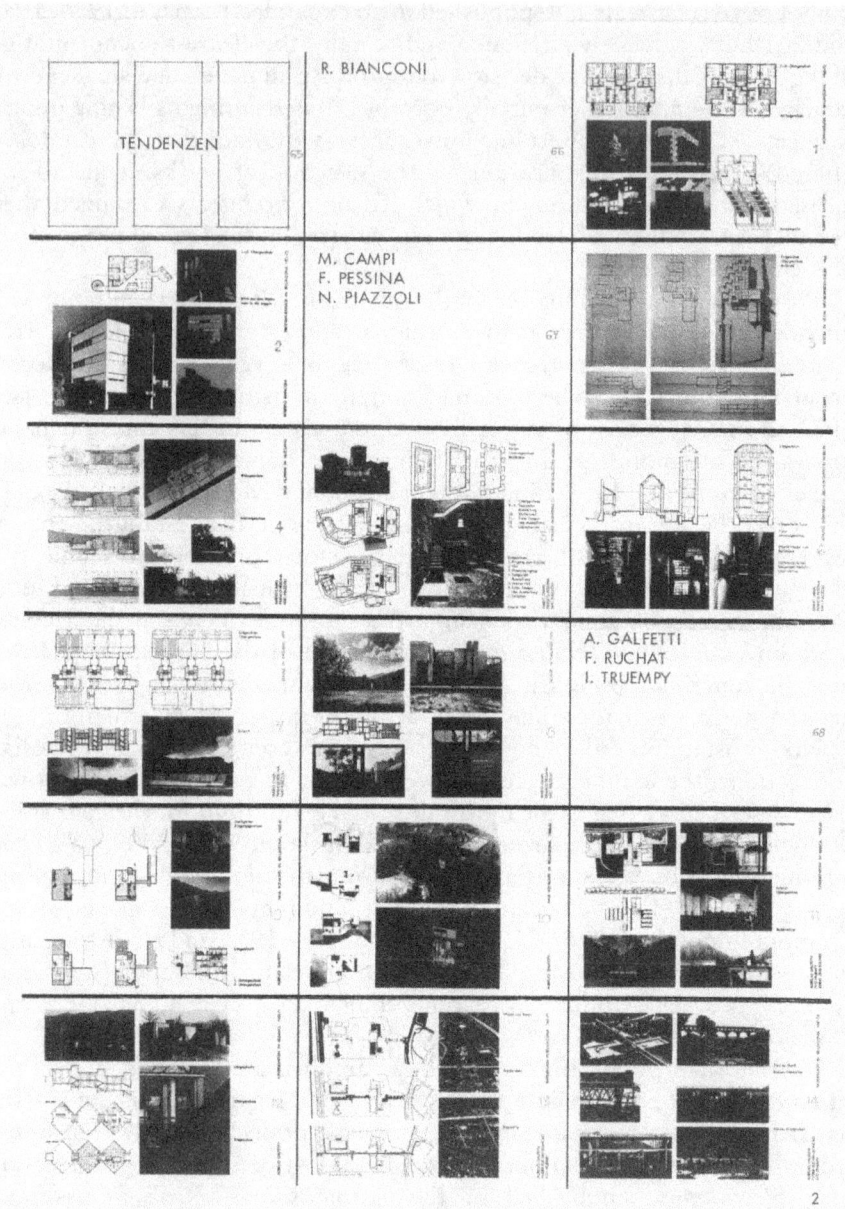

FIG. 4.2 ETH Zurich, gta Organisationsstelle für Ausstellungen der Architekturabteilung. First of the five A4 inventory sheets showing the exhibition panels in reduced size. The original wall panels, 90cm × 120cm, and the landscape A4 catalogue pages shared the same graphic layout for all projects. Source: Courtesy of gta Archiv, Zurich.

FIG. 4.3 A+U Architecture and Urbanism *9 (1976)*. *Cover: Bruno Reichlin and Fabio Reinhart, Casa Tonini, Toricella (1972–4). Featuring private houses from the exhibition, this monographic issue of* A+U, *edited by Toshio Nakamura, indicates how quickly Ticinese architecture gained an international currency through the agency of the exhibition. Source: Courtesy of* A+U, *Tokyo.*

international channels, Ticinese architecture became a global brand for critical regionalism and remained a staple of high-profile publications, exhibitions and architectural tours throughout the 1980s and beyond.

Black cats in the night-time

The fascination with Ticinese architecture was by no means unanimous. Huet's *Formalisme – Realisme* anthology included a tetchy review of the *Tendenzen* exhibition by Italian critic Francesco Dal Co, as well as a response crafted by Steinmann and Reichlin (Dal Co 1977; Reichlin and Steinmann 1977). Like Huet and Frampton, Dal Co overlooked the curators' slight provisos of demarcation from the Italian *Tendenza*. He bemoaned the term's 'debasement' through its overuse and transposition to a provincial cultural context (Dal Co 1977: 58, AT). To Dal Co, the Ticinese production was no more than a 'conscientious interpretation' of Le Corbusier and Aldo Rossi, while the exhibition's narrow curatorial angle opened 'a blatant gap between reality and its "representation"' (Dal Co 1977: 58–9, AT). Steinmann and Reichlin gave a detailed reaction to this critique, which can be summarized in their rebuff – 'dans la nuit de la critique, tous les chats sont noirs' (Reichlin and Steinmann 1977: 59). And yet, Dal Co did raise an important point. Tremendous efforts had been required to inscribe all projects, despite marked differences of approach, within the unifying intellectual framework of the exhibition. It was in this context that the theoretical interpretation took a turn away from the actual architecture. In the night of theory, the Ticinese projects became themselves 'black cats', shadowy reflections of the Italian discourse.

In truth, Ticinese architecture at this time was neither stylistically nor qualitatively homogeneous. Formal and personal affinities swayed from project to individual project. While the works of Galfetti, Ruchat, Trümpy and Snozzi had strong Corbusian overtones, Carloni and Collettivo 2 channelled Frank Lloyd Wright; Botta, Kahn, Scarpa and Vacchini, Mies van der Rohe. Peppo Brivio's mannerism balanced Reichlin's and Reinhart's abstract Palladianism and the Terragni-inspired *razionalismo* of Campi and Pessina (Tschanz 1998: 46; Fumagalli 1995: 32) (see Fig. 4.4).

A common dimension could be found, rather, in the striking contrast between the projects' parochial locations and their artistic and intellectual ambitions. In a canton of less than three thousand square kilometres, with a quarter of a million inhabitants, the buildings rooted themselves by laying claim to a synthesis between various modernist and vernacular traditions (Risch 1975: 815). This recognition invited reflections on Ticino's status as an isolated cultural territory, split between its political allegiance to the rest of Switzerland and its historical, linguistically reinforced, orientation towards Italy (Frampton 1978: 3).

The cultural continuity of the modernist/vernacular legacy gave rise among Ticinese architects to a strong generational self-understanding (see Fig. 4.5). The participants shared a concern with architecture's role in transforming society, and a centrist sense of social engagement, sharply veering towards the political left in Carloni's and Snozzi's membership of the Partito Socialista Autonomo (Bachmann 1986: 67). Another common characteristic in this otherwise disparate architectural neighbourhood was the practitioners' interest in collaborations, which had set up a fluid professional network. Short- and medium-term partnerships and alliances were formed; temporary pacts were brokered over the duration of a competition or project.[5] This collaborative manner of practice was rooted in the tension between the cultural periphery in which the architects practised and the central locations of the architectural discourses they adhered to, in Zurich, Milan or Venice.

FIG. 4.4 *Aurelio Galfetti, Casa Rotalinti, Bellinzona (1960–1), as shown on original exhibition panel (detail). Source: Courtesy of Aurelio Galfetti, Lugano, and gta Archiv, Zurich.*

Catalogue as manifesto

In this context, the exhibition catalogue offered a text-based platform through which Steinmann, Ronner and the Ticinese protagonists built up an overarching argument for the laconic and disjointed visual material on display. Ronner surveyed the cultural and historical context of Ticino's architecture, emphasizing its origins in the local modernist tradition and pondering its professional and cultural connections to ETH (Ronner 1976: 3–8). Conversely, Steinmann presented the paradox of autonomy as being central to this production:

> One essential common denominator of these architects is their clear conception of the relationship of architecture with these mentioned

conditions [existing hegemonies and ideologies] and also the recognition that architecture is a discipline which possesses its own internal laws[,] i.e., which is autonomous . . . the meaning of architecture defines itself in relation to its own tradition.

STEINMANN 1976a: 155

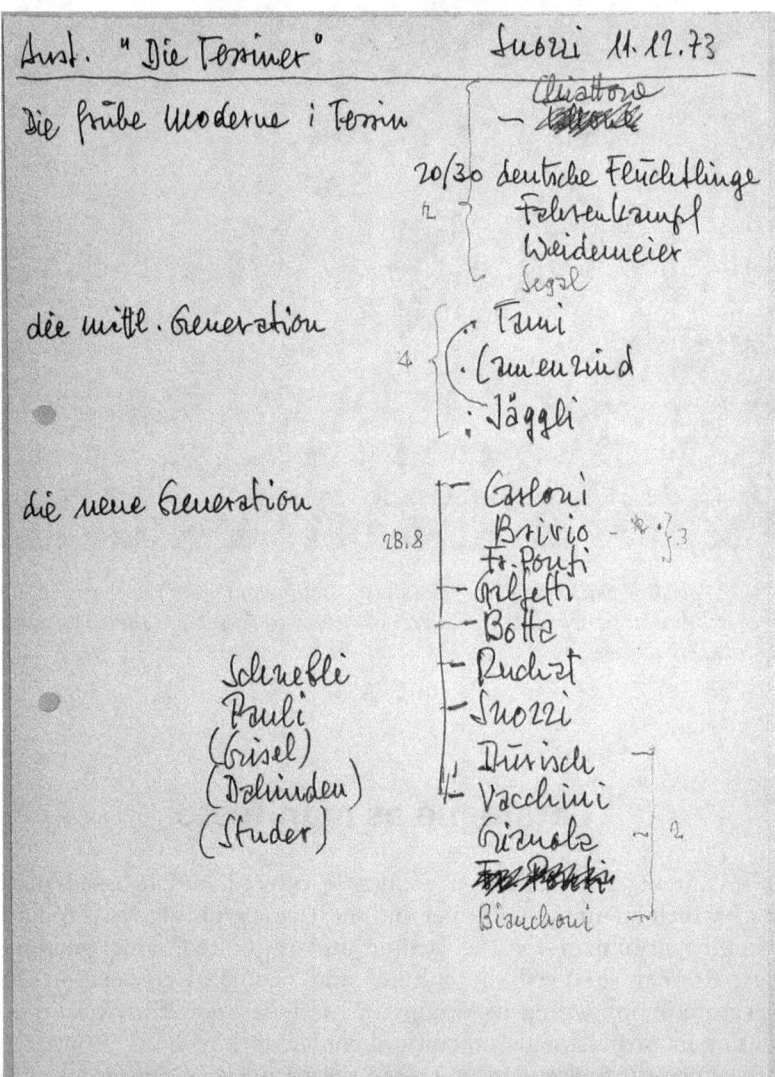

FIG. 4.5 Die Tessiner: *Provisional exhibition title and notes of meeting with Luigi Snozzi, 11 December 1973. The notes (attributed to Heinz Ronner) from this preparatory discussion reveal the historical self-understanding of Ticinese architects within a regional modernist genealogy. Source: Courtesy of gta Archiv, Zurich.*

In line with Steinmann's notion of 'criticism and design as activities that are structurally related', participants were invited to reflect on their work in writing (Hays 1998: 252).[6] Their attitudes towards this task were as varied as their buildings, and the diversity of voices to emerge from this exercise indicated the plurality of positions. While Galfetti, Ruchat-Roncati and Trümpy gave a factual description of the Bellinzona public baths, refraining from explicit ideological statements, Giancarlo Durisch used references to contemporary and modern art – Paul Klee, Henry Moore, Roy Lichtenstein, Walter de Maria, Sol Le Witt and Alfred Jensen – to break down the radical design of his house and studio in Riva San Vitale. The analogies were based on his 'conviction that every cognitive-creative process, in particular architectonic ones, are part of one intellectual sphere' (Durisch 1976: 160). Campi, Pessina and Piazzoli's reluctance to commit to paper their intuitive method for the Montebello Castle project was palpable in their statement, 'We mean to point out the difficulties we have experience [sic] in expressing an architectural event with the analytical tools of the written word' (Campi, Pessina and Piazzoli 1976: 162).

Conversely, the same tools were rather more enthusiastically deployed by other participants to justify their architectural designs. Reichlin and Reinhart assigned to their Tonini House a sophisticated *concetto*, quoting literary sources as diverse as Edgar Allan Poe, Paul Valéry, Walter Benjamin and Alberti (Reichlin and Reinhart 1976: 163). Botta's text on the Morbio Inferiore gymnasium articulated a design method centred on the notion of 'costruire QUEL SITO' ('building THAT SITE'), as he emphasized with the use of capital letters (Botta 1976: 145, 160).[7] Nevertheless, it was Snozzi, echoing his teaching experience at ETH, who provided the clearest didactic statement of the principles deployed in design processes. He listed the reference to architectural history; a critical reappraisal of *Neues Bauen*'s social ambitions; the study of city and territory as fields of architectural intervention; the reliance on typological and morphological analysis; and architecture's primary focus on the 'problem of form':

> The designer must approach the problems of architecture starting from form. Thus, other approaches (sociological, economic, etc.), which in recent years have provided architects with an avenue of escape from their true responsibilities, must be excluded. It is my contention that the failure of the architect in contemporary interdisciplinary work is due mainly to his lack of depth in his own discipline.
>
> SNOZZI 1976: 164[8]

Snozzi thus implicitly criticized the dominance of sociological studies in ETH teaching during the 1960s and early 1970s. Intended as a corrective to this polemical conceptual climate, this position was aligned with the methodological agenda articulated by Aldo Rossi in his recent ETH post

(Hanisch and Spier 2009: 659–67; Moravánszky and Hopfengärtner 2011; Davidovici 2012: 52–66).

This aversion to all things non-architectural manifested itself in the lack of curatorial interest in the specific historical, political and technological contexts of the built Ticinese production. Apart from Ronner's introduction, the catalogue made little attempt to situate the work in the background of practice. Remarkably, the cantonal programme for the construction of educational buildings in the late 1960s and early 1970s, through which most of the public projects had been commissioned, was not mentioned, nor did the texts highlight the contradiction between the architecture's socially transformative aims and its actual conditions – favourable, at best, to individual experiments with middle-class villas. Such commentaries would arise in the mid-1980s, after the formal furore had abated, and even then, by literary critics and historians rather than architects (Bachmann 1986: 67). Local intellectual Virgilio Gilardoni best formulated the paradox of the new Ticinese architecture, which, despite its professed political credentials

> ... is no solution for the collective, like for example the Höfe of Red Vienna. The working class for which these had been built exists no longer in that sense, neither do projects for such solutions. For this reason, the new Ticinese architecture is also not revolutionary. The merit of these architects was to find a solution for the family house that is neither bourgeois nor petit bourgeois.
> GILARDONI quoted in BACHMANN 1986: 67, AT

From *Tendenza* to *Tendenzen*

Any architectural exhibition offers knowledge transfers between practice and theory, mediated through the graphic reproduction and textual interpretation of built projects. In the case in point, the built, graphic and written materials constructed a fluid historical sequence emphasizing Ticino's status as a 'frontier-culture' between Italy and German-speaking Switzerland (Frampton 1978: 3). In assessing the cultural effect of the *Tendenzen* exhibition, one can identify three overlapping sets of exchanges between the built production and its theoretical framework. The first, prior to the exhibition (*c.* 1965–75), comprised the absorption of Italian *Tendenza* theory into the built production of the Ticino. The second stage (*c.* 1975–7) took place at the time of the exhibition and immediately afterwards, when an autonomous narrative, departing from the built architecture, became a theoretical contribution to international debates around realism. The third stage (*c.* 1976–86) represents the reabsorption of this body of realist theory by the built production of German-Swiss architecture – and beyond – through its reformulation as general design method, freed from the socio-economic and cultural preconditions of the Ticino.

The exhibition narrative connected the built architecture with the earlier theoretical discourse of the Italian *Tendenza*. First coined by Ernesto Rogers in 1946, in its original sense this term pertained to the cultivation of historical conscience, denoting a personal engagement with the pursuit of cultural continuity (Rogers 1997a: 88–90). In 1969, Rossi linked the term *Tendenza* to a formal agenda, which he described as a 'shared stylistic will' – *volontà di stile* – sometimes identifiable among artists active in a certain region at a certain time (Rossi 1969: 7–15).[9] Rather than their contemporaneity, Rossi maintained, it was this deliberate

> ... stylistic will that allows one to analyse forms and the world of forms so as to arrive at an autonomous construct. This conception of art as pure speculation on appearance, as research into the existent forms of architecture, opens one of the most important avenues of modern art. Moreover, this combination of architectural objects, forms, materials is meant to create a potential reality of unexpected developments, to bring up different solutions, to construct the real.
>
> ROSSI 1969: 9, AT

Although, in this specific text, the possibility of a shared and rather vague *Tendenza* was postulated in relation to the architects of eighteenth-century Veneto, Rossi implicitly set up this specific historical episode as a potential model for examining contemporary work. The use of *Tendenza* in its current accepted use, as referring to the predominant northern Italian architectural discourse of the 1960s and 1970s – with Rossi himself at its centre – was eventually thematized during the 15th Triennale of Milan in 1973. 'For the Tendenza,' wrote Massimo Scolari,

> ... architecture is a cognitive process that in and of itself, in the acknowledgment of its own autonomy, is today necessitating a refounding of the discipline; that refuses interdisciplinary solutions to its own crisis; that does not pursue and immerse itself in political, economic, social, and technological events only to mask its own creative and formal sterility, but rather desires to understand them so as to be able to intervene in them with lucidity.
>
> SCOLARI 1973, translated in HAYS 1998: 131–2

The Swiss association with this attitude, as hinted in the title of the exhibition, was forged in the Ticino, due to the shared language and geographical proximity that enabled frequent professional and academic exchanges. The plural in the exhibition's title indicated the heterogeneity of formal vocabularies and ideological approaches in Ticinese architecture. Yet the appellation *Tendenzen*, translatable as 'trends', was also a convenient shorthand for stating its intellectual and ideological affinities with the Italian discourse. Parallels could be clearly drawn, such as the attempt to define the variegated Ticinese production through the lens of architectural autonomy. Scolari's formulation of *Tendenza* design principles – 'the strict relationship to history, the predominance of urban studies, the relation between building typology and urban morphology, monumentality, and the importance of form' (Scolari 1973: 139) – re-emerged almost unchanged in Luigi Snozzi's catalogue texts and his 'points of reference' for design:

> a) Reference to history; b) Reference to the 'New architecture' [Neues Bauen] as the last unifying element in architectural history ... c) The analytical study of the city in all its topographical, historical and formal components; d) The study of typology and morphology.
>
> SNOZZI 1976: 164

It comes as no surprise that, in order to defend the new architecture's legitimacy, the curator highlighted distinctions between the Italian *Tendenza* and its Swiss counterparts, placing the latter under the sign of a '*répétition differente*' (Steinmann 1976a: 156).

The flight of theory

Of all the texts in the catalogue, Steinmann's essay was the most conjectural. Its title, 'Reality as History: Notes for a Discussion of Realism in Architecture', was calibrated to transcend the local situation and invite a purely theoretical stance (Steinmann 1976a). A number of subsequent translations and republications – as revised and expanded in *A+U* in 1976, and as included in K. Michael Hays's *Architecture Theory Since 1968* – suggest moreover that the relevance of this text was reinforced precisely through its freedom vis-à-vis specific historical conditions (Steinmann 1976b; Hays 1998: 248–53). Rather than explaining the development of the Ticinese works in the fullness of their actual context, Steinmann used them to punctuate an original reflection on the nature of architectural reality in general (Hays 1998: 246). Territorial particularities were minimized. References to Rogers and Rossi, albeit frequent, lost their visibility among the multiplicity of sources from art and literature, including French structuralism, Bertold Brecht, Edgar Allan Poe, Arnold Hauser, Le Corbusier, Roy Lichtentsein and Peter Handke.

Steinmann's theoretical statement thus transgressed the territorial, cultural and disciplinary context of the Ticino, or indeed Switzerland, to be framed as a universal – Western – dilemma of creative endeavour. Concentrating on architecture as a 'problem of form' (Snozzi 1976: 164), this approach promoted a dialectically understood autonomy, whereby the discipline recognized its internal, historically generated laws over the conditions of its production. Architecture was rational, Steinmann contended, inasmuch as it defined itself in relation to its own traditions and techniques. This 'auto-reflexivity' guaranteed its cultural intelligibility: 'If architecture makes reference to itself in this way, then history ... is not merely a vast depository of experiences already made, but is rather the place where the meaning of architecture defines itself' (Steinmann 1976a: 156). Rather than generating new meaning, or abandoning meaning altogether, the architect built upon historically established associations to integrate the design into its cultural setting.

At the centre of this argument stood the notion of *répétition differente*, an artistic procedure through which the architectural intervention is attached to a typological or morphological tradition, while simultaneously communicating its own 'historicity' (Steinmann 1976a: 156). In the Italian context, the necessity of repetition in new architecture had already been promulgated by Rogers in the early 1950s in an attempt to secure the intelligibility of architecture and thus preserve its continuity within culture. Rogers, too, understood repetition as a creative act – in the sense of a 'dynamic continuation rather than passive copying' (Rogers 1997b: 92–5, AT). Correspondingly, Rossi explained his notion of artistic *Tendenza* as a 'mixture of description and deformation, of invention and knowledge' (Rossi 1969: 7, AT).

The use of French in Steinmann's formulation indicates a further connection to Gilles Deleuze's significant volume, *Difference and Repetition* (1968), a philosophical reflection on the nature of reality. For Deleuze, repetition was one manner of intellectual interaction between virtual and concrete aspects of reality; difference was thus intrinsic to it. Contemplation, he argued, would 'make something new of repetition itself ... [M]aking repetition as such a novelty [was both] a freedom and a task of freedom' (Deleuze 2014: 7). This notion slips very quickly into a hall of mirrors in which thought and praxis, historical precedent and creative gesture are connected through the fecund act of mimesis.

In the case in point, a chain of 'different repetitions' connects Italian ideology and Ticinese architecture, Ticinese architecture and German-Swiss theory, German-Swiss theory and German-Swiss architecture. In 1991, looking at the 'new directions' emerging as a result of this echoing process in the architecture of northern Switzerland, Steinmann would again place *répétition differente* at the core of the phenomenon. He aptly described it as 'a repetition that brings out the difference: the result being at the same time the object and the critique of the object' (Steinmann 1991; Steinmann 2003: 98, AT). The idea of an architecture that preserved the continuity with culture, while adducing its own critique of it, still underlines much of Swiss production today.

One of the greatest merits in Steinmann's theoretical construct in the 1970s was to have drawn a connection between rationalism, history and the vexed question of architectural realism – a theme reprised in the eponymous issue of *archithese* he co-edited with Bruno Reichlin in 1976. In the same issue, a sceptical Rossi, arguing against the institutionalization of neorealism in Italy, had questioned the extent to which architecture, as opposed to art, literature and film, could reflect reality (Rossi 1976: 25–6). Steinmann's revised conclusion to his essay, published in *A+U* in 1976, seemed to respond directly to Rossi's challenge:

> Architecture is not able to designate the real ... directly, but only indirectly, by repeating forms which draw their meaning from appropriate socialized experiences – connotations. Architecture is able to connote the real, but not denote it ... If we now propose the question of realism in architecture, we notice that we must return to architecture for the answer: there we find the confirmation that the meaning of architecture derives from its relationship to itself, its autoreflexivity.
>
> STEINMANN 1976b: 34

This notion of architectural realism can be seen as a *répétition differente* of the theoretical field developed by Rogers, later by Rossi and Scolari and then adopted by Ticinese architects – mainly by Reichlin and Reinhart, Rossi's assistants and collaborators. While reflecting on their concerns with history, territory and autonomy, Steinmann used these notions to develop an original understanding of architectural realism. The theme was soon elaborated in the 1976 *archithese* editorial 'On the inherent reality of architecture', co-authored with Reichlin (Reichlin and Steinmann 1976: 3–11, AT). Together, they argued that realism implied an empirical understanding of architecture, whose ultimate aim was to be constructed and enjoyed in a material sense. The emphasis on built projects in the exhibition can be understood in the same sense. It was guided by the conviction that the 'inherent reality of architecture', in the terms of its own traditions, was sufficient to ensure its integration with the surrounding culture.

Difference through repetition

The *Tendenzen* exhibition marked a pivotal moment in the cross-fertilization of Italian theory on both sides of the Alps. Its autonomous theoretical construct formed the basis of the design methodology that was later adopted and adapted in northern Swiss architecture. Its first proponents were the generation of those born around 1950, who were ETH students at the time. Using the mimetic procedures of *répétition differente*, the intellectual transfer from Italian and Ticinese architecture anchored itself in the design methodology of German-Swiss practice, in particular in the morphological, typological and historical analysis of a project's location: 'taking stock of the site in terms of its architectural, and hence cultural, continuity' (Lucan and Steinmann 2001: 10). After a short period of implementation – with varying degrees of literalness – of the Platonic forms and northern Italian typologies of Rossi's architecture, his ETH students turned to the reworking of the local formal and typological motifs, as seen in the ordinary yet atmospheric propositions of *Analoge Architektur* (Lucan 2001: 44–51).

From reading the complex architectural and cultural 'realities' of sites, in the early 1980s Swiss architects started to produce heterogeneous designs that directly responded to multifaceted contexts, such as Diener & Diener's St Alban Tal (1981–6) and Herzog & de Meuron's Photographic Studio Frei (1981–2) (see Fig. 4.6). Gradually, semiological subtexts and literal interpretations of historical forms became secondary to the seductive material qualities of constructed architecture, leading in the late 1980s and early 1990s to an emphasis on the object-like qualities of buildings – as seen in Herzog & de Meuron Ricola Storage in Laufen (1986), Diener & Diener's Administration Building in Picassoplatz (1987–93) or Peter Zumthor's Thermal Baths in Vals (1996). In 1991, Marcel Meili saw Swiss architecture as oscillating between autonomy and culture: 'our incursions into the world of the ordinary and the everyday constitute a search for collective meanings ... this research attempts to recover the traces of an identity in the affected mobility of our contemporary culture' (Meili 1991: 22, AT).

Developing his research at the interface between design and criticism, Steinmann became one of the most important commentators on the Swiss architecture of this generation. As editor of *archithese* between 1980 and 1986, he pursued a number of strategies in order to connect present practice and reflection onto the past. Using the journal's thematic format, he produced monographic issues on historical figures attached to regional contexts, in Switzerland and abroad (Hans Schmidt, Franz Scheibler, Haefeli Moser Steiger, Kay Fisker), initiated discussions and interviews with contemporary Swiss architects and investigated the cultural associations of construction materials as architectural and art media – concrete, timber, glass. Characteristically, Steinmann endorsed the articulation of concepts as a way to sustain formal production, and examined the cultural resonance of images and built forms. His surveys of contemporary architecture covered projects of many stripes, from the high-tech projects of Theo Hotz to the deliberately ordinary houses of Michael Adler; but most actively he promoted the work of emergent practices such as Herzog & de Meuron, Peter Zumthor, Diener & Diener, Burkhalter Sumi and Gigon Guyer (Steinmann 2003).[10] In the late 1990s, his position as a spokesperson of Swiss architecture was challenged by the growing divergence of approaches. However, his insistence that design decisions must be based on some form of explicit intellectual positioning, already fully formed by 1975, left an indelible mark on the conceptual turn of subsequent Swiss architecture. As such, Steinmann's written oeuvre about built things contains an interesting paradox. By compelling architects to articulate their ideas in writing, he became associated with a theoretical stance that appropriated their built works in the construction of its own legitimacy.[11]

FIG. 4.6 *Diener & Diener, St Albal-Tal, Basel (1981–6)* – répétition differente *in German-Swiss architecture. Different aspects of this residential complex respond to various found conditions on the site. The facades are a synthesis of interwar Basel modernism, Swiss Timber modernism and industrial vernacular. Source: Courtesy of Diener & Diener, Basel.*

At its time, the *Tendenzen* exhibition outlined critical boundaries between Switzerland's culturally distinct regions, between the practice and criticism of architecture and between its concrete embodiments and their representation in text and images. Its legacy is still perceptible in current

Swiss production, described by Andrea Wiegelmann as oscillating between 'two antipodes: on the one side an autonomous, self-referential, occasionally ironic architecture; on the other, an analogous position' (Wiegelmann 2017: 74, AT). To be sure, the attempt to bring this architecture under one identifiable banner would be as futile as trying to subsume the plurality of the Ticinese *Tendenzen* under a singular intellectual format. However, one should not underestimate the power of theoretical production to conceptualize a more complex reality into seductive, easily digestible interpretations. The *Tendenzen* exhibition illustrates the effort to bridge a formally heterogeneous production through a coherent theoretical construct. The attempt to extract a general theory out of Ticinese architecture did not sufficiently address its historical and cultural conditioning, or its inability to transcend its middle-class clientele and artisanal status. Rather, the exhibition and its theoretical justification were instrumental in the creation of a 'Ticino school' myth, which was outlived by the autonomous theory and design methods it helped generate.

Notes

1. All translations of non-English quotes, henceforth marked AT, are the author's own. All non-marked quotes are taken from English-language editions.
2. The exhibition installation, catalogue production and its subsequent rehangings throughout Europe were coordinated by Thomas Boga; Steinmann was responsible for its intellectual content.
3. The catalogue's international demand is apparent in the expansion of print runs: from 500 copies in the first edition (1975) to 738 in the second edition (1976), which included the translation in Italian and English of the texts originally published in German, to 1,500 copies for the third edition (1977). The continued demand of the catalogue and its legendary status was demonstrated by the 2010 facsimile reprint of 1,500 copies.
4. Regarding the Swiss reaction to Rossi, Steinmann recounts that he was invited by Heinz Ronner to curate the exhibition on Ticinese architecture during the dinner following the vernissage of Aldo Rossi's (and John Hejduk's) show at ETH Zurich in December 1973. Ronner's personal interest in Ticinese architecture is revealed in notes of the meetings he had in late 1973 and during 1974 with Luigi Snozzi on this topic (gta Archiv, ETH Zurich).
5. For example, the Bellinzona public baths (Aurelio Galfetti, Flora Ruchat and Ivo Trümpy, 1967–70) and the competition entry for the EPFL Lausanne campus in Dorigny (Mario Botta, Tita Carloni, Aurelio Galfetti, Flora Ruchat and Luigi Snozzi, 1970). ETH alumni were more naturally drawn towards joint endeavours.
6. Subsequently, Steinmann's career as editor of *archithese* (1980–6) was focused on articulating the intellectual positions of Swiss practitioners, whom he repeatedly encouraged to justify the ideas behind the production of forms. Also see Salm and Steinmann, 2016.

7   'The architectonic intervention does not provide the opportunity of building on a SITE, but rather provides the tools for building THAT SITE.'
8   This emphasis on the autonomy of architecture, as opposed to other forms of knowledge, would have had a considerable impact on Swiss architectural training due to the long-term involvement of Ticinese actors with ETH, as well as EPFL Lausanne. Some of the original protagonists of the Tendenzen exhibition, Fabio Reinhart, Dolf Schnebli, Flora Ruchat and Mario Campi, were or became professors at ETH.
9   Aldo Rossi, 'L'architettura della raggione come architettura di tendenza', in Manlio Brusatin (ed.), *Illuminismo e architettura del '700 Veneto': Catalogo della mostra, 31 Agosto–9 Novembre 1969,* Venice: Castelfranco Veneto, 1969, 7–15. The author is grateful to Luca Ortelli for bringing this text to her attention.
10 For an overview of these contributions see, e.g., the essays 'Neuere Architektur in der Deutschen Schweiz' (1991), 93–109; 'Die Gegenwärtigkeit der Dinge' (1994), 111–31; 'Die Unterwäsche von Madonna' (1997), 209–25, collected in Steinmann 2003.
11 I thank editor Ricardo Agarez for bringing this paradox to my attention. After retiring from teaching the history and theory of architecture at EPFL Lausanne (1987–2007), Steinmann returned to practice in a collaborative project with Diener & Diener for the expansion of the Stadtmuseum Aarau (2007–15). He is currently President of the Basel Stadtbildkommission, which controls the design quality of architectural projects in the city.

References

Bachmann, D. (1986), 'Gründer, Schüler, Epigonen', *du: Die Zeitschrift für Kunst und Kultur* 46, no. 8: 66–72.

Boga, T. and M. Steinmann (eds) (1975), *Tendenzen – Neuere Architektur im Tessin,* Zurich: ETH Zurich.

Boga, T. and M. Steinmann (eds) (1976), *Tendenzen – Neuere Architektur im Tessin,* 2nd edition with translations in Italian and English, Zurich: ETH Zurich.

Boga, T. and M. Steinmann (eds) (2010/1977), *Tendenzen – Neuere Architektur im Tessin,* reprint of 3rd edition, Basel: Birkhäuser.

Botta, M. (1976), 'Academic High School in Morbio Inferiore: Intervention Criteria and Design Objectives', in T. Boga and M. Steinmann (eds), *Tendenzen – Neuere Architektur im Tessin,* 160, Zurich: ETH Zurich.

Campi, M., F. Pessina and N. Piazzoli (1976), 'Montebello Castle in Bellinzona', in T. Boga and M. Steinmann (eds), *Tendenzen – Neuere Architektur im Tessin,* 162, Zurich: ETH Zurich.

Cohen, J.-L. (1998), 'The Italophiles at Work', in K. M. Hays (ed.), *Architecture Theory since 1968,* 508–20, Cambridge, MA: MIT Press.

Dal Co, F. (1977), 'Critique d'une exposition', *L'architecture d'aujourd'hui* 190: 58–60.

Davidovici, I. (2012), *Forms of Practice: German-Swiss Architecture 1980–2000,* Zurich: gta Verlag.

Deleuze, G. (2014), *Difference and Repetition*, trans. Paul Patton, London: Bloomsbury, 7.
Disch, P. (ed.) (1991), *Architektur in der Deutschen Schweiz 1980–1990*, Lugano: Verlag ADV.
Durisch G. (1976), 'House in Riva San Vitale', in T. Boga and M. Steinmann (eds), *Tendenzen – Neuere Architektur im Tessin*, 160, Zurich: ETH Zurich.
Frampton, K. (1978), 'Mario Botta and the School of the Ticino', *Oppositions* 14: 1–25.
Fumagalli, P. (1995), 'L'architettura degli anni Settanta nel Ticino', *Kunst + Architektur in der Schweiz = Art + architecture en Suisse = Arte + architettura in Svizzera* 45, no. 1: 28–35.
Hanisch R. and S. Spier (2009), '"History is not the Past but Another Mightier Presence": the founding of the Institute for the History and Theory (gta) at the Eidgenössische Technische Hochschule (ETH) Zurich and its effects on Swiss architecture', *Journal of Architecture* 14, no. 6: 667–70.
Hays, K. M. (ed.) (1998), *Architecture Theory since 1968*, Cambridge, MA: MIT Press.
Huet, B. (ed.) (1977), 'La "tendenza", ou l'architecture de la raison comme architecture de tendance', *L'architecture d'aujourd'hui* 190: 47–70.
Lucan, J. (ed.) (2001), *A Matter of Art: Contemporary Architecture in Switzerland*, Paris: Centre Culturel Suisse; Basel, Boston and Berlin: Birkhäuser.
Lucan, J. and M. Steinmann (2001), 'Obsessions: Conversation between Jacques Lucan and Martin Steinmann', in J. Lucan (ed.), *A Matter of Art: Contemporary Architecture in Switzerland*, 8–25, Paris: Centre Culturel Suisse; Basel, Boston and Berlin: Birkhäuser.
Meili, M. (1991), 'Ein paar Bauten, viele Pläne', in P. Disch (ed.), *Architektur in der Deutschen Schweiz 1980–1990*, 22–7, Lugano: Verlag ADV.
Moravánszky A. and J. Hopfengärtner (eds) (2011), *Aldo Rossi und die Schweiz: Architektonische Wechselwirkungen*, Zurich: gta Verlag.
Nakamura, T. (ed.) (1976), *A+U* 69, no. 9: 23–145.
Reichlin, B. and F. Reinhart (1976), 'Two Houses', in T. Boga and M. Steinmann (eds), *Tendenzen – Neuere Architektur im Tessin*, 163, Zurich: ETH Zurich.
Reichlin. B. and M. Steinmann (1976), 'Zum Problem der innerarchitektonischen Wirklichkeit', *archithese* 19: 3–11.
Reichlin. B. and M. Steinmann (1977), 'Critique d'une critique', *L'architecture d'aujourd'hui* 190: 58–60.
Risch, G. (1975), 'Tendenzen: neuere Architektur im Tessin', *Schweizerische Bauzeitung SIA-Heft* 93, no. 9: 815–16.
Rogers, E. N. (1997a), 'Elogio della tendenza', in *Esperienza dell'architettura*, 88–90, Milan: Skira. Originally published in *Domus* 216 (1946).
Rogers, E. N. (1997b), 'Continuità', in *Esperienza dell'architettura*, 92–95, Milan: Skira. Originally published in *Casabella-Continuità* 199 (1953).
Ronner, H. (1975), 'Zur Lage der Architektur im Tessin', in M. Steinmann (ed.), *Tendenzen – Neuere Architektur im Tessin*, 3–8, Zurich: ETH Zurich.
Rossi, A. (1969), 'L'architettura della raggione come architettura di tendenza', in M. Brusatin (ed.), *Illuminismo e architettura del '700 Veneto': Catalogo della mostra, 31 Agosto–9 Novembre 1969*, 7–15, Venice: Castelfranco Veneto.
Rossi, A. (1976), 'Une éducation réaliste', *archithese* 19: 25–6.

Scolari, M. (1998/1973), 'The New Architecture and the Avant-Garde', in K. M. Hays (ed.), *Architecture Theory since 1968*, 126–45, Cambridge, MA: MIT Press.
Snozzi, L. (1976), 'Design Motivation', in T. Boga and M. Steinmann (eds), *Tendenzen – Neuere Architektur im Tessin*, 164, Zurich: ETH Zurich.
Steinmann, M. (1976a), 'Reality as History: Notes for a Discussion of Realism in Architecture', in T. Boga and M. Steinmann (eds), *Tendenzen – Neuere Architektur im Tessin*, 2nd edition with translations in Italian and English, 155, Zurich: ETH Zurich.
Steinmann, M. (1976b), 'Reality as History: Notes for a Discussion of Realism in Architecture', *A+U* 69, no. 9: 31–4.
Steinmann, M. (1991), 'Neuere Architektur in der Deutschen Schweiz', in P. Disch (ed.), *Architektur in der Deutschen Schweiz 1980–1990*, 10–17, Lugano: Verlag ADV.
Steinmann, M. (1998/1976), 'Reality as History: Notes for a Discussion of Realism in Architecture', in K. M. Hays (ed.), *Architecture Theory since 1968*, 248–53, Cambridge, MA: MIT Press.
Steinmann, M. (2003), *Forme Forte. Écrits / Schriften 1972–2002*, Basel, Boston and Berlin: Birkhäuser.
Steinmann, M. and K. Salm (2016), 'Ich wollte Architekten zum Nachdenken über ihre Arbeit bringen', radio interview, SRF, Monday, 13 June 2016, https://www.srf.ch/kultur/kunst/ich-wollte-architekten-zum-nachdenken-ueber-ihre-arbeit-bringen.
Tschanz, M. (1998), 'Tendenzen und Konstruktionen', in A. Meseure, M. Tschanz and W. Wang (eds), *Schweiz*, 45–53, Munich: Prestel.
von Moos, S. (1969), 'New Directions in Swiss Architecture?', in J. Bachmann and S. von Moos (eds), *New Directions in Swiss Architecture*, 11–40, New York: Brazilier.
Wiegelmann, A. (2017), 'Justierungsprozesse', *archithese* 2: 74–8.

PART TWO
Imprints and Undercurrents

CHAPTER FIVE

Royston Landau and the Research Programmes of Architecture

Jasper Cepl

Introduction

In architectural discourse, Royston Landau (1927–2001) ranks among the most original figures of his time (see Fig. 5.1). As Head of the Graduate School at the Architectural Association from 1974 to 1993, he played a decisive role in architectural education.[1] Though the Graduate School with its shorter and much smaller programmes never became as important as the Diploma School – which we likely have in mind when talking about the AA – Landau contributed his share to enhancing the institution's lively atmosphere. Francis Duffy, in his obituary for the *Guardian*, asserts that Landau was among those who turned the AA 'from a fine, but limited, professional school of architecture into an international powerhouse' (Duffy 2001). In an obituary for the *Architects' Journal*, Dennis Sharp gets more specific, when he describes Landau's importance by acknowledging the 'considerable intellectual clout' Landau had given to AA's Graduate School (Sharp 2001).

While his role as an educator would have given reason enough to examine his life and work, the purpose of this chapter is to draw attention to his writings. Rather than exploring the educational settings Landau belonged to, it will re-evaluate the *ideas* he brought into them. As in his writings, Landau contributed tremendously to reflecting on the architectural culture to which he belonged. He was looking for new ways to understand its structures, and introduced ideas from other disciplines to do so.

FIG. 5.1 *Portrait of Royston Landau (1988). Photographer: Valerie Bennett. Source: Courtesy of Architectural Association Photo Library.*

Particularly fruitful were his inquiries into the philosophy of science, which generally had a huge impact on architectural discourse after 1945, and particularly in the early 1960s, when architectural academia first developed an interest in the philosophy of Karl Popper (1902–94) and later in the further developments of the debate, namely in the writings of Thomas Kuhn (1922–96) and Imre Lakatos (1922–74).[2] But in critically applying their ideas to architecture, few others went as far as Landau or his friend Stanford Anderson, whose efforts will also be discussed. In architecture, most of those who referred to the philosophy of science were happy with quoting a bit of Popper and remained rather uncritical.

Architecture and philosophy in the twentieth century

Landau's was not the first or only attempt to secure arguments from the philosophy of science. In the 1920s, the Bauhaus, under Hannes Meyer, had established contacts with the neo-positivist *Wiener Kreis*, from which Popper's – similar, yet decisively different – arguments sprang (see Galison 1990; Krukowski 1992). In this context, the idea of *Neue Sachlichkeit* has been put in parallel with philosophical discourse (see Dahms 2004). Yet, while there is substantial research on the close ties then established between architecture and the philosophy of science, no such attention has been paid to the developments after 1945. Some of the lacunae in our understanding may hopefully be filled in here.

While in the 1920s, architecture and philosophy had first aligned in a common quest for modernity, at the time Landau started to build his arguments times had changed. Modern architecture was well established and what was needed now was doubt rather than reassurance. In contrast to the neo-positivist stance cherished by the Bauhaus, the arguments now imported from Popper's thinking served to build a critical approach to modernity. They helped to understand modern architecture as a series of experiments that needed to be critically studied if progress was to be hoped for. And while Meyer et al. had been interested in making architectural practice more scientific, Landau (and his peers) wanted to understand more clearly what architects did. Meyer had wanted to reinvent practice; Landau wanted to understand it, and improve it along the way. In this context, Popper offered essential support.

Karl Popper and the architects

To architects, Popper's ideas about the 'logic of scientific discovery', just as his support of an 'open society', offered forceful arguments for reconsidering the role of the architect – both in his relationship to history and tradition and in light of contemporary attempts to turn the design process into an activity governed by procedures of factual analysis and synthetic decision-making.

With his forceful rejection of induction, Popper became one of the most important references in the area of 'design research', because his claim that science progressed as an interplay of 'conjectures and refutations' allowed the re-establishment of a notion of creativity that was now quasi scientifically grounded: to move ahead, the designer needed an idea just as much as a scientist needed a theory or a hypothesis. This helped to overcome earlier, futile attempts to arrive at designs in a process leading from analysis to synthesis.

But unlike most others in architecture then inspired by the philosophy of science, Landau also carefully studied those who built on Popper's work to elaborate it, such as Kuhn, or, most importantly, Lakatos. The latter's *Methodology of Scientific Research Programmes* (1978) became the prototype for Landau's inquiries into the structures of architectural discourse.

Enter Stanford Anderson

Landau's initial interest in Popper had been inspired by a chance encounter at the end of the 1950s, when he met Stanford Anderson (1934–2016), who became his most important ally in the quest of introducing the advances in the philosophy of science into architectural discourse. They met in an architecture office in San Francisco, where both were working at the time. Landau had come to the US after graduating from the AA, where he had studied from 1952 to 1954 (after a stint at the Bartlett, where he had begun his studies) (Landau 1954; Duffy 2001; Sharp 2001). He stayed in the US until 1960, working in various offices.

At the time he met Landau, Anderson, though still studying architecture at Berkeley, was already pondering a PhD, yet uncertain whether to tend to philosophy or art history. While he finally decided in favour of history, he was still equally interested in philosophy (see Anderson, quoted in Frank 2010: 214–15). At Berkeley he also studied with Paul Feyerabend, who introduced him to Popper in the autumn of 1958 (see Anderson 1965: 327, n. 15). Feyerabend, an Austrian by birth, had just come from England, where he had studied and worked with Popper. He came to stay at Berkeley, where he increasingly moved away from his teacher to eventually oppose him – assuming a position of methodological anarchism, which he most fervently advocated in his *Against Method* of 1975. But at the time, he must have been an apostle of Popper's ideas: Anderson later recalled that he and Landau 'enthusiastically pursued Popperian studies' (Anderson, quoted in Frank 2010: 214) at the time. Alas, it remains unclear what these discussions were about, and we only find evidence of their substance a few years later, after Landau had returned to London.

Exploring the 'Context for Decision Making'

Back home, Landau started to teach at the AA. There, he organized a conference on 'The Context for Decision Making in the Arts and Sciences' in February 1963 – with Anderson as one of the key speakers. The conference explored what architecture could learn from the philosophy of science, and namely from Karl Popper. Landau even invited two close confidants of Popper's – Ernst Gombrich (1909–2001) and William Bartley (1934–90) – to win his audience over.

In 1965, Landau published papers arising from that conference in a series of articles in the *Architectural Association Journal*. In a brief introduction, he emphasized that the common feature of the papers was their relatedness to Popper's 'critical approach' (1965b: 212).[3] Though Landau does not specify what he meant by this – he was probably alluding to *The Critical Approach to Science and Philosophy*, a *Festschrift* for Popper, published in 1964, which he cites in his writings – his introduction shows what he hoped Popper's ideas would provide for architectural discourse.

Landau argued that there was a 'crisis in architectural knowledge' caused by its 'accelerating expansion'; in the light of 'growing complexities', he continued, 'responsible decision making' had 'gradually become more and more difficult' (1965b: 212). According to Landau, the architect faced a 'dilemma':

> ... either he must attempt to recognize the ever-increasing knowledge of the present age and set himself the task of building all that is known into his problems and then responding to this knowledge in his designs, a task which, using present techniques, is complicated and ungainly, or else he is obliged to seriously oversimplify the state of knowledge by using an arbitrary system in selecting what he considers to be most relevant.
>
> LANDAU 1965b: 212

For Landau, practice had shown the limits or even the unfeasibility of an analytical approach based on accumulating facts. Trying to find a new approach to the problem of design, he argued that 'there appeared to exist, within the philosophic and scientific disciplines, highly articulated theoretical systems, as well as attitudes towards knowledge, which could help to establish a basis for reconsideration' (Landau 1965b: 212). He highlighted Popper's 'advocacy' that scientific knowledge was 'a special case of ordinary knowledge and that the order governing the growth of scientific knowledge need not be considered exclusive to science' (Landau 1965b: 212). Based on the license Popper had granted to apply his arguments to fields outside of its original realm, Landau and his allies now set out to reconsider the knowledge of the architect by looking for an order like the one Popper had found in scientific discovery.

Anderson on modern traditions

The wealth of inspiration Popper had provided is particularly evident in the ideas discussed by Anderson, who in the meantime had entered Columbia University to work on a PhD about Peter Behrens and who at the time of the conference briefly also taught at the AA, before starting to work at MIT later in 1963. Anderson's paper was titled 'Architecture and Tradition That Isn't "Trad, Dad"' (1965) – a reference to Reyner Banham's article, 'Coventry Cathedral – Strictly "Trad, Dad"' (1962), an unfavourable account of one of Britain's most notable rebuilding efforts. Opposing Banham's 'modernist' view of tradition as something debilitating that architects had to overcome, Anderson suggested that tradition was 'a necessary, common dynamic ground upon which we operate' (Anderson

1965: 326). He posited that architects should rather be criticized for 'their self-righteous belief in their independence from tradition', and demurred: 'This supposed independence often led them into blind submission to traditions which they might otherwise have critically observed and overthrown' (Anderson 1965: 326).

Anderson justified the need for a critical analysis of tradition by quoting from Popper's essay, 'Towards a Rational Theory of Tradition', in which the author had explained that in society traditions provided the same kind of order that theories provided in science: 'Just as the invention of myths or theories in the field of natural science has a function – that of helping us to bring order into the events of nature – so has the creation of traditions in the field of society' (Popper 1963: 123, quoted in Anderson 1965: 328). To this quote Anderson added a footnote, to clarify that the 'creation of traditions' was not quite to the point, and explained, 'Just as the scientist invents a new theory, but must see that the community accepts it before it is effective; so also in social or cultural matters, one invents a new theory or a new way of doing things but must await more general acceptance before it is "traditional"' (Anderson 1965: 328, n. 18). Though Anderson himself does not make this very clear, his comment explained how modern architecture may have arrived at the false assumption that it had left tradition behind. Modern architecture had inevitably established a new tradition, once its ideas had become accepted; a tradition that had become a driving force, even if many were unwilling to acknowledge this.

To explain his point, Anderson sketched out how Popper's logic of conjecture and refutation could illuminate the traditions of the Modern Movement. He claimed that it would help to evaluate and readjust modern architecture's agenda, if one saw the conjectural nature of its proposals, something he felt had not been properly done:

> In architecture, in the twentieth century, we have not lacked for conjectures, nor for criticism. But I would suggest that we have failed to establish a rational attitude towards our conjectures and criticism. What are only conjectures have been put forward as utopian panaceas and supported with absolutist fervour. Corroboration is always sought; never falsification.
>
> ANDERSON 1965: 330

Applying Popper's logic of scientific discovery to architecture thus allowed Anderson to reclaim a productive relationship with the past, by showing that twentieth-century architecture was bound to its own traditions. To illustrate his claim, Anderson described the developments in mass housing as a series of conjectures, from the *Mietskaserne* to Park Hill in Sheffield, then one of England's latest and most ambitious council housing estates (which we may not find as enticing as Anderson did in his day, though one could say that, in terms of mass housing, at least it's a better conjecture than the *Mietskaserne*).

Landau on induction and design method

Anderson would further develop the arguments sketched out here in his writings on modern architecture's history. Similarly, Landau gave a first hint at what would keep occupying him, namely: the question of how contemporary practice could be framed intellectually. Though he hadn't himself contributed to the 'Context for Decision Making' conference, he now added his ideas on the topic in the last instalment of the series. As stated in a brief introduction to his contribution, he had further developed his thinking in what is described as 'a follow-up seminar called "The Philosophy of Science – its relevances to architecture"'.[4] In 1964, he had presented the first version of his thoughts at MIT, where Anderson had started to teach in the meantime. In the essay that he eventually published as 'Towards a Structure for Architectural Ideas' (Landau 1965b), he shed more light on the issues he had raised in his introduction to the series.

Taking his cue from the 'thesis that a version of the problem of induction exists in the relationship between facts and designs' (Landau 1965b: 7), he first referred to Francis Bacon to illustrate the origins of the concept in philosophy. Distancing himself from the 'design-from-facts inductivists' (Landau 1965b: 11), Landau drew on Popper's theories to further explain why he thought design could not be based on gathered information. Here he raised the question of whether design in architecture could be considered 'a summation of a particular set of facts' and argued against this idea that this would preclude 'the possibility of the content of the design being greater than the content of the facts' (Landau 1965b: 9). He furthermore doubted that it was possible 'to define *all* the relevant data' for a design, and added that 'even if a building amounted to a complete summation of facts, and no more, and even if such a summation were possible, then the result would be a building that was obsolete a moment after it was completed, for it would have been built out of a fact situation which could not acknowledge that which it did not know' (Landau 1965b: 9).

Landau appealed to Popper to 'suggest the "conceptual" or "hypothesis" schema as an alternative' and, referring to D. G. Thornley (1963), showed that, in fact, deductive reasoning was already apparent in design discourse. Like Anderson before him, Landau then showed that traditions, as explained by Popper, played a vital role in solving design problems. Though, as Landau was predominantly occupied with refuting the idea of induction in design, in the text itself Popper did not feature as prominently as in Anderson's essay. It was the footnotes – in which Popper is the most quoted author – that showed the great influence his writings had had on Landau's argument.

Enter Imre Lakatos

These footnotes also showed that Landau had sought the personal advice of Lakatos—who became an increasingly important influence at that time (Landau 1965b: 7, n. 1).[5] Though it took some years for Lakatos's ideas to take the place of Popper's,[6] in the long run it was mainly Lakatos who provided guidance, for both Landau and Anderson.

At the time Landau first met him, Lakatos hadn't fully elaborated his own concepts, but by the beginning of the 1970s he would develop a model to describe how scientific communities were held together by 'research programmes' that provided them with a basic agenda – a 'hard core' – but also directed their activities in what Lakatos called 'heuristics'. Thereby Lakatos, whose ideas will be examined in greater detail below, offered a model that could be adopted to understand the inner workings of architectural discourse more precisely. His concept of 'research programmes' offered a way to disentangle the premises and the actions, something Popper's rather solitary conjecture/refutation scheme hadn't been able to explain. The 'research programme' also allowed the exploration of the structure in what Popper had simply subsumed as 'tradition': it could both explain the historical and structural dimension of scientific discovery more clearly and hence also offer new perspectives to explore architectural 'discovery' as well.

Anderson later applied Lakatos's ideas to architectural history, looking for research programmes in modernism. His approach was showcased in *Design Studies* in 1984, with a selection of three studies, one done by Anderson, the others by two students under his tutelage.[7] Introducing the work he and his students Libero Andreotti and Vasilia A. Metallinou had done, Anderson explained that they had sought to investigate 'whether a qualified version of Imre Lakatos's methodology of scientific research programmes may provide an explanatory and normative model of design processes' (Anderson 1984a: 147).[8] While he conceded that they hadn't demonstrated a full-fledged application of this idea, he still expressed the hope that this work could 'provide an anticipation' (Anderson 1984a: 150) of an analysis according to Lakatos's methodology.

In his own essay, Anderson tended to the early work of Le Corbusier, trying to explain how Le Corbusier, through a series of designs, arrived at a research programme that was outlined in his 'Five Points of a New Architecture'. Andreotti explored Kahn's 'remarkably Lakatosian design theory', as Anderson described it in his introduction (Anderson 1984a: 150), while Metallinou gave an account of 'Regionalism as an Architectural Research Programme in the Work of Dimitris and Suzana Antonakakis' (Anderson 1984b; Andreotti 1984; Metallinou 1984).

At the same time, Landau – in what he also called 'positional analysis' – turned the concept into a method that would help understand the values and beliefs implicit in contemporary practice. By 1984, the year in which

Anderson showed how to apply Lakatos to architectural history, Landau was able to analyse contemporary practice with a full-fledged Lakatosian approach (which also incorporated Foucauldian discourse analysis and other influences).[9] As will be shown in greater detail below, Landau picked up Lakatos to explore the 'pluralism' apparent in contemporary architecture, and the problem of 'relativism' that ensued, and set out to explain the coexistence of 'approaches' and how those were structured.

Interlude: the future of practice

Though, taking his cue from his interest in practice, Landau first tended to an inquiry about the changes and challenges the profession faced at the time. He gave a well-informed account of the latest developments in his *New Directions in British Architecture*, published in 1968 (see Fig. 5.2). It was a remarkable book that set out both to describe 'the logic of a situation' and to explore the 'new directions' (Landau 1968: 15) that deserved the name, even if they questioned what architecture was, as did the projects by Archigram or Cedric Price, which Landau foregrounded.

New Directions was the only book Landau wrote, but in a steady stream of articles, and through guest-editing journals, he kept contributing to architectural discourse. In September 1969, he guest-edited an issue of *Architectural Design* entitled 'Despite popular demand ... AD is thinking about architecture and planning', in which he collected contributions by the likes of Anderson, Lakatos and Popper, as well as by Nicholas Negroponte, Gordon Pask and Cedric Price. A 'sequel' issue, for October 1972, on 'Complexity (or how to see the wood in spite of the trees)', further explored the potential of systems theory (Landau 1972a, b). Apart from that, he contributed to the 'sector' section that was part of *Architectural Design* from January 1970 to November 1973. Steve Parnell summarizes that Landau was 'effectively *AD*'s "cybernetics" correspondent' (Parnell 2011: 296).

After his appointment as Head of the Graduate School in 1974, Landau at first remained concerned with such new approaches to practice. In an *Architectural Design* issue that he edited on 'The individual in an institutionalised world' in 1976, a brief CV states that he was interested in 'problems of housing in complex organisational settings' (*Architectural Design* 46: 75). With Cedric Price, who was a close friend, he seems to have been working on a book on *Housing in a World of Change*, which was announced in the same issue of *Architectural Design* but never came to fruition (Landau, 1976a, b).[10]

Instead, Landau eventually chose to return to his earlier interests in the general structure of discourse – maybe because focusing on reflection rather than action was more in line with the agenda of a graduate school. The questions Landau had brought to the fore with 'The Context for Decision Making' conference in 1963 again became the focus for much of his later

FIG. 5.2 Cover of Landau's New Directions in British Architecture (1968). Jacket design by Toshihiro Katayama.

work: how can we understand how architects decide when designing, and how are they reasoning in general? He returned to these concerns with a new level of understanding, adopting Lakatos's model of the structure of science and using it to clarify how architects set up their agendas.

Lessons from Lakatos

Lakatos had wanted to find a model for science that was more refined than Popper's (rather simplistic) logic, which had rightly been criticized, mainly by Kuhn and Feyerabend. Kuhn's *The Structure of Scientific Revolutions* (1962) had shown that scientific communities, in fact, did not behave the way they ought to according to Popper's 'conjecture and refutation' scheme, but that they were rather reluctant to change their course, even in light of counter-evidence; while Feyerabend had argued that there wasn't much logic in scientific discovery anyway. Either way, both critics offered nothing productive for Popper's cause: while Kuhn had rather dealt with the sociology of science, Feyerabend was willing to altogether ditch the idea of looking for structure in the production of knowledge.

To overcome such attacks on Popper's systematic inquiry, Lakatos was looking for a better model to explain the inner workings of real-life science. He briefly explained his attempt to frame scientific discourse as follows:

> First I claim that the typical descriptive unit of great scientific achievements is not an isolated hypothesis but rather a research programme. Science is not simply trial and error, a series of conjectures and refutations ... Newtonian science, for instance, is not simply a set of four conjectures – the three laws of mechanics and the law of gravitation. These four laws constitute only the 'hard core' of the Newtonian programme. But this hard core is tenaciously protected from refutation by a vast 'protective belt' of auxiliary hypotheses. And, even more importantly, the research programme also has a 'heuristic', that is, a powerful problem-solving machinery, which, with the help of sophisticated mathematical techniques, digests anomalies and even turns them into positive evidence. For instance, if a planet does not move exactly as it should, the Newtonian scientist checks his conjectures concerning atmospheric refraction, concerning the propagation of light in magnetic storms, and hundreds of other conjectures which are all part of the programme. He may even invent a hitherto unknown planet and calculate its position, mass and velocity in order to explain the anomaly.
>
> LAKATOS 1978: 4

Lakatos also differentiated between 'positive' and 'negative' heuristics that either provide rules for what to do or what to leave in the practice of science, and he claimed that all theories 'are born refuted and die refuted' (1978: 5).

More important than the logic of conjecture and refutation was whether a theory could predict new observations one would not have made without it. The difference between a 'progressive' and a 'degenerating' research programme was that in the former, 'theory leads to the discovery of hitherto unknown novel facts', while in the latter, 'theories are fabricated only in order to accommodate known facts' (Lakatos 1978: 5).

This explanation allowed Lakatos to fill the black box in Kuhn's argument with light: Kuhn had argued that, in the history of science, calm periods of 'normal science' were occasionally interrupted by turbulent times in which a 'paradigm shift' would eventually produce a new agenda for science – but he had not been able to convincingly describe the inner workings of these processes. Now Lakatos's model explained how science behaved in time: as long as a programme produced new insights, its hard core was protected and would not be questioned. It provided the agenda to stick to – despite its unresolved contradictions. Changes were necessary when this no longer was the case.

For Anderson and Landau, it was but a small step from here to an intellectual history of architecture that explained the succession of its ideas along similar lines. Like scientists, architects would need something to believe in, something that would direct their work and keep them on track even if under attack, or in light of failures. But did they not have research programmes as well – research programmes they were trying to explore in a series of designs?

Programmes in 'History and Theory'

The full impact of Lakatos's philosophy of science on Landau's thinking showed in the context of a new programme in 'History and Theory', established at the AA Graduate School in 1980 (see Fig. 5.3).[11] For this, Landau teamed up with Micha Bandini, who also became his partner until his death (Landau died of a heart attack in 2001, at the age of 74).[12] Together they also researched 'the underlying philosophies of current British architecture', sponsored by the RIBA:[13] it is in this context that Landau developed his most valuable ideas. As Landau outlined in a short note on 'Relativism and the Critical Present', published in the AA's *Projects Review* for 1982–3, he was particularly concerned with the proliferation of movements that coexisted in contemporary architecture, which he saw troubled by the potential arbitrariness that ensued:

> The topic of a pluralistic architectural world, with the problem of relativism looming over it, seems to suggest a criticism of the direction in which much in architecture appears to be going today – with the emergence of large numbers of small, low content, self-referential, relativistic movements, indifferent or unaware of the dimensions that

history has shown architecture to be capable of, and which are just as oblivious to history as they are to their own imminent demise.

LANDAU 1983: unpaginated

Between 1981 and 1984, Landau published a series of articles, in which he set out to provide a proper framework to analyse these trends with the help of Lakatos's *Research Programmes*, even if he would not criticize them as bitterly as here.

In his 'Notes on the Concept of an Architectural Position', published in *AA Files* 1 in 1981, Landau argued firmly along the lines of Lakatos's methodology. He suggested that an 'architectural position' was like a programme, and used Lakatos's model to shed light on the coexistence of different agendas in contemporary architecture. To explain his notion of an 'architectural position', Landau stated that architects 'hold a great variety of belief systems which they use in the production of their architecture and which are expressed in different ways' (1981–2: 112).

Comparing Léon Krier and Peter Cook, Landau outlined how both had very particular basic beliefs – a hard core – that remained unquestioned and provided the questions that had to be explored, as well as sets of rules telling them what to do or to leave, and what to test out in a series of designs. Landau asked, 'Could the positions of Leon Krier or Peter Cook be said to have inviolable statements or beliefs which they would be totally unwilling to abandon, and which would be present throughout their body of work?'

FIG. 5.3 *Group photo of faculty and participants in the 'History and Theory' programme at the AA, with Roy Landau on the left and Micha Bandini in the middle of the back row. Source: Architectural Association,* Projects Review 1982–83.

(1981–2: 112). He argued that Krier's 'axioms' amounted to a hard core that was 'constantly present': 'that urban architecture must be spatially articulated (in a specified way), and must take its forms from vernacular building and classical architecture and must be designed to be built by an anti-industrial building force ... and so on' (1981–2: 112). Cook's programme, he claimed, was 'neither expressed in the same way' nor was it 'of the same sort as Krier's', but, 'he – Cook – appears, however, to have a continuing commitment to an architectural exploration created out of a necessity to constantly re-invent new architectural forms, to be original, to use functionalism as a restraint and to maintain a love–hate relationship with technology' (1981–2: 112).

As a model for describing an architect's overarching agenda, the 'research programme' allowed Landau to explain the relationship between basic beliefs and individual action, and hence between theory – both explicit and implicit – and practice. As the comparison between Krier and Cook shows, it also served him as a method to explain differences in approach. Over the following years, Landau continued to elaborate on these ideas.

In 1984, in an issue of *UIA International Architect* (see Fig. 5.4) which showcased the work of his Graduate School, Landau gave the most comprehensive version of his adoption of Lakatos's approach. He again set out to analyse 'the programme of action' which resulted from an 'approach' or a 'position', this time being more specific about the consequences, that is, the heuristics involved. Landau now held that the negative heuristic that instructed the investigator 'never to tamper with the hardcore' was in fact 'very common in all architectural thinking', and explained:

> All architectural programmes have rules which forbid the holder from asking certain questions. The avant-garde has always rejected the conventional wisdom (precisely because it was conventional) and hence history; just as the architectural Modernists, who originated as part of the avant-garde, were to reject both history and that historical manifestation, decoration. The Post-Modernists reject Modernist principles and are formulated on that rejection. Thus, the programmes achieve direction from knowing where they do not wish to go.
>
> LANDAU 1984: 7

The positive heuristic, Landau continued, contained 'the operating rules about what the programme is looking for', and again, going for a similar juxtaposition, he explained that in 'a Leon Krier type of programme, the formal language will be stylistically specified: classical, axial, hierarchical, etc.', while the formal language of 'British high-tech' architecture included 'directives to display technological virtuosity, although not ... with a functional or economic compatibility' (1984: 7).

Seen in this way, describing an architect's position as if it were a research programme offers an interesting perspective: it directs us towards what

FIG. 5.4 *Cover of* UIA International Architect, *comprising the documentation of Landau's work on 'The Culture of Architecture: A Historiography of the Current Discourse' (1984).*

Landau later called 'dogmatic knowledge' (Landau 1996: 64).[14] Arguing that 'all programmes of action will contain two general classes of thought' (1996: 63), he then differentiated between a 'positional hardcore' on the one hand and 'rejection rules' and 'operational rules' on the other (1996: 64).

Landau thus succeeded in showing how positions depend on different values and beliefs, how these lead to different courses of action and how individual designs are embedded in systems of values. Though Landau never managed to bring his inquiry into comprehensive form, he made valuable suggestions for the still ongoing, and recently more topical, research into the 'forms of knowledge' employed by artists or designers. That was Landau's interest: to find out what the knowledge of the architect is made of.

Coda

Today Lakatos's impact on architecture most clearly echoes in Patrik Schumacher's argument that parametricism as a 'style' was equal to a 'research programme' (Schumacher 2008: 12). Drawing heavily on Lakatos, he clearly described the agenda of the AA's Design Research Lab (DRL) along the lines of a research programme, down to the details of the heuristics involved, for instance claiming that:

> The defining heuristics of parametricism are fully reflected in the taboos and dogmas of the DRL design culture:
> *Negative heuristics: avoid familiar typologies, avoid platonic/hermetic objects, avoid clear-cut zones/territories, avoid repetition, avoid straight lines, avoid right angles, avoid corners . . .*
> *Positive heuristics: hybridise, morph, deterritorialise, deform, iterate, use splines, nurbs, generative components, script rather than model . . .*
>
> SCHUMACHER 2008: 12; ellipses and italics in the original

While Schumacher sets out to impregnate his architecture and make it unassailable – you cannot judge the success or failure of an individual design, as it is part of a research programme, and so on – Landau himself was less narrow-minded. For him, Lakatosian thinking rather provided a framework that offered a kind of enlightenment and allowed critical examination of contemporary architecture in order to understand how theory and practice were intertwined. And even if Landau was in the centre of the debate, he was no ruthless advocate of avant-gardism; rather, he was interested in exploring the mechanisms of the profession, a profession in which all sorts of agendas seemed to coexist. For this quest, drawing on the philosophy of science proved extremely productive.

Though I should close by conceding that the questions Landau addressed in his much more hands-on field remained less easy to answer than in the more clearly outlined area of scientific research. After all, Lakatos was looking at a profession dedicated to improving our understanding of the (presumably immutable) laws of nature – while Landau tried to unveil the much less predictable rules of cultural productions. Disentangling their mechanisms was much more complicated than understanding natural science, where defining the problem situation is much simpler, and scientific communities will hence agree on a research programme more easily.

The positions held by groups of architects or even by individual designers will always remain more volatile. That being said, if one does consider parametricism as a research programme, wouldn't one have to say that it is a degenerating one, while others – say, sustainability – will certainly have a longer lease of life? Seriously asking this question is beyond the scope of this chapter, though it hopefully suggests that considering changing agendas in architecture along the lines of research programmes may still prove fruitful.

In the end, we may be well advised to pick up where Landau (and Anderson) left off.

Notes

1 Before assuming that role, Landau had taught at the AA, the University of Pennsylvania (1969–73), MIT and the Rhode Island School of Design. The establishment of the graduate school was part of a restructuring of the AA, which had been taken over by Alvin Boyarsky in 1971. For an account of these developments, see Jencks 1975. On Boyarsky, see Sunwoo 2012, with further references. By selecting Boyarsky, the AA had effectively decided to reinvent itself as a global player, independent from its locus, and set out to transform itself into a centre for avant-garde experimentalism. At the same time, the AA established a Graduate School that was first run by Paul Oliver, before Landau took over, having worked with Boyarsky before: Landau had contributed a 'Systems Seminar' to Boyarsky's IID Summer Session in 1970. See Sunwoo 2009: 42.
2 See Cepl 2018.
3 'All the papers to be published in this series, with the exception of Jack D. Cowan's "Some Principles Underlying the Mechanisation of Thought Processes" [see pp. 251–9 of the volume], are related in some degree to the critical approach of Karl Popper' (Landau 1965b: 212).
4 This only seems to be documented through this quotation from the (editor's?) introduction to Landau's essay. See Landau 1965b: 7.
5 Landau also acknowledged the support of Alan Musgrave (b. 1940), another important philosopher of science at the time.
6 In the *Architectural Design* issue he guest-edited in September 1969, Landau included an excerpt (Lakatos 1969) of Lakatos 1968–9.
7 That Anderson would keep exposing his students to Lakatos is apparent in the thesis work supervised by him. It is documented in https://dspace.mit.edu.
8 On Lakatos, see also Anderson 2011.
9 Landau also gave a brief description of Lakatos's methodology in general (Landau 1982). At the time, Landau also began to refer to Michel Foucault, who seems to have directed his focus back to the question of meta-levels, in relation to understanding discourse rather than contributing to it. Yet, while Foucault's ideas may have renewed his interest in the philosophy of science, the ideas he had picked up from Lakatos in the 1960s remained more important in the long run.
10 At the end of both articles an identical note stated that the book was to be published by Braziller.
11 Which is briefly described in the *AA Files* (1981–2: 111) as 'concerned with major architectural historians and their works, architectural theories both historical and current, and the problem of the architectural use of history'.
12 See Duffy 2011. On Bandini and her collaboration with Landau, see also the brief CV in *UIA International Architect* 1984: 3.

13 See a biographical note in *AA Files* 1981–2: 111: 'She has recently received an RIBA Research Award to carry out a study, together with Roy Landau, of the underlying philosophies of current British architecture.'
14 'Dogmatic knowledge, which by definition is not open to questioning, and which the philosopher Imre Lakatos called the hardcore of a programme, is what the programme is all about' (Landau 1996: 64).

References

AA Files 1 (Winter 1981–2).
Anderson, S. (1965), 'Architecture and Tradition that isn't "Trad, Dad"', *Architectural Association Journal* 80: 325–30.
Anderson, S. (1984a), 'Architectural Design as a System of Research Programmes', *Design Studies* 5: 146–50. Reprinted, merged with Anderson 1984b, in M. K. Hays (ed.) (1998), *Architecture Theory Since 1968*, 490–505, Cambridge, MA: MIT Press.
Anderson, S. (1984b), 'Architectural Research Programmes in the Work of Le Corbusier', *Design Studies* 5: 151–8.
Anderson, S. (2011), 'Rational Reconstructions and Architectural Knowledge', in K. Faschingeder, K. Jormakka, N. Korrek, O. Pfeifer and G. Zimmermann (eds), *Architecture in the Age of Empire / Die Architektur der Neuen Weltordnung: 11th Internationales Bauhaus-Kolloquium, 2010*, 163–75, Weimar: Universitätsverlag.
Andreotti, L. (1984), 'Conceptual and Artefactual Research Programmes in Louis I Kahn's Design of the Phillips Exeter Academy Library (1966–72)', *Design Studies* 5: 159–65.
Architectural Design 46 (1976).
Banham, R. (1962), 'Coventry Cathedral – Strictly "Trad, Dad"', *New Statesman* 63: 768–9.
Cepl, J. (2018), 'Architectural Design in the Interplay between *Conjectures and Refutations*: Karl Popper and the Architects', in S. Hildebrand, D. Mondini and R. Grignolo (eds), with Bruno Pedretti, *Architettura e saperi: Architecture and Knowledge*, 207–15, Mendrisio: Mendrisio Academy Press.
Dahms, H. (2004), 'Neue Sachlichkeit in the Architecture and Philosophy of the 1920s', in S. Awodey and C. Klein (eds), *Carnap Brought Home: The View from Jena*, 357–75, Chicago: Open Court.
Duffy, F. (2001), 'Royston Landau: Power behind an International Architecture School', *Guardian*, 20 November, https://www.theguardian.com/news/2001/nov/20/guardianobituaries.highereducation.
Frank, S. (2010), *IAUS. The Institute for Architecture and Urban Studies: An Insider's Memoir*, Bloomington, IN: Authorhouse.
Galison, P. (1990), 'Aufbau/Bauhaus: Logical Positivism and Architectural Modernism', *Critical Inquiry* 16: 709–52.
Jencks, C. (1975), '125 Years of Quasi Democracy', in J. Gowan (ed.), *A Continuing Experiment: Learning and Teaching at the Architectural Association*, 149–59, London: Architectural Press.
Krukowski, L. (1992), 'Aufbau and Bauhaus: A Cross-Realm Comparison', *Journal of Aesthetics and Art Criticism* 50: 197–209.

Kuhn, T. S. (1962), *The Structure of Scientific Revolutions*, Chicago: University of Chicago Press.
Lakatos, I. (1968–9), 'Criticism and the Methodology of Scientific Research Programmes', *Proceedings of the Aristotelian Society, New Series* 69: 149–86.
Lakatos, I. (1969), 'Sophisticated Versus Naive Methodological Falsificationism', *Architectural Design* 39: 482–3 (an excerpt of Lakatos 1968–9).
Lakatos, I. (1978), 'Introduction: Science and Pseudoscience', in I. Lakatos, *The Methodology of Scientific Research Programmes*, ed. J. Worral and G. Currie, 1–7, Cambridge: Cambridge University Press.
Landau, R. (1954), 'Central Criminal Court', *AA Journal* 69: 183–8.
Landau, R. (1965a) 'The Context for Decision Making: Introduction', *Architectural Association Journal* 80: 212.
Landau, R. (1965b), 'Towards a Structure for Architectural Ideas', *Arena: Architectural Association Journal* 81: 7–11.
Landau, R. (1968), *New Directions in British Architecture*, New York: George Braziller.
Landau, R. (1972a), 'Complexity and Complexing', *Architectural Design* 42: 608–10.
Landau, R. (1972b), 'On Russell Ackoff's Strategies of Management', *Architectural Design* 42: 635–6.
Landau, R. (1976a), 'Introduction: Individuals and Institutions', *Architectural Design* 46: 76–7.
Landau, R. (1976b), 'The Server and the Served in Housing', *Architectural Design* 46: 102–4.
Landau, R. (1982a), 'Methodology of Research Programmes', in B. Evans, J. A. Powell and R. J. Talbot (eds), *Changing Design*, 303–9, Chichester: John Wiley & Sons.
Landau, R. (1982b), 'Notes on the Concept of an Architectural Position', *AA Files* 1 (Winter 1981–2): 111–14.
Landau, R. (1983), 'Relativism and the Critical Present', *Architectural Association: Projects Review 1982–83* (unpaginated).
Landau, R. (1984), 'The Culture of Architecture: A Historiography of the Current Discourse', *UIA International Architect* 5: 6–9.
Landau, R. (1996), 'Architectural Discourse and Giedion', *Journal of Architecture* 1: 59–73.
Metallinou, V. A. (1984), 'Regionalism as an Architectural Research Programme in the Work of Dimitris and Suzana Antonakakis', *Design Studies* 5: 166–74.
Parnell, S. (2011), 'Architectural Design, 1954–1972: The Architectural Magazine's Contribution to the Writing of Architectural History', PhD dissertation, University of Sheffield, Sheffield, http://etheses.whiterose.ac.uk/id/eprint/14585.
Popper, K. R. (1963), 'Towards a Rational Theory of Tradition', in K. Popper, *Conjectures and Refutations: The Growth of Scientific Knowledge*, 120–35, London: Routledge and Kegan Paul.
Schumacher, P. (2008), 'Style as Research Programme', in T. Verebes (ed.), *DRL Ten: A Design Research Compendium*, 11–13, London: AA Publications.
Sharp, D. (2001), 'Remembering AA Intellectual and Teacher Royston Landau', *Architects' Journal*, 25 October, www.architectsjournal.co.uk/home/remembering-aa-intellectual-and-teacher-royston-landau/184948.article.
Sunwoo, I. (2009), 'Pedagogy's Progress: Alvin Boyarsky's International Institute of Design', *Grey Room* 34 (Winter 2009): 28–57.

Sunwoo, I. (2012), 'From the "Well-Laid Table" to the "Market Place:" The Architectural Association Unit System', *Journal of Architectural Education* 65, no. 2 (March): 24–41.
Thornley, D. G. (1963), 'Design Method in Architectural Education', in J. C. Jones and D. G. Thornley (eds), *Conference on Design Methods: Papers Presented at the Conference on Systematic and Intuitive Methods in Engineering, Industrial Design, Architecture and Communications, London, 1962,* New York: Macmillan.
UIA International Architect 5 (1984).

CHAPTER SIX

Theoretical A/gnosticisms: Paul Tillich, Colin Rowe and the Theology of Architecture

Karla Cavarra Britton and Kyle Dugdale

What are the categories within which architectural knowledge is best contained? This is, no doubt, a fraught question, not only for our generation, and not only for architects. The French *Encyclopédistes* of the eighteenth century are justly famous for having attempted to collect and systematize the entirety of human knowledge within the constraints of the printed page, launching a trajectory of classificatory enthusiasm that would lead in due course to the monumental *Encyclopédie méthodique* (Paris, 1782–1832). A truly massive undertaking, its 200 volumes constitute a correspondingly heavy and unwieldy vehicle of knowledge.[1]

But there exists a more succinct document that registers a similar ambition. A single sheet of paper precedes the first volume of the original *Encyclopédie, ou dictionnaire raisonné des sciences, des arts et des métiers* (Paris, 1751). This sheet represents the *Système figuré des connoissances* [sic] *humaines*, its title printed in large capital letters at the top of the page (see Fig. 6.1). The reader must deploy a double fold-out to reveal its full contents, for although the book within which it is enclosed is a distinctly large volume, its dimensions are evidently insufficient to encompass the grand scheme of reality. This single sheet represents, after all, the diagrammatic framework of all human knowledge. It is for good reason that this register of humanity's enlightenment is known more informally – adopting a term with biblical resonance – as the 'Tree of Knowledge'.

As in the Book of Genesis, so here, too, the tree offers both knowledge and power. For the *Système* participates in the broader ambition of the

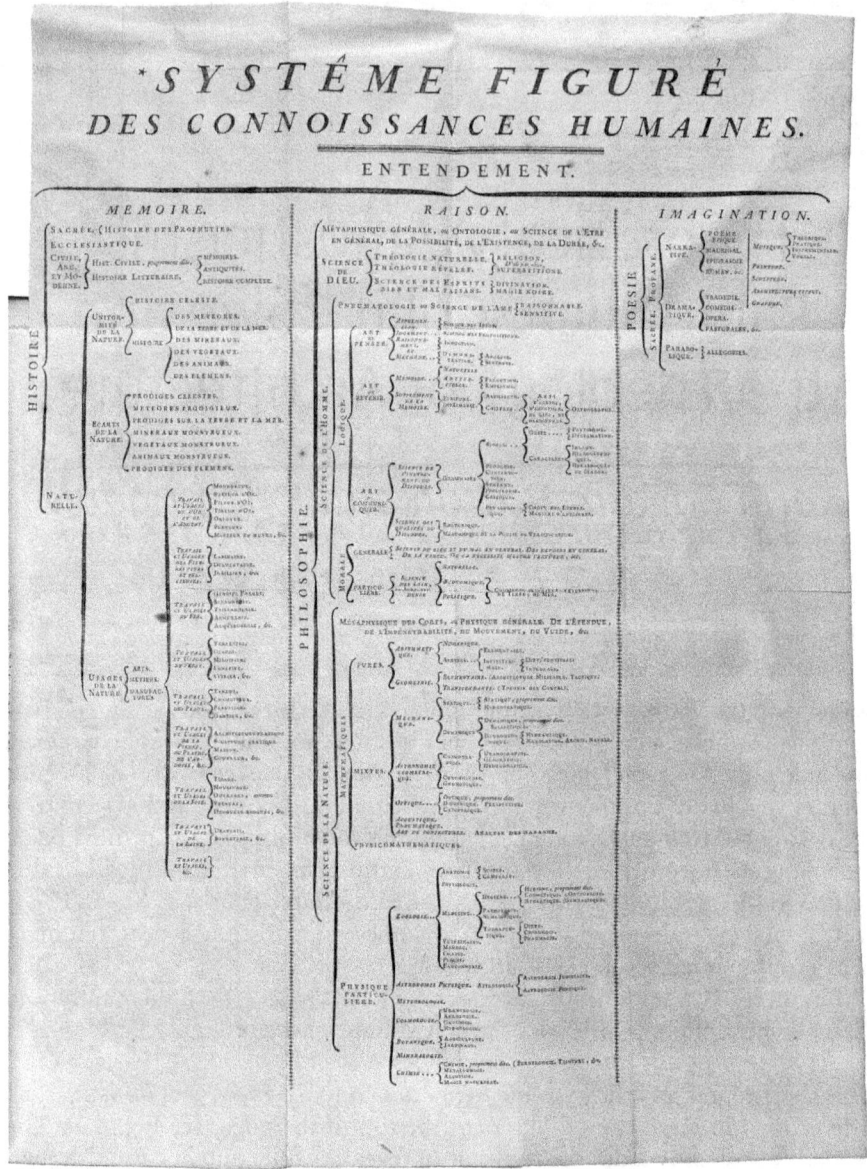

FIG. 6.1 *The* Système figuré des connoissances [sic] humaines, *from the* Encyclopédie, ou dictionnaire raisonné des sciences, des arts et des métiers, *Vol. 1 (Paris, 1751). Source: Beinecke Rare Book and Manuscript Library, Yale University.*

Encyclopédie, identified by Roland Barthes as 'an impious fragmentation of the world', whereby reality is '*reduced*, tamed, familiarized ... *divided*' (1980: 28, 39). Categorization, that is, promises control. Accordingly, each field of human knowledge is here duly assigned to one of three distinct categories placed side by side in an uneven array. Memory, reason and imagination are the three – but the most prominent of these is reason. Theology, famously, plays only a limited role in this scheme: divine revelation, once authoritative, is now rendered heavily subordinate to human reason, and is represented by a brief and discreet entry inserted before the more elaborately explicated sciences of man and of nature. Carefully calculated, this recalibration of priorities proved prophetic of an emerging modernity that no longer sought to assess the material world against the measure of the spiritual.

Yet the creators of this all-encompassing scheme struggled to locate the discipline of architecture. Refusing to assign it to any one of the available headings, they chose instead to disperse it under all three, subdivided into the categories of *architecture pratique* (under *mémoire*), *architecture militaire* (under *raison*) and *architecture civile* (under *imagination*).[2] Architecture's once-presumed unity thus gives way to an unholy trinity. And yet this, too, seems forced. Is reason the only governing impetus for military architecture? Does its civil counterpart cede all authority to the imagination?[3] It is perhaps symptomatic of a larger failure that in the process of such typographic fragmentation the recurring word 'architecture' is itself liable to be obscured by the crease of the constraining fold-out – by the very materiality of its fragmented categorization (see Fig. 6.2).

Subsequent generations have each adopted their own categories within which to organize architectural knowledge. Twentieth-century modernity proved no exception, and today it is often taken for granted that architectural knowledge can most usefully be divided between the domains either of design and technology or of history and theory. With minimal effort one might draw correspondences to the triad of memory, reason and imagination. The standard course listings of contemporary schools of architecture offer multiple examples of such categorization, their structures rarely more sophisticated than those of their disciplinary predecessors. Alternatively, one might look to job advertisements for architectural faculty, or to the categories used by national accreditation boards, the presumed arbiters of contemporary practice, who occasionally – and somewhat arbitrarily – substitute the word 'culture' for 'history/theory'. *Design/technology* and *history/theory*: one of these domains is held to be primarily material in its expression, the other is deemed amenable to more intangible and esoteric speculations. Today's dominant assumption, in other words, is that 'history and theory' are the obvious categories within which to assess the distinctively intellectual claims that are held to govern architectural knowledge.

This chapter addresses a different category: neither the history of architecture nor the theory of architecture, but the theology of architecture –

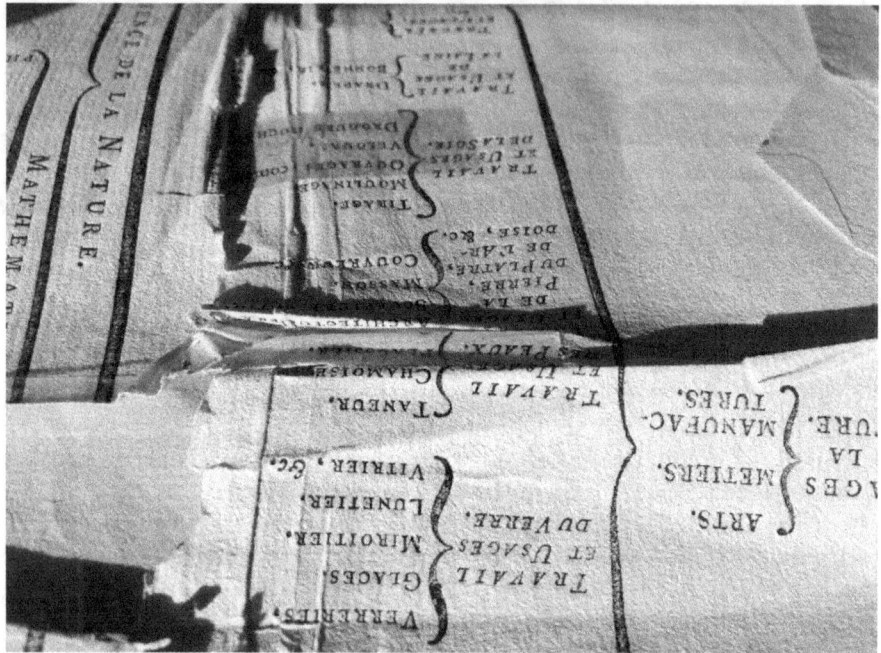

FIG. 6.2 Système figuré des connoissances humaines, *detail. Source: Yale University Library; photograph by authors.*

a category that is typically absent from standard classifications of architectural knowledge. It brackets its argument with two talks: an address given at the Museum of Modern Art in 1964 by the theologian Paul Tillich, published more widely in 1987, and a 1979 lecture delivered in London by Colin Rowe on the occasion of the publication of *Collage City*, reported in turn in K. Michael Hays's *Architecture Theory Since 1968* (1998: 88) (see Fig. 6.3). Both talks claim, albeit with different purposes in mind, that the essence of modernity's architectural knowledge cannot be contained within familiar boundaries, and that its interpretation must therefore be pursued through categories that transcend predictable boundaries between architecture's material and immaterial concerns. They seek, in other words, to challenge the tidy distinctions established by the *Système figuré*.

Tillich

The Reformed theologian Paul Tillich's convictions regarding the theology of architecture are foundational to this discussion. Modern art and architecture were essential to Tillich's existentialism, for they provided for him an entrée into dimensions of human experience that are otherwise inaccessible, even

FIG. 6.3 *Paul Tillich (1958) and Colin Rowe (1992). Photographs © Philippe Halsman / Magnum Photos and Valerie Bennett.*

through prayer or scripture. In the post-war period, he embraced the Museum of Modern Art in New York City as a place that provided the material means for probing these questions of human existence. The 'disruptedness' that he saw evidenced in the museum's sculpture garden, and in its collection of works of expressionism, surrealism, cubism and futurism, penetrated the depths of reality, speaking of truths that could not be found elsewhere. The expressionist element, for Tillich, breaks the surface of reality; it 'pierces into its ground; it reshapes it, reorders the elements in order more powerfully to express meaning', so as to become an expression of 'ultimate concern' – which is precisely the category through which Tillich expresses the fundamental relationship of humanity to God (1965/1987: 177).

Tillich grew up in Germany in the world of the Lutheran Church, and had a fascination with architecture from an early age. At one time he thought of becoming an architect, and he saw philosophy with its emphasis on modalities and the imagination as closely linked to the processes of architectural design. Tillich's repeated statements on architecture and theology appeared in essays such as an extended piece in *Architectural Forum* in 1955 and addressed the themes of contemporary Protestant architecture and its ability to speak of 'consecration' and honesty (1955/1987). His deep appreciation for architecture's responsibility to communal and spiritual wellbeing is most fully underscored by his chosen burial site in a park that bears his name in the bucolic Midwestern town of historical utopian heritage, New Harmony, Indiana. Here in the midst of a wooded grove, Tillich is interred adjacent to the masterfully landscaped enclosure of the Roofless Church designed by Philip Johnson and dedicated in 1960. The brick-walled enclave is marked by a startling mushroom-shaped parabola dome that encloses Jacques Lipchitz's cubist sculpture titled Notre Dame de Liesse. The landscape of the Roofless Church is reminiscent of Johnson's skilful interweaving of nature and enclosure evident in his composition of both the Glass House and the sculpture garden of the Museum of Modern Art. This dual orientation also magnified Tillich's appreciation for New Harmony as he expressed it in 'Estranged and Reunited', the address he delivered at the dedication of Paul Tillich Park. In it, he held up the possibility of overcoming the estrangement from true being, from the self and from those with whom we live, that he regarded as the essential dilemma of modern humanity. Echoing this sentiment, the park now includes an inscription from one of Tillich's books, *The Shaking of the Foundations*, where he observed, 'Man and nature belong together in their created glory, in their tragedy, and in their salvation' (Tillich 1948: 83; Owen 2015: 248).

Tillich's convictions regarding the redemptive qualities of art and architecture were derived from his own life experience, especially his service as a chaplain in the trenches of the Western Front during the First World War and then his flight from Hitler's Germany in the 1930s. Tillich was dismissed from his faculty position at the University of Frankfurt in 1933, shortly after Hitler had assumed power, and then emigrated to the United States. Following his move to Union Theological Seminary in New York City (at the invitation of Reinhold Niebuhr), he discovered in the Museum of Modern Art a new intellectual home that provided him with the impetus for deepening his visually-based theology. Growing out of his revelatory encounter with the art and architecture of the Bauhaus, Tillich became increasingly committed to seeing MoMA as a space for understanding modern art's potential to foster theological understanding. In addition to texts written for various occasions at the Museum, Tillich established (alongside Alfred Barr of MoMA and the theologian Marvin Halverson) the Society for the Arts, Religion, and Contemporary Culture (ARC) – an organization intended to provide a liaison between the arts and institutional religion. For Tillich, the Museum was 'home' because it was aesthetically 'good' (in the sense of being intellectually honest and spiritually revelatory), and represented all that for which he had stood and fought when his country was being 'conquered by forces of evil' (1964/1987: 246).

In particular, Tillich argued that the arts can provide access to an essential human experience that is not a surrogate for religious experience, but a deepening of it. Unlike the forms of 'secular spirituality' that are often associated with contemporary art museums, which tend to understand the aesthetic experience of art as a contemporary substitute for religion, the architecture of the Museum provided Tillich with 'the space and the frame' for encountering the reality of the world as it really is. The experience of the Museum is incorporated into, rather than substituted for, the religious. As Tillich states of the arts, 'they open up a dimension of reality which is otherwise hidden . . . Only the arts can do this; science, philosophy, moral action and religious devotion cannot' (1964/1987: 247). Significantly, Tillich saw the arts as offering not only a focus on the good and the beautiful, but also an exploration of the more demonic, uncertain and even tragic aspects of human experience, which for him led toward religious concern itself. Uncertainty is the point where religion and art intersect, and where art, in its pointing to the truth about the human condition, expresses that intimacy which is religious.

Tillich's essay 'Contemporary Protestant Architecture' (1962) stands behind his convictions about the importance of the contemporary art museum in general, and the Museum of Modern Art in particular. This brief essay offers not only a succinct framework for the reading of the contemporary character of Protestant architecture, but also a forceful plea from a theologian's perspective for the centrality of creativity and the evolution of form for modern art and architecture. As a theological stance, Tillich presents his conviction regarding the necessity of an ethical posture on the part of the contemporary artist and/or architect. He draws a direct relationship between the creative activities of the artist/architect as a means of drawing human attention more closely to an understanding of God. While the essay sets out to systematize and categorize contemporary Protestant architecture, Tillich pushes beyond that subject to argue for the importance more generally of the architect's commitment to innovation in design and to the possibility of 'breaking through to the new'. Tillich's argument essentially makes a theological claim that the artist/architect must be held responsible for revealing the power of the creator in the contemporary period, and so cannot rely on the mere replication of forms from the past. For the artist and historian Albert Christ-Janer, who edited the book in which Tillich's essay appeared, Tillich's argument is nothing less than 'a new perspective on the controversy between traditional and modern styles in church building' (Tillich 1962: 122). Yet it is even more than that, for Tillich argues that if the architect 'is asked to imitate the style of a period which is not his own, his creativity is undercut and his honesty of self-expression is destroyed' (1962: 123). In short, if the architect does not strive for the new, '[h]e has ceased to be a mirror to his contemporaries and instead prevents them from awareness of their actual being. He deceives them – even though often they like to be deceived.' In this regard, Tillich warns, 'an element of risk is unavoidable in the building of sacred places, just as a risk must be taken in every act of faith' (1962: 125).

Architecture may therefore be seen as central to Tillich's theological understanding, for architecture has the capacity to express both our human finitude and our innate openness to the infinite – think of the effect on Tillich of Johnson's Roofless Church (Tillich 1985/1987). In the museum building itself, architecture serves the purpose of creating a space that is symbolically evocative of the transcendent dimensions of human experience (specifically including the tragic and even demonic) to which art itself can allude. Rather than being a place of comfort or retreat, it is a place that challenges and deepens our understanding of the existential dimensions of human experience. Rather than standing as a surrogate for the religious building, the architectural form of the museum more authentically stands alongside it as both building types address the full reality of the human condition.

Rowe

Colin Rowe – architect, historian and critic – is a figure who is doubtless more familiar to other architects than is the theologian Paul Tillich. Unsurprisingly, Rowe and Tillich are not frequently compared or contrasted.[4] And yet they may be read as sharing an overlapping set of interests in what might best be described, borrowing a phrase used by Rowe, as 'the ethical posture of modern architecture' (1979: 2). To put it more explicitly, if architecture may be seen as central to Tillich's theological understanding, theology may, in turn, be seen as central to Rowe's architectural understanding. This is evident, for instance, in his 1979 Cubitt Lecture, delivered at London's Royal Institution on the occasion of the publication of *Collage City* – a book that articulated ideas that Rowe had been developing for several years prior.[5]

Rowe's talk is entitled 'The Present Urban Predicament: Some Observations', and despite the modest tone of its subtitle, it offers nothing less than an exegesis of architectural modernity's fundamental beliefs, with an attendant diagnosis of what is held to be its terminal condition.[6] Combining a now familiar 'obituary for modern architecture' (Hays's description) with an attendant personalization of modernism's aims, Rowe speaks of modern architecture's redemptive aspirations and of her ambitions (she is deemed feminine) for society's 'moral regeneration'. Modern architecture hoped, according to Rowe's assessment, that society 'would, by the influence of her example, become redeemed of errors' – and here he sets up a contrast between 'external charms' and 'inherent virtues . . . the ethical posture of modern architecture' (1979: 2). Rowe adopts, quite self-consciously, a theological vocabulary – deployed with a dose of irony that could also be read as an implicit critique of Tillich. In fact, he characterizes modernism's aspirations using the language of the 'New Jerusalem', arguing that modernism was 'motivated by a quasi-religious sentiment not well understood' (Rowe 1979: 2–3, quoted in Hays 1988: 88). If this assertion is to be taken seriously, it follows not only that the domain of architecture has expanded to fill the vacuum left by modernity's extraction of theology from the chambers of human knowledge, but also, somewhat paradoxically, that the modern condition can *only* be fully understood if studied with the tools of the theologian.

For an even more explicit statement of a similar idea we might turn to a familiar passage from *Collage City* itself, in which, at the opening of the chapter entitled 'Utopia: Decline and Fall', the authors write, 'Modern architecture is surely most cogently to be interpreted as a gospel – as, quite literally, a message of good news; and hence its impact' (Rowe and Koetter 1978: 11). The discourses of architecture and theology here seem to map onto one another; or, to be more precise, architecture takes upon itself a role that was once assigned to theology. And indeed, this statement is in turn bracketed by direct quotations from biblical texts: on the previous page the reader encounters, by way of an epigraph, an apocryphal passage from the Second Book of Esdras; and a few lines later this is supplemented by a familiar passage about camels and needles, from the Gospel of Luke.

There is more – much more – along these lines in the pages that follow: talk of the architect as saviour, of the discipline's messianic passion, and so on. All of this is offered in the context of an assessment of twentieth-century architecture's fundamental motivations and purposes. And here too the reader encounters the suggestion that modernity can only be properly understood if the history of architecture and the theory of architecture are supplemented with an understanding of the theology of architecture.

Rowe's position of the 1970s evidently survived intact his experience of the 1980s. By the early 1990s, when he published *The Architecture of Good Intentions*, it had crystallized into a fully-developed theory, articulated explicitly in a chapter bearing the suitably theological title 'Eschatology' – the study of the 'last things' (Rowe 1994: 30–43).[7] Summarizing his assessment of modernism's sense of mission (one is reminded of Tillich), and rehearsing its frequent invocations of the architect as saviour, Rowe concludes, 'It is only this eminently dramatic and ultimately Hebraic conception of history in terms of architectural sin and architectural redemption which provides any real accommodation for the emotional preconditions of modern architecture's existence' (1994: 41). Rowe here presents the trajectory of modern architecture's development as comprehensible only within the larger context of attitudes that are ultimately theological in their conception.

The implications of such an assertion for the study of architecture are, of course, legion; and they can be pursued into almost any of the many subcategories into which one might be inclined to organize the complexities of architectural knowledge. How, for instance, are we to make sense of Rowe's framing of modern architecture's dreams of a future utopia as visions of the fulfilment of a biblical paradise? This is a variant, no doubt, of Robert Smithson's recombination of 'extreme past and future' (1966: 27) – and it stands to reason that the discipline of theology has a longer history of wrestling with this problem than does the discipline of architecture. That is not even to begin to question the consent of Manfredo Tafuri, who in his 1980 essay on 'The New Babylon' offers the witness of early twentieth-century modernity (Wohler 1924: 328) in support of a contemporary assessment of the 'aspiration toward the metaphysical' (Tafuri 1987: 175). And any interpretation of genealogy as a legitimizing tool to locate contemporary history within a longer, grander narrative cannot run very far without stumbling, sooner or later, over the biblical genealogies that legitimize the grandest architectural narrative of all – which leads, as Rowe would surely recognize, from the architect's imagining of Adam's hut in paradise, through a series of biblical architectures of growing ambition, to a final consummation in the New Jerusalem of the future. This offers, in some regards, a perfect foil to what has been described as 'the causality, objectivity and teleology of history, notions which are inherent to the modern thinking'.[8]

Rowe's assessment is thus clearly related yet distinctly different to that of Tillich. If Tillich insists on modern architecture's potential to address 'man's ultimate concern', Rowe counters with the claim that modern architecture fails to deliver on its promise to do precisely that – to address humanity's most fundamental existential condition. And this failure is tied, by Rowe, to the failure of modernism itself.

To weigh the relative merits of these positions lies outside the scope of this chapter; for now, we wish only to suggest that such weighing cannot be accomplished without a willingness to engage the discipline of theology.

Gnostic/agnostic

If one of the central questions framing the concept behind this book was, in fact, the question of how to pursue 'historical research on something as intangible as theory, or in a broadened sense, the knowledge of architecture', one of the possible answers might involve a rapprochement between the ranks of architectural and theological thinkers. There exist, in fact, elective affinities in both directions, as even a cursory glance at the work of Tillich and of Rowe would suggest; but such affinities are rarely mobilized. There are prominent exceptions, to be sure: one might point to scholarship exploring the relationship between the Dominican friar Marie-Alain Couturier and concepts of the sacred as understood by Le Corbusier (whose name, incidentally, appears under the *Oxford English Dictionary* definition of the word *daemonic*), or tracing the intellectual influence on Ludwig Mies van der Rohe of the Catholic priest Romano Guardini or of the philosopher Jacques Maritain.[9]

Other names could certainly be added to this list. But these studies remain exceptional; architectural thinking has preferred, on the whole, to maintain a posture of comfortable agnosticism in regard to architecture's theological imbrications. Such refusal to engage is doubtless also tied to the ideological leanings of modernism's most vocal protagonists; and it is all the more evident the closer one approaches the discipline's fundamental motivations and promises. This tendency is acknowledged by Rowe, who writes in 1994 that architecture's redemptive claims do not seem 'seriously to have engaged the scrutiny of the polemicists/apologists/critics/'historians' of the so-called modern movement ... For these are very embarrassing themes for the would-be rationalist either to recognize or discuss: and, preferably, they should be invisible' (1994: 32).[10]

Should more be done to confront such embarrassments? To do so is, of course, not so easily achieved; there are very real pedagogical, disciplinary and institutional challenges involved. Prior generations' convictions have, as Rowe reminds us, often proved illusory, and their bravest hopes for the possibility of architecture's ethical function have frequently been abandoned – and not always without good cause. Renewed efforts in this direction would do well to proceed with caution. Moreover, their promoters must learn to do business with a realm of knowledge that cannot readily be contained within the categories either of design/technology or of history/theory, any more than architecture can be limited to a single branch of the categories of memory, reason and imagination. Instead, they must engage with deliberate seriousness a subject that has often been treated as a heretical subtext to the legitimate narrative of mainstream architectural dogma, or else relegated to the status of a sort of Gnosticism – an esoteric form of knowledge that cannot readily be discussed without lapsing into a realm of mystery and imprecision that stands in stark opposition to the solid and precise material of modernity's architecture.[11] That this caricature, at least, is untenable, can be amply demonstrated by the study of architecture's recent history. But the underlying attitude has a long heritage, tidily documented in the *Système figuré*. Adjacent to its single-line entry for natural theology stands the world 'RELIGION'; and printed close by, in capital letters of equal size that align with the entry for revealed theology, its authors insert the word 'SUPERSTITIONS', introduced by three dismissive words printed in italic typeface: '*d'où par abus*' (see Fig. 6.4).

The dismissal is absolute. Just as divine revelation is no longer considered a legitimate source of knowledge, so its study no longer holds pride of place in the grand scheme of human enterprise. Furthermore, there is no space of overlap between theology and other categories of endeavour. And yet, as Barthes insists in his analysis of the *Encyclopédie*, such attempts at fragmentation fall foul of reality – these efforts to assert control result,

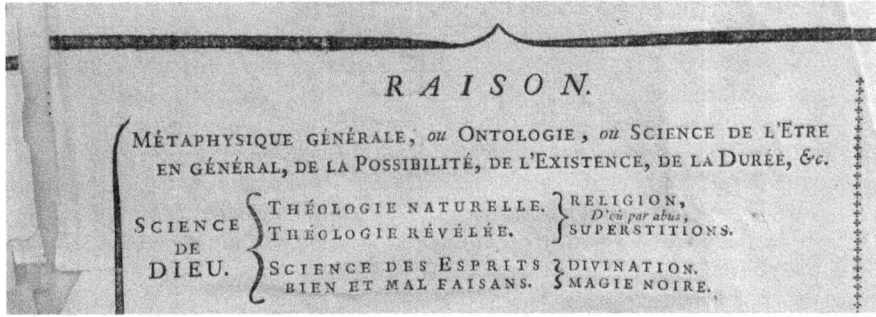

FIG. 6.4 Système figuré des connoissances humaines, *detail. Source: Yale University Library; photograph by authors.*

sooner or later, in failure. 'In a word, the fracture of the world is impossible' (Barthes 1980: 39). If Tillich and Rowe are to be taken seriously, the study of theology may yet come to reclaim its legitimate place within the discipline of architecture.

Notes

We are grateful to the readers of our manuscript for their encouragement and critique. The credit for improvements is theirs, the blame for surviving infelicities ours.

1   For more on this, the 'ultimate in Encyclopedism', which 'now sits unread and forgotten on remote shelves of research libraries', see Darnton (1979: 395).
2   There is a further entry for naval architecture. For a fuller discussion, see 'Architectures in the *Encyclopédie*' in Parcell (2012: 193–205).
3   For d'Alembert's own acknowledgement of the limitations inherent to the design of the *Système*, see Parcell (2012: 195).
4   For a point of contact one might look to the scientist and philosopher Michael Polanyi, whose work was influential on both Rowe and Tillich. See Hays (1988: 90, n. 3) and Gelwick (2008–9). Not insignificantly, texts by both Tillich and Rowe appear in Hejduk and Williamson (2011).
5   The manuscript for *Collage City* had been in circulation from 1973: see Hays (1988: 88).
6   In the body of his text, Rowe proposes an alternate title: 'Object Fixation: Cause and Cure' (1979: 21).
7   The author notes that this book was shaped from the contents of the 1982 Preston H. Thomas Lectures at Cornell, themselves the development of lectures delivered as early as 1967 (Rowe 1994: 6). The chapter is reproduced in Hejduk and Williamson (2011: 252–62).
8   Quoted from the call for papers for the conference, 'Theory's History 196X–199X: Challenges in the Historiography of Architectural Knowledge', Brussels, 9–10 February 2017. An early version of this text was originally presented as a paper at this conference.
9   For recent work, see Heynickx and Symons (2017), the introduction to a special issue that aims to address 'hidden, forgotten, neglected and, at times, repressed connections' (Heynickx and Symons 2017: 255) between architecture and theology. The authors note that it is especially the influence of more orthodox forms of doctrine that has tended to suffer neglect in accounts of modernist architecture's formation. On Mies and Maritain, see, in the same issue, Heynickx (2017), tracing the influence of old ideas seemingly 'stamped out by the dominant narratives of intellectual and cultural progress' (Heynickx and Symons 2017: 268).
10 Rowe adds, in the same breath, that 'the would-be rationalist is never, very seriously, agnostic' – but here he is speaking of a naive belief in the redemptive power of architecture.

11 See also the introduction (1–9) to Hejduk and Williamson (2011), which presents religion as 'Modern architecture's blind spot' (8) and victim of the 'secularizing rhetoric of Modernity' (2). The authors take for granted that religion is 'constructed' (2) – in other words, that religion is understood in the image of architecture.

References

Barthes, R. (1980), 'The Plates of the *Encyclopedia*', in *New Critical Essays*, trans. Richard Howard, 23–39, New York: Hill and Wang.
Darnton, R. (1979), *The Business of Enlightenment: A Publishing History of the Encyclopédie, 1775–1800*, Cambridge, MA: Belknap Press of Harvard University Press.
Diderot, D. and J. le Rond d'Alembert (eds) (1751–72), *Encyclopédie, ou dictionnaire raisonné des sciences, des arts et des métiers*, 28 vols, Paris: Briasson.
Gelwick, R. (2008–9), 'The Christian Encounter of Paul Tillich and Michael Polanyi', *Tradition and Discovery: The Polanyi Society Periodical* 35, no. 3: 7–20.
Hays, K. M. (ed.) (1998), *Architecture Theory Since 1968*, Cambridge, MA: MIT Press.
Hejduk, R. and J. Williamson (eds) (2011), *The Religious Imagination in Modern and Contemporary Architecture: A Reader*, New York: Routledge.
Heynickx, R. (2017), 'Conceptual Debts: Modern Architecture and Neo-Thomism in Postwar America', *The European Legacy: Toward New Paradigms* 22, no. 3: 258–77.
Heynickx, R. and S. Symons (2017), 'A Matter of Interactions: Religion and Architectural Modernism, 1945–70', *The European Legacy: Toward New Paradigms* 22, no. 3: 251–7.
Owen, J. Blaffer (2015), *New Harmony, Indiana: Like a River, Not a Lake*, Bloomington: Indiana University Press.
Panckoucke, C.-J. (ed.) (1782–1832), *Encyclopédie méthodique*, 206 vols, Paris: Panckoucke.
Parcell, S. (2012), *Four Historical Definitions of Architecture*, Montreal: McGill-Queen's University Press.
Rowe, C. (1979), *The Present Urban Predicament: Some Observations*, Second Thomas Cubitt Lecture at the Royal Institution, London: Thomas Cubitt Trust. Reprinted, with minor edits, in *Architectural Association Quarterly* 11, no. 4 (1979): 40–48, and reproduced with accompanying images in *Cornell Journal of Architecture* 1 (Fall 1981): 16–33, and (with slight adjustments) in C. Rowe (1996), *As I was Saying: Recollections and Miscellaneous Essays*, ed. A. Caragonne, Cambridge, MA: MIT Press, 3:165–220.
Rowe, C. (1994), *The Architecture of Good Intentions: Towards a Possible Retrospect*, London: Academy Editions.
Rowe, C. and F. Koetter (1978), *Collage City*, Cambridge, MA: MIT Press.
Smithson, R. (1966), 'Entropy and the New Monuments', *Artforum* 4, no. 10: 26–31.
Tafuri, M. (1987), 'The New Babylon: The "Yellow Giants" and the Myth of Americanism', in *The Sphere and the Labyrinth: Avant-Gardes and Architecture from Piranesi to the 1970s*, trans. Pellegrino d'Acierno and Robert Connolly,

171–89, Cambridge, MA: MIT Press. Originally published as 'The New Babylon: I "giganti gialli" e il mito dell'americanismo', in *La sfera e il labirinto: Avanguardie e architettura da Piranesi agli anni '70*, 211–35, Turin: Einaudi, 1980.

Tillich, P. (1948), *The Shaking of the Foundations*, New York: Charles Scribner's Sons.

Tillich, P. (1955/1987), 'Theology and Architecture', in *On Art and Architecture*, 188–98. Originally published in *Architectural Forum* 103, no. 6 (December 1955): 131–6.

Tillich, P. (1962), 'Contemporary Protestant Architecture', in A. Christ-Janer and M. Mix Foley (eds), *Modern Church Architecture*, 122–5, New York: McGraw-Hill.

Tillich, P. (1964/1987), 'Address on the Occasion of the Opening of the New Galleries and Sculpture Garden of the Museum of Modern Art', in *On Art and Architecture*, 246–50. Originally published in *Criterion* 3, no. 3 (Summer 1964): 39–40.

Tillich, P. (1965/1987), 'Religious Dimensions of Contemporary Art', in *On Art and Architecture*, 171–88. Edited from the typescript for a lecture sponsored by the Program in Religious Studies, University of California, Santa Barbara, 1965.

Tillich, P. (1985/1987), 'Dwelling, Space, and Time', in *On Art and Architecture*, 81–5. First published in English (edited by Betty Meyer) under the title 'Domestic Architecture, Space, and Time', *Faith and Form* (Fall 1985): 11–12. Originally published as 'Das Wohnen, der Raum, und die Zeit', *Die Form* 8 (1933): 11–12.

Tillich, P. (1987), *On Art and Architecture*, ed. John Dillenberger and Jane Dillenberger, New York: Crossroad.

Wohler, G. (1924), 'Das Hochhaus im Wettbewerb der Chicago Tribune', *Deutsche Bauzeitung* 58, no. 54: 325–30.

PART THREE
Vehicles

CHAPTER SEVEN

Cedric Price's Chats: Orality and the Production of Architectural Theory

Jim Njoo

'Non-Plan – A True Mirror of Social Appetites?' was the title of a talk given by the British architect Cedric Price in 1997 at the Courtauld Institute of Art in London, as part of a debate on indeterminacy in architecture and urbanism. The point of departure was a polemical article that Price had co-authored in 1969 with Reyner Banham, Paul Barker and Peter Hall entitled 'Non-Plan: An Experiment in Freedom' (Banham et al. 1969). Published in the social enquiry weekly *New Society*, the original text outlined a radical proposal to experiment a deregulated 'bottom-up' approach to planning via selected 'control-free' sites in the UK, promoting as it were a self-organized citizen-driven form of urbanism.[1] In the passage, however, from conference to publication, Price's contribution appears to have radically departed from his original presentation, notably in terms of its form. Retitled 'Cedric Price's Non-Plan Diary' (2000), the final article consisted of a montage of images, personal quotes and critical reactions, resembling more a scrapbook than an academic article. Indeed, the first image presents an excerpt of a page from one of Price's own scrapbooks circa 1970, a kind of archival *mise en abyme*. Was this simply the expedient of an architect who couldn't be bothered to rewrite his paper for publication?

This was not the first time that a lecture by Price had been published as a montage of images and textual fragments. In the autumn of 1975, for example, he delivered a three-part lecture at London's Art Net, an art and architecture gallery run by Archigram's Peter Cook and journalist Rebecca Collings, which was later published under the title 'Cedric Price: Aiming to Miss. Notes based on the three lectures given at Art Net November 1975'

(1976). Rather than an abridged transcription, the published text presents a collection of selected quotes and aphoristic 'notes'. But whose notes are these: Price's or the editor's? When were these notes prepared: before the lectures, during or after?

A similar question of post-production – and reproduction – arises in the 1980s with the publication of various talks that Price gave at the Architectural Association (AA) in London. Although the translation here from talk to text still followed a principle of montage, Price experimented with new iterations, adding subtitles, captions and afterthoughts. In the publication of one series, Price offers this prefatory reflection on the passage from speech to writing, from talk to text:

> Translation from the spoken to the written word destroys immediacy, but enables reference. The music played at the live delivery consisted of 'Take Five', by the MJQ and Ravel's 'Bolero'. Primarily theses chats were a MANIFESTO in the making.
>
> PRICE 1990: 27

While this statement by Price certainly highlights his interest in process and live performance, I want to contest the suggestion that he simply conceded a documentary role to textual discourse. In this chapter, I will argue that the passage from spoken to written language, from 'immediacy' to 'reference', as Price calls it, is far more complex, and that Price himself was profoundly engaged in exploring the interactions of orality and literacy in his production of theory. By the term 'orality', I am referring here to the definition of the oral historian Walter Ong in his critical work, *Orality and Literacy: The Technologizing of the Word* (1982). Ong defines 'orality' as verbal expression in oral culture. However, as he points out, it is not possible to return to the purely oral tradition of preliterate times. In today's condition of mediated or 'secondary' orality, we must consider how speech and writing are inevitably interrelated activities, not isolated forms of communication. As he argues, orality and literacy continue to be deeply interdependent, even in a society increasingly dominated by literacy. A public lecture, for example, although spoken, is often mediated through writing, whereas a personal letter, although written, is spoken-like in many respects. This is all the truer today with instant text messaging and chat rooms, since such forms of writing can be likened to face-to-face conversations (Olson and Torrance 1991; Olson et al. 2006) (see Fig. 7.1).

A glance at Price's lecture notes reveals that he often used textual fragments such as quotes or short articles as a way to map out his talks during the process of their elaboration. One such note from the 1990s is particularly revealing: a text collage composed of a selection of quotes on the topic of time. The quotes have been recopied by hand, and then photocopied and collaged on top of an excerpt of a reprinted text by Price from a proposal for a Japanese design competition entitled 'A Style for the

CEDRIC PRICE'S CHATS 121

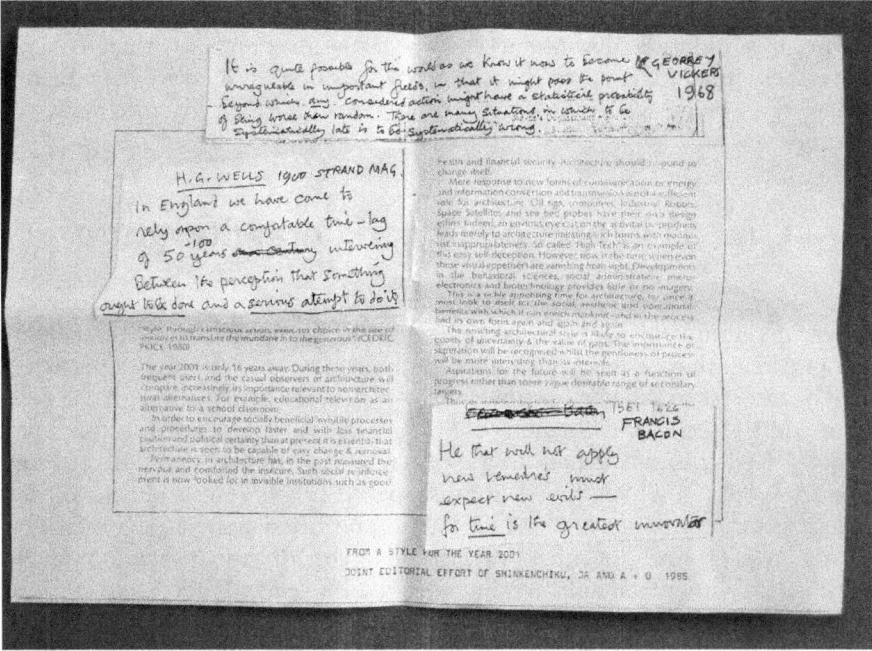

FIG. 7.1 *Cedric Price, lecture notes c. 1994, Cedric Price Fonds. Source: Courtesy of the Canadian Centre for Architecture.*

Year 2001' (Maki 1985). The collage charts an imaginary conversation between Price the architect, Francis Bacon the philosopher, H. G. Wells the writer, Geoffrey Vickers the systems scientist, and possibly the competition jury as well (composed of Fumihiko Maki, Hiroshi Hara and Aldo Rossi): a conversation on time, but also in and over time, not unlike Price's 'Non-Plan Diary'.

Price was interested in the social intimacy of conversation, or what he often referred to as 'chats': casual open-ended conversations implying the active participation of his audience. He used the word 'chats' not only in reference to his public lectures, but also in relation to other discursive contexts such as his articles and weekly design columns or his discussions with clients and project collaborators, which he occasionally taped for future reference.[2] His dialogic understanding of discourse was therefore not bound to speech alone, but translated into various forms of expression, including writing. In this sense, his approach to architectural theory was very much concerned with *process* in the same way that he considered process to be an integral part of architectural design and production.

For this discussion, I will focus on three ways in which 'chats' may be interpreted as emblematic of Price's emphasis on process and dialogue: oral literature, conversation theory and live improvisation. Although I will discuss each perspective with regards to a particular issue and in terms of a different disciplinary source, it is also my intention to show how these dialogic approaches toward discourse and ultimately theory, rather than being wholly distinct, are fundamentally intertwined with one another.

Chat as genre: orality and oral literature

Price often cited literature as a key source of inspiration, ranging from the travel adventures of Dickens to contemporary horror fiction (Price 1985a). Despite his rather eclectic taste in literature, it is possible to trace a persistent line of interest in what might be called 'oral literature'. Although the term commonly refers to a wide range of oral art forms – epics, ballads, folk tales, songs – I wish to use it here in a much more restrictive sense to reference literary works in which 'talk' – that is, speech or dialogue – plays a central role in promoting a sense of the interaction we often associate with face-to-face conversation.[3] In other words, this part of my discussion is not concerned with texts that are intended to be read aloud, such as those produced in the context of oration or theatre.

In the mid-1980s, Price began his fourth weekly column series entitled 'Starting Price' for the London trade tabloid *Building Design* (1985b).[4] Unlike previous columns, this new series was primarily devoted to letter correspondence with readers. As a form of oral literature, letters fascinated Price. Reflecting on one of his favourite books, *The Natural History of Selborne* by the Reverend Gilbert White, Price speculated that it 'achieved an excellence in that genre [i.e. history writing] possibly because it was not meant for public consumption but merely as a private commentary – in the form of numerous letters – to a friend whose opinions and comments White welcomed and respected' (1978: 63). Although column journalism does address itself to the public, one of its peculiarities is its ability to forge a sense of community and proximity with its readership through its regular interaction with everyday events. Many of Price's readers were indeed friends whose opinions and comments he welcomed and respected. However, as Price's editor Paul Finch claims, no one ever did write in – Price invented all the questions himself (Finch 2014). Price's column was in this sense a fictional dialogue in the tradition of literary journalists like Charles Dickens, Price's favourite author, who notably began his career as a reporter, publishing his first texts as journalistic sketches of everyday life (see Fig. 7.2).[5]

Fictional dialogue – or what could be called in the case of Price, 'chat fiction' – promotes a sense of involvement on the part of the reader. The published initials of the authors' names and their simplified street addresses in Price's columns are like clues in a detective novel. As literary scholar Bronwen Thomas argues, fictional dialogue aims to 'create life in the

FIG. 7.2 Cedric Price, 'Starting Price' column, Building Design, 5 April 1985. Source: Courtesy of Building Design.

reader' by posing a challenge, 'not only in the sense of simply working out who is saying what to whom, but also in attempting to figure out what they mean and what their impact is for their interlocutors'. It asks the reader to actively participate and critically engage in the '(re)construction of meaning' (2012: viii).

This characteristic of fictional dialogue also attracted other authors in the history of architectural theory to whom Price made explicit reference, notably in terms of writing style (Price 1979: 60). An important precedent in this context was the English theorist, critic and historian John Ruskin, whose writings Price greatly admired. From 1871 to 1884, for example, Ruskin published a series of public letters, *Fors Clavigera: Letters to the Workmen and Labourers of Great Britain*, with the aim of stimulating critically-motivated reading practices amongst the British working class. Similar to Price, Ruskin explored the accessibility, immediacy and economy of serial publication and the use of different print genres for his arguments.[6] At the same time, he perpetuated an epistolary tradition whose rhetorical power flourished in nineteenth-century England, notably in the expanding context of news periodicals and the tradition of political pamphleteering carried on by social commentators like William Cobbett, Samuel Taylor Coleridge or Thomas Carlyle (Palmegiano 2012; Stoddart 1995). Drawing on these sources, Ruskin developed a sense of proximity with the social sphere of his readers very similar to Price's columns, publishing for example their letters, as well as those of the popular press with whom he also corresponded. Although there is no evidence to lay claim that Ruskin's letters were fictional dialogues, English scholar Judith Stoddart has highlighted Ruskin's dexterity for moving from fact to fantasy and 'blending the various modes of the discourse in order to question their difference' (1995: 155). In *Fors Clavigera*, Ruskin indeed combines multiple 'voices' – political theory, fairy tales, social gossip – and dramatizes this discursive style in the manner of a Dickens serial novel. Through this stylistic range and 'aliveness', Ruskin attempted to reach a very different audience than the educated elite that constituted the core of his earlier readership. It was no longer simply a matter of *what* to write but to *whom* to write and *how* to best address this intended public.

The use of dialogue in architectural writing, fictional or otherwise, was not only an English phenomenon. In the 1870s, for example, the French architect and theorist Viollet-le-Duc published a series of pedagogical texts on art and architecture, adopting for each book the form of a fictional dialogue to better address his young readers.[7] His first book, *Histoire d'une maison* (1873), is the dialogue between an architect and his nephew who decide to build a house together: a lesson on architecture, but also a tale of the emotions and the 'patient research' involved in its pursuit. As the architectural historian Laurent Baridon (2014) claims, Viollet-le-Duc wrote these books as a compensation for his ejection as a professor at the École des Beaux-Arts in Paris, in other words as a fictional dialogue between himself and his students. But Viollet-le-Duc also wrote these stories in a period when the art of conversation played an important role in the developing literary form of the popular novel, and in a time, too, when literacy itself was becoming a mass phenomenon.[8]

Viollet-le-Duc's *Histoire* series would serve as an inspiration for another architectural fiction, *Kindergarten Chats on Architecture, Democracy and Education* by the American architect Louis Sullivan (1934),[9] which was first published weekly in the *Interstate Architect and Builder* magazine from 1901 to 1902[10] before being re-edited as a book in 1934, ten years after Sullivan's death – not unlike Ruskin's letters which were republished in collective volumes starting in 1871. If Viollet-le-Duc's stories still echo something of the classical oral tradition of Socratic dialogue, Sullivan's *Chats* mark a shift towards a more informal jocular style of writing, anticipating Price's more playful prose. And like Price's columns, Sullivan published his *Chats* in a weekly trade magazine. However, as Sullivan asserted in a letter to his editor, 'I am writing for the people, not for the architects' (1904: 244). For Sullivan, like Viollet-le-Duc and Ruskin before him, and Price later on, fictional dialogue was a way to reach a wider audience, to come closer to 'the people'.

Chat as epistemology: cybernetics and conversation theory

This brief historical survey of fictional dialogue in architectural writing brings to light another key motivation at the heart of Price's conversational approach to theory. The question of education – or what Price preferred to call *learning* – is perhaps the most fundamental theme of Price's entire oeuvre. While significant attention has been devoted to his projects dealing with education, such as the Potteries Thinkbelt or Polyark, relatively little mention has been made of his own personal experience of teaching, such as his work as a tutor at the AA in London.

In 1980, for example, Price ran a studio course there entitled 'The Exchange'. As part of a 'two-way consultancy', as he qualified it, Price proposed his 'services' (somewhat promiscuously) to staff and students alike who could solicit his expertise on demand once a week, thereby introducing professional practice protocols into the academic setting of the AA; or just the opposite, since studio meetings could now possibly take place outside academic boundaries in the style of negotiations between future 'clients' who at the same time acted as 'consultants' (Price 1980a). In this way, Price challenged the institutional threshold separating theory and practice in terms of academic and professional milieus, and emphasized the value of social interaction as part of a two-way process of learning (see Fig. 7.3).

A critical influence on Price's thinking about learning came from his involvement with cybernetics. This can be traced back to the Fun Palace project and more particularly his relationship with Gordon Pask (1928–96), whom Price and client Joan Littlewood invited to chair the project's 'Cybernetics Subcommittee' and who later went on to teach at the AA.[11] Cybernetics was first defined in the 1940s as the scientific study of control and communication in living organisms and machines (Wiener 1948). Pask

FIG. 7.3 *Cedric Price, 'The Exchange', AA Prospectus 1980–81. Source: Courtesy of AA Publications.*

came to cybernetics in the 1950s with a more specific ambition: to stimulate learning like a nervous system through the use of electronics (Pickering 2010). One of his first applications was a 'Self-Adaptive Keyboard Instructor' to teach typing and card punching using an artificial intelligence machine. Pask saw cybernetics as a performative epistemology, in the sense that it advanced a way of knowing that was fundamentally geared to *doing*. To describe this, Pask distinguished between two types of observers: the 'scientific observer' whose hypothesis-testing method submits the object of study, or 'assemblage' as he called it, to the terms of a pre-defined language or agenda, and the 'participant observer' or cybernetician whose interactive-exploratory method aims to 'learn' from the assemblage in order to best determine what kind of enquiry might be relevant (Pickering 2010: 343–6).

One of Pask's key contributions to cybernetics was to have linked this idea of 'learning' to a question of orality, what he called 'conversation theory'. Although most cyberneticians tend to understand Pask's use of the term 'conversation' as a metaphor (Pangaro 1993; Glanville and Müller 2007), I would argue that Pask's conception of 'conversation theory' is more fundamentally rooted in oral culture than its various accounts or applications typically suggest. For example, Pask's first engagement with cybernetics was the development of an interactive sound and light machine named *Musicolour* that allowed the sound of a performer's voice and instrument to control a light show. What was particularly innovative was the fact that the internal parameters of the machine's circuitry were not constant, but could evolve according to the interactions of the performance (Pickering 2010: 313–17). In other words, Musicolour was able to 'learn' from the performer and vice versa, with the aim of achieving a synesthetic 'conversation' of sound and light.

Pask pursued his 'conversation theory' by developing 'adaptive learning systems' in which users and learning machines would develop what he called a 'common language' through dialogic interactions (Pickering 2010: 344). One of the ways through which Price developed this idea in his teaching was the use of 'contracts' (1980b, 1994): his students had to define through 'negotiation' not only their project task (its purpose and intentions), but also the means, techniques and even criteria of evaluation. The 'contract' was renegotiated after midterm, and the revised version signed again by both parties. This pedagogic device, which he introduced in the early 1980s, reflected Price's engagement with self-education methods, but it also questioned the ideological shift from social to liberal attitudes in education that was being played out at the AA in the aftermath of the May 1968 revolution (Sunwoo 2012) (see Fig. 7.4).

During the late 1950s, Pask and Musicolour toured England like a musical revue, making appearances in clubs, holiday camps, dance halls, private balls and theatres (Pickering 2010: 317–19). It is through this connection to performance that Pask caught the attention of another enthusiast of play and pedagogy, who would also have a major impact on Price: the theatre director Joan Littlewood.

Chat as performance: popular theatre and the art of improvisation

Littlewood (1914–2002), who is widely recognized as one of Britain's most influential theatre directors and a pioneer in the renewal of popular theatre in the second half of the twentieth century, treated text, that is to say script writing, only as a point of departure and never as a blueprint for performance (Holdsworth 2006). One of her major contributions to revolutionizing theatre practice in England was the use of improvisation as part of the creative process and as an integral part of live performance. According to performance art historian Nadine Holdsworth, Littlewood 'responded to

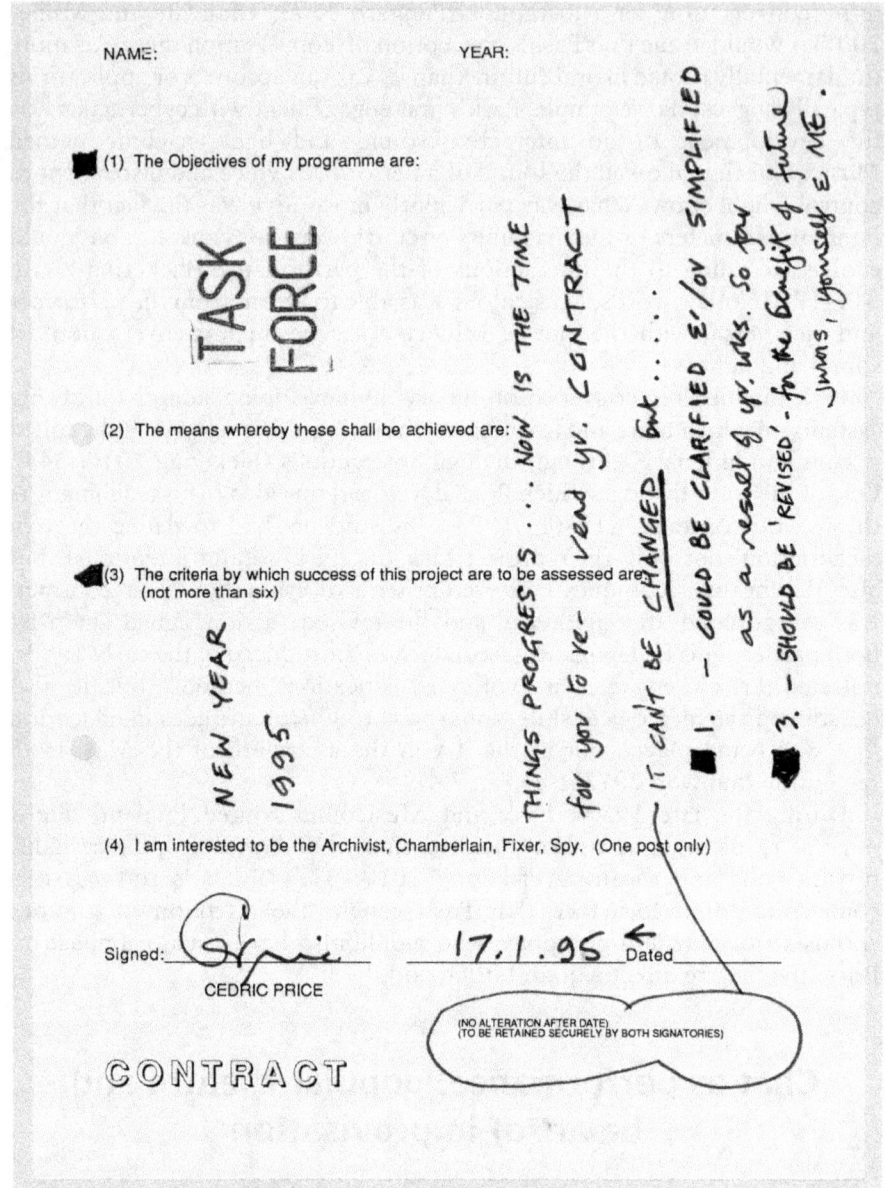

FIG. 7.4 Cedric Price, Task Force 'Contract', AA Diploma Unit 12a, 1994–5, Cedric Price Fonds. Source: Courtesy of the Canadian Centre for Architecture.

the enacted, live event and the creative interaction between text and performance' (2006: 69–70).

The Fun Palace project was the brainchild of Littlewood, who essentially enlisted Price's collaboration as a designer. It was a way for her to reinvent the idea of a 'people's theatre' and depart from traditional theatre practice not only in terms of architecture or staging, but also as a disciplinary field, opening up culture, science and education to everyone. However, Littlewood's impact on Price went well beyond the Fun Palace, notably in terms of Price's own public 'performances'. For example, Samantha Hardingham, author and editor of a recent anthology of Price's work, offers this apt description of Price's public lectures:

> Central to his success – as any performer will know – was precision and timing, deployed more often than not to great comic effect ... What his audiences were exposed to – and what Price was attempting to conjure – was a form of scholarly architectural edu-tainment, designed to make listeners work as hard as the speaker.
>
> HARDINGHAM 2016, 2: 10

As Hardingham suggests, the spontaneity of Price's talks was carefully crafted. For his AA lectures and many others, Price used small 3in. × 5in. index cards on which he made shorthand notes – a word, a letter, a name – suggesting that like a stand-up comedian, he had more or less assimilated his material to allow for a great deal of improvisation and dialogue. The architect Bernard Tschumi, who was a tutor at the AA in the 1970s, suggests that Price would even shuffle his cards and then develop an argument or lecture out of the random sequence of the resulting questions or comments (2014). Furthermore, Price welcomed interruptions and always anticipated a form of audience feedback as an essential part of his lectures. For one series, he even designed a special notebook to encourage the audience to take notes – preferably in point form or as a scrapbook for news – since his talks were often developed over several weeks (Price 1983).

One of the principles of theatrical improvisation involving audience participation is the abandonment of what is known as the 'fourth wall': the virtual separation between the actors and the audience. A critical model for Littlewood's and, I would argue, Price's removal of this implicit barrier was the popular musical hall, the variety act from which the now familiar heckling of the stand-up comedian originated. Stand-up comedy was in itself a violation of the 'fourth wall', since stand-up comedians were first introduced as a way to entertain the audience during scenery and costume changes, typically standing *in front* of the stage curtain, in other words, in the space of the audience (Double 2012). Price was very close to the British comedy scene. As a student at Cambridge in the mid-1950s, he discovered the famous 'Smokers' concerts at the Footlights drama club, one of Britain's most successful comedy venues where such legendary acts as *Beyond the*

FIG. 7.5 *Entertainer at Borough Music Hall, Southwark, London, 1859, Mander and Mitchenson Collection. Source: Courtesy of the University of Bristol/ArenaPAL.*

Fringe or *Monty Python* had their beginnings.[12] He maintained close ties with his college friend Jonathan Miller of *Beyond the Fringe* fame[13] and was also a long-term companion of the actress-writer Eleanor Bron, one of the original comedians at London's *The Establishment Club*, the jazz and comedy club that launched the British satire boom of the 1960s (Carpenter 2009) (see Fig. 7.5).

It was the atmosphere of these sites of popular entertainment – the music hall, the jazz and comedy club – and the casual 'live' mix of jokes, gossip, commentary, smoking, food and drink that Price tried to capture in his in-situ performances or 'chats' and made his choice of venues, at times, so significant. These ranged from spectacular events like his Detroit Think Grid lecture in the fittingly motorized setting of a local drive-in theatre (see Fig. 7.6) to more everyday rituals such as his early morning 'breakfast chats' (Finch 2014) or lunchtime talks in the AA bar where no one was expected to stop and be quiet – and they weren't (Hardingham 2016, 2: 10). Like Littlewood's rehearsals, these improvised chats were a form of dialogic training. One of Price's most loyal chat guests, Alistair McAlpine, called it 'mental gymnastics' (Hardingham 2016, 1: 303).

FIG. 7.6 'Lecture Given At Drive-In Theatre', Ann Arbor News, 30 October 1968, Cedric Price Fonds. Courtesy of the Canadian Centre for Architecture.

Conclusion: orality, autonomy and architectural theory

In conclusion, I would like to return briefly to my initial question concerning the form of Price's 'Non-Plan Diary' and the possible discrepancy between talk and text. Printed text is commonly considered to be the privileged medium of architectural theory (Crysler, Cairns and Heynen 2012). Even the history of architectural theory tends to be based on the study of texts. The rare moments in which orality has been discussed as a part of architectural theory's history has been primarily to support the dominant narrative that architectural discourse, like society in general, has followed a path from orality to textuality.[14] In this chapter, I have challenged this assumption with reference to the seminal work of the oral historian Walter Ong (1982), but also by drawing on ideas developed in literary criticism, performance art theory and cultural studies. One of the defining characteristics that Ong associates with oral forms of communication is that they are 'situational'. As Ong advances, 'oral cultures tend to use concepts in situational, operational frames of reference that are minimally abstract in the sense that they remain close to the living human lifeworld' (48–9). To consider orality in the context of architectural theory is to question not only the hegemony of textuality, but also its presupposed 'autonomy', which has insinuated itself into the larger discourse of architectural autonomy. In examining Price's chats, I have tried to scrutinize not only the complex interrelationship of orality and textuality that exists – and persists – but also the situational and operational frames of reference which are intrinsic to their very meaning. Like Walter Benjamin's 'storyteller' (1936) or Roland Barthes' 'pleasure of the text' (1973), Price's chats point to a more *performative* understanding of textuality bound to social and material processes or what has also been called 'tacit' theory (Crysler, Cairns and Heynen 2012; Avermaete et al. 2020) – a relatively unexplored territory in the historiography of architectural knowledge. Seen from this angle, Price's 'Non-Plan Diary' appears to be less of a divergence between talk and text than a prescription for indeterminacy and participation.

Notes

1 Simon Sadler, interview with the author, 27 December 2017. On the wider ideological context and legacy of the 'Non-Plan' concept, see Sadler and Hughes (2000) and Barker (1991).

2 See, for example, Price, 'Chat: Fun Palace' (1971). In the office filing system, Price's *Building Design* columns are listed under 'BD chats', whereas several audiocassette recordings of office discussions, client meetings and public lectures are also labelled 'chats'. Cedric Price Fonds, Canadian Centre for Architecture, DR2004:1462 and DR2003:0008.

3 See Ong (1982), 10–16. The author underlines the ambiguities of the term 'oral literature' and the indiscriminate primacy it gives to literacy.

4 Price ran nine columns in all: eight for *Building Design* (1975–97) and a final series for the *Architects' Journal* (1998–9). See Hardingham (2016) and Njoo (2018).

5 See Drew (2003). On literary journalism, see Keeble and Wheeler (2007).

6   See Maidment (1981), 196–7. On similar issues of readership, see Rose (2014). For a more comprehensive analysis of *Fors Clavigera*, see Stoddart (1995).
7   Viollet-le-Duc published four books (1873–9) in the 'educational and recreational collection' of the Éditions Hetzel. See Baridon (2014).
8   See, for example, Kacandes (2001).
9   On the influence of Viollet-le-Duc's writing on Sullivan, see Menocal (1981).
10 Sullivan published fifty-two 'chats' in the *Interstate Architect and Builder* from 16 February 1901 to 8 February 1902.
11 On the relationship between the Fun Palace and Cybernetics, see Lobsinger (2000), Mathews (2005) and Pickering (2010: 361–3). On the exchanges of Pask and Price at the AA, see Furtado (2007). The author wishes to thank Ben Sweeting for his help with and insights on cybernetic theory.
12 Gordon Pask, who was a medical student at Cambridge in the early 1950s, collaborated on the Footlights comedy revue as a writer. See Pickering (2010).
13 See Obrist (2003: 82).
14 See, for example, Carpo (2001).

References

Avermaete, T., J. Gosseye, K. Havik, H. Mattsson, J. Mack, T. Anstey, C. Grafe, G. Postiglione, G. Caramellino, A. Schnell, L. Schrijver, P. Rawes and M. Buchert (2020), 'TACK/Communities of Tacit Knowledge: Architecture and its Ways of Knowing', research and training programme, https://tacit-knowledge-architecture.com/.
Banham, R., P. Barker, P. Hall and C. Price (1969), 'Non-Plan: An Experiment in Freedom', *New Society*, 21 March, 435–43.
Baridon, L. (2014), 'Écrire pour enseigner: Enseigner pour reformer', in L. de Finance and J.-M. Leniaud (eds), *Viollet-le-Duc: les visions d'un architecte*, 150–5. Paris: Cité de l'architecture, Norma.
Barker, P. (1991), 'Non-Plan Revisited: Or the Real Way Cities Grow – The Tenth Reyner Banham Memorial Lecture', *Journal of Design History* 12, no. 2: 95–110.
Barthes, R. (1973/1975), *The Pleasure of the Text*, trans. R. Miller, New York: Hill and Wang.
Benjamin, W. (1936/2006). 'The Storyteller: Reflections on the Works of Nikolai Leskov', in D. J. Hale (ed.) and H. Zohn (trans.), *The Novel: An Anthology of Criticism and Theory 1900–2000*. Malden, MA: Blackwell.
Carpenter, H. (2009), *That Was Satire that Was: The Satire Boom of the 1960s*, London: Faber & Faber.
Carpo, M. (2001), *Architecture in the Age of Printing: Orality, Typing, Typography, and Printed Images in the History of Architectural Theory*, Cambridge, MA: MIT Press.
Crysler, C. G., S. Cairns and H. Heynen (eds) (2012), *The SAGE Handbook of Architectural Theory*, London: SAGE.

Double, O. (2012), *Britain Had Talent: A History of Variety Theatre*, Basingstoke: Palgrave Macmillan.
Drew, J. M. L. (2003), *Dickens the Journalist*, Basingstoke: Palgrave Macmillan.
Finch, P. (2014), 'Breakfast with Cedric', in 'Cedric Price: The Dynamics of Time', *Volume* 42: 3.
Furtado, G. (2007), 'Envisioning an Evolving Environment: the Encounters of Gordon Pask, Cedric Price and John Frazer', PhD diss., University of London.
Glanville, R. and K. H. Müller (eds) (2007), *Gordon Pask, Philosopher Mechanic: An Introduction to the Cybernetician's Cybernetician*, Vienna: Echoraum.
Hardingham, S. (2016), *Cedric Price Works 1952–2003: A Forward-Minded Retrospective*, London: Architectural Association; Montreal: Canadian Centre for Architecture.
Holdsworth, N. (2006), *Joan Littlewood*, London: Routledge.
Hughes, J. and S. Sadler (eds) (2000), *Non-Plan: Essays on Freedom, Participation and Change in Modern Architecture and Urbanism*, Oxford: Architectural Press.
Kacandes, I. (2001), *Talk Fiction: Literature and the Talk Explosion*, Lincoln: University of Nebraska Press.
Keeble, R. and S. Wheeler (eds) (2007), *The Journalistic Imagination: Literary Journalists from Defoe to Capote and Carter*, London: Routledge.
Krukowski, S. (1993), 'Louis Sullivan's *Kindergarten Chats* or Form really does follow Function', http://www.rasa.net/writings/kindergardenchats.html.
Lobsinger, M. L. (2000), 'Cybernetic Theory and the Architecture of Performance: Cedric Price's Fun Palace', in S. W. Goldhagen and R. Legault (eds), *Anxious Modernisms: Experimentation in Postwar Architectural Culture*, 119–37, Montreal: Canadian Centre for Architecture; Cambridge, MA: MIT Press.
Maidment, B. (1981), 'Ruskin, *Fors Clavigera* and Ruskinism, 1800–1900', in R. Hewison (ed.), *New Approaches to Ruskin: Thirteen essays*, 194–213, London: Routledge, Kegan Paul.
Maki, F. (1985), *A Style for the Year 2001*, Tokyo: Shikenchiku.
Mathews, S. (2005), 'The Fun Palace: Cedric Price's experiment in architecture and technology', *Technoetic Arts: A Journal of Speculative Research* 3, no. 2: 73–91.
Menocal, N. (1981), *Architecture as Nature: The Transcendentalist Idea of Louis Sullivan*, Madison: University of Wisconsin Press.
Njoo, J. (2018), 'L'architecte en conteur: Cedric Price et le langage de l'expérience', in C. Younès and C. Bodart (eds), *Au tournant de l'expérience. Interroger ce qui se construit, partager ce qui nous arrive*, 179–93, Paris: Hermann.
Obrist, H. U. (ed.) (2003), *Re: CP*, Basel: Birkhäuser.
Olson, D. R., D. Bloome, A. H. Dyson, J. P. Gee, V. Purcell-Gates and G. Wells (2006), 'Orality and Literacy: A Symposium in Honour of David Olson', *Research in the Teaching of English* 41, no. 2: 136–79.
Olson, D. R. and N. Torrance (eds) (1991), *Literacy and Orality*, Cambridge: Cambridge University Press.
Ong, W. J. (1982/2002), *Orality and Literacy: The Technologizing of the Word*, London: Routledge.
Palmegiano, E. M. (2012), *Perceptions of the Press in Nineteenth Century British Periodicals: A Bibliography*, London: Anthem Press.
Pangaro, P. (1993), 'Pask as Dramaturg', in R. Glanville (ed.), *Systems Research* 10, no. 3: 135–42.

Pickering, A. (2010), *The Cybernetic Brain: Sketches for a New Future*, Chicago: University of Chicago Press.
Price, C. (1971), 'Chat: Fun Palace', *Architectural Design* 41 (April): 231–2.
Price, C. (1976), 'Cedric Price: Aiming to Miss. Notes based on three lectures given at Art Net November 1975', *Net* 2.
Price, C. (1978), 'Some Excellent Ideas', *Pegasus* 15: 63–4.
Price, C. (1979), 'Filling the Space: Recent Books on Architecture', *Encounter* 59 (October). Reprinted in Hardingham 2016, 2: 321–5.
Price, C. (1980a), 'The Exchange', *AA Prospectus 1980–81*, 44.
Price, C. (1980b, 1994), AA 'Contracts': Intermediate Unit 6 and Diploma Unit 12a, Cedric Price Fonds, Canadian Centre for Architecture, Montreal, DR2006:0109, DR2004:1011:001:001 and DR2004:1008:003:002.
Price, C. (1983), notebook, Cedric Price Fonds, Canadian Centre for Architecture, Montreal, DR2004:1521.
Price, C. (1985a), 'Horror Stories with a Bonus', *Building Design*, 18 October, 10–16.
Price, C. (1985b/2016), 'Starting Price' and 'Closing Price', *Building Design*, 19 April–19 December 1986. Reprinted in Hardingham 2016, 2: 382–8.
Price, C. (1990), 'Cedric Price Talks at the AA', *AA Files* 19 (Spring): 27–34.
Price, C. (1997), 'Non-Plan – A True Mirror of Social Appetites?', Association for Art History conference, Courtauld Institute of Art, London, 4–6 April, Cedric Fonds, Canadian Centre for Architecture, Montreal, DR2004:1527.
Price, C. (2000), 'Cedric Price's Non-Plan Diary', in J. Hughes and S. Sadler (eds), *Non-Plan: Essays on Freedom, Participation and Change in Modern Architecture and Urbanism*, 22–31, Oxford: Architectural Press.
Rose, C. (2014), 'John Ruskin's *Fors Clavigera*: The Educator as Hero', BA thesis, University of California Los Angeles, http://escholarship.org/uc/item/2cg5r8z6.
Schudson, M. (1996), *The Power of News*, Cambridge, MA: Harvard University Press.
Stoddart, J. (1995), *Ruskin's Culture Wars: Fors Clavigera and the Crisis of Victorian Liberalism*, Charlottesville: University of Virginia Press.
Sullivan, L. (1901/1979), 'Letter to Lyndon P. Smith', 22 February, in L. Sullivan, *Kindergarten Chats and Other Writings*, ed. I. Athey, appendix A: 244, New York: Dover.
Sullivan, L. (1934), *Kindergarten Chats on Architecture, Democracy and Education*, Lawrence, KS: Scarab Fraternity Press.
Sunwoo, I. (2012), 'From the "Well-Laid Table" to the "Market-Place": The Architectural Association Unit System', *Journal of Architectural Education* 65, no. 2: 24–41.
Thomas, B. (2012), *Fictional Dialogue: Speech and Conversation in the Modern and Postmodern Novel*, Lincoln: University of Nebraska Press.
Tschumi, B. (2014), video interview with Jan Nauta, *Cedric Price Memory Bank*, http://www.cedricprice.com/#/memory-bank.
Viollet-le-Duc, E. E. (1873), *Histoire d'une maison*, Paris: Hetzel.
Wiener, N. (1948), *Cybernetics: or Control and Communication in the Animal and the Machine*, Cambridge, MA: MIT Press.

CHAPTER EIGHT

Alternative Facts: Towards a Theorization of Oral History in Architecture

Janina Gosseye, Naomi Stead and Deborah van der Plaat

This book is concerned with the mobility of ideas and concepts in architecture – the ways in which knowledge moves, how it shifts and transforms through that movement, how ideas mean different things in different places to different people at different times. In this context, the place of oral history in architecture is complex: stories derived from oral history are, by definition, highly particularized and highly local. Their specificity to a given place and time is part of their power, yet also party to their marginalization – oral histories are often dismissed as trivial, just as they bring into question fundamental issues of the 'truthfulness' of distinct kinds of architectural knowledge.[1]

Oral history is mobile in its being *dialogic*, both literally and figuratively, and with all the malleability that term implies. At the literal level, it is evinced in dialogue between an individual and an interviewer, but more than this, across an individual's life, stories have often been continually reshaped – as they are told and retold, edited and performed and narrativized, and transformed in and through that process (Portelli 1998). In oral history, meaning is negotiated through polyvocal, interpersonal, dialogical movement back and forth between people, in shuttling, flickering, changeable motion. Oral histories are also mobile to the same extent that individuals themselves are: stories are embodied, and carried, through time and space, through both history and memory, on migratory journeys through the self.

Oral history is thus always already social – in exploring the link between personal life and epochal times, between individual experience and historic events. Likewise, it is always already spatial – taking account of the places and spaces in which personal events took place, and made a small part of history (Ohmann 2001).

In this context, and if we think of the potential of oral history as either a conduit or a mechanism for the transmission of knowledge, the complexities immediately mount. This chapter is concerned, in part, with the ways in which oral history challenges and complexifies the primacy of establishment figures – such as architects or theorists – in defining and architectural ideas. Such figures are themselves not the obvious subjects of oral history, which has long been framed and celebrated as a mode of history 'from the ground up' – valorizing precisely those people who have *not* been authorized to speak about architecture or architectural knowledge. Yet, at the same time, architectural culture has been profoundly characterized by oral modes: of conversation, critique, gossip, lecture, spoken aphorism and so on. Orality has been a profound influence, even as it has often been overlooked in the dissemination of knowledge and ideas in architecture. At the same time, oral history as a discipline and a practice has been both underutilized and underexamined.

One might say that in its current state of theorization, oral history, as a method in architecture, is itself mobile or in flux. Its value or significance is not universally acknowledged but is rather under investigation; its theoretical framework is still mutable, currently under negotiation; and its role in the carriage and movement of architectural knowledge is not yet established. Oral history has not found a home in architecture – or not yet.[2] This chapter is an endeavour to trace the method's movement from other disciplines into architecture, and its attempts to settle there.

The hot breath of the architect down the historian's neck

Given this chapter's subject matter, it seems appropriate to start with an anecdote. In 2015 a respected architectural historian wrote a scholarly essay about one of Australia's newest state art museums. The building was located in a semi-tropical region of the country, and much of the surrounding rhetoric tended to frame it in terms of an apparent place-specificity – of an architecture emerging from the climatic, material and cultural conditions of its site. The historian's essay questioned this. It asked if the building's purported 'regionalist' place-specificity was perhaps more an article of rhetoric on the part of the architects, or perhaps an artefact of media construction, or possibly evidence of a thoroughgoing state approach to cultural policy. The paper was an example of critical history. It advanced an interpretative position set forth by and specific to a critical author, and supported this position with both primary and secondary sources. The author, however, deliberately chose not to interview the architects – both were (and are) still alive, and in practice. The paper was double-blind peer-reviewed and published by Australia's leading scholarly society in architectural history.

Nine months after the essay was published, the architects wrote back, producing their own 'refereed paper' – in reality, a paper that had been read by a select group of supporters to whom they had sent it – and publishing it on their website, on social media and also via email to a selection of high-profile architects and architectural scholars in Australia. Their text, they stated, would 'redress and correct the inaccuracies and fundamental research deficiencies' that 'plagued' the architectural historian's original work. Accusing the author of a 'circular logic' that had led to preconceived outcomes, they demanded the retraction of the paper, which (they alleged) made 'painfully plain the pitfalls of failing to interrogate primary sources: the key protagonists involved in the project's design and realisation'.

The dispute between the architects and the author was bitter and protracted. The architects first demanded the retraction of the paper, then that their text be published alongside the original piece, later that an 'erratum' be published, and finally that the paper be extensively revised based on a number of what they described as 'factual errors'. While the author of the original piece maintained that these were not factual errors but rather differences of opinion and interpretation, minor clarifications were duly made to the text and it was eventually republished, with a note to this effect.

The point of relaying this painful story here is to demonstrate how 'yesterday's breath can be felt down today's historian's neck'.[3] Disciplinary distinctions between criticism and history, indeed the practice *of* critical history, and the historicization of the recent past are all revealed to be risky in advance of the (both literal and figurative) death of the architectural author. These practices not only open questions about the status of architects as primary evidential sources – even *the* primary source – and the weight given to the intentions they claim for a built work, but also about what constitutes architectural knowledge and who possesses it. Who can speak for and about buildings?

Oral history and architectural authorship

The discipline of architecture is often said to be characterized by a rigid separation between the domains of practice and knowledge production: between architectural design and architectural theory. The method of oral history, which first attached itself to interviewing in 1942 (Ritchie 2011), offers scholars a unique opportunity to bridge this divide: to access the knowledge embedded in the act of design; what has also been called 'tacit knowledge' (Niedderer 2007; Polanyi 1964; Polanyi 1966). It is then no surprise that in architecture, oral history as a method is commonly used to record the stories of architects as well as their perspective on buildings and their design intentions. However, a side effect of this use of oral history as a method in architecture is that it often reinforces the notion of the heroic designer – even if involuntarily. Architecture remains a strongly authorized practice, in the sense that the mythic author-figure remains very much alive, and also that the legitimization to speak for and about buildings is still attached to author figures. Architects are often also at pains to shape and protect their legacy and to dictate how their work and persona will be written into history. All of this makes the use of oral history methods in architecture a complex proposition.

While many historians have argued that oral history has the potential to counter more singular and conventional modes of history writing (Abrams 2010; Portelli 1998), in architecture there seems to be a tacit understanding that when the 'author' of a building is still alive, he or she should be the first port of call. Valorizing the architect's intentions above all else, oral history thus commonly reinforces rather than critiques the metanarratives that characterize the discipline, one of which is the myth of the genius or master designer. Historically, invention and innovation have been presented as solitary ventures, and this is a perception that continues to be cultivated in architecture, as the name of the principal architect often obscures the multiple hands and voices that have a stake in the design. Clients are chief among this category.

In the 1996 book *The Sex of Architecture*, Alice Friedman writes, 'Notably missing from the history of modern architecture is any substantive discussion of the role of women clients as collaborators in design or catalysts for architectural innovation. This failure of attention, together with the overvaluing of the individual architect as innovator, has contributed to the 'star system' and distorts our understanding of the design process' (Friedman 1996: 217). Using her analysis of the important role that Truus Schröder played in the design of the Schröder house – an analysis that is heavily reliant on interviews with Mrs Schröder – as an example, Friedman suggests that reinserting the role of the client – be they male or female – into historical inquiry results in a strikingly different narrative from the familiar surveys of architecture.

But other voices, other potential sources of architectural knowledge, are also commonly lost: the focus on architects and their professional culture[4] often comes at the expense of accounts that are personal and individual; those who use, occupy and construct buildings are seldom part of the conversation (Gosseye 2014). And yet, use, occupancy and construction can provide an intimate insight into a building's social and cultural 'life'.[5] Sociologists such as Georg Simmel, and philosophical theorists such as Paul Ricoeur and Maurice Halbwachs, have long stressed the interdependence between physical places and social realms and the capacity of buildings to produce mental geographies (Halbwachs 1992; Ricoeur 1991; Ricoeur 2000). It could be argued that insight into social realms – the 'life' in and of architecture – is more likely to occur by verbal means than by relying on more conventional forms of architectural evidence, such as the textual and the visual. If this premise is accepted, then the use of oral history merely to record architects' own stories seems like a missed opportunity.

The risk of using oral history in architecture is thus that the method may simply amplify existing mythologies – assembling yet more evidence towards a hagiography of the 'great man' behind the 'great architect' (and we use these gendered terms deliberately). And yet, as the methodological biases of professional history have come under review in recent decades, leading to a reevaluation of oral history and recognition of oral history's ability to give voice to 'other' stories, architecture's wariness of alternative voices remains strong.

Because of the historic (rather limited) use of the method of oral history in architecture, the impact that valorizing and including these particular sources of architectural knowledge might have on our architectural theory is as yet unknown. The scholarly literature in the area is also underdeveloped: while there are accounts of architectural scholars using oral history, the literature analysing or theorizing oral history as a method in architecture, or the implications of its use, is still only small. This chapter is an attempt towards building this body of theoretical literature. Tracing some of the lineage of oral history research in architecture, and drawing upon the theory of oral history as it has been set out in other disciplines,[6] this text interrogates whether a broader, more inclusive use of oral history, as a vehicle of architectural knowledge, might alter our insights into architectural theory and history.

Oral history and architectural knowledge

The designated use of oral history as a method in architectural history can be traced to the mid-1990s – in the sense that only then were attempts made to structurally and systematically frame an extended architectural history text explicitly around oral history interviews. In 1994, the book *The Oral History of Modern Architecture* appeared, a publication that had been a long time in the making. Its prehistory dates back to 1953 when an eager young American architect by the name of John Peter set off with his tape recorder to talk to those whom he described as 'the greatest architects of the twentieth century'. Peter interviewed Frank Lloyd Wright, Marcel Breuer, Buckminster Fuller, Eero Saarinen, Walter Gropius, Mies van der Rohe, Louis Kahn, I. M. Pei and many more, and after several decades realized that he had a considerable archive of these 'greatest architects' and compiled a small selection of his more than seventy interviews into a book.

Acknowledging that the oral history method had at that time rarely been applied to architecture, and that the technique was more commonly reserved for the creation of micro-histories rather than metanarratives, Peter, in the introduction to his book, writes that he opted for the method of oral history as he wanted to produce a different type of history. Not a history of modern architecture told by historians and critics – those on the 'outside' – but a history of modern architecture relayed by those 'on the inside': the modern masters. Peter spent considerable energy to ensure that those interviewed were truly authorities in modern architecture and argues that the result of his efforts is 'history alive', stating, 'There is a distinctive quality to the spontaneity of thoughts expressed in speech' and 'something uniquely moving in hearing the spoken words of these people' (Peter 1994: 10). It is worth noting that he meant this literally. The book was accompanied by a CD ROM, allowing readers to also listen to the interviews. This 'orality', the ability to hear the actual voices of these canonical figures, is in fact one of the strengths of the book, which, as we will show, also exhibited significant conceptual flaws.

Some were quick to point these out. In March 1995, a few months after Peter's book appeared, architectural critic Julian Holder published a pulverizing review in the British *Architects' Journal*, titled 'Modernist "heroes" with little to say'. In this piece, Holder labels Peter's publication as nothing more than hero-worship, 'an out-of-date homage to the leaders of the Modern Movement and their famous – and not so famous – acolytes'. He concludes that 'essentially "the greatest" have nothing very interesting to say' (Holder 1995: 45).

While in early post-war America oral history targeted both the lives of everyday people and the 'great men', Britain employed oral history much more as a means of rescuing the voices of the labouring people – those who had no voice in past historical narratives. By the 1980s, this approach prevailed on both sides of the Atlantic and oral history became the method of choice amongst scholars of the twentieth century, seeking to uncover the experiences of a number of groups who had traditionally been disregarded by conventional histories (Abrams 2016: 15).[7] In this sense, Holder was right: Peter's book was out of date; time had caught up with him and the work no longer corresponded with prevailing ideology in the method of oral history.[8]

However, by telling the story from the inside, and thereby implicitly asserting the authority of the architect and chronicling the story of 'great men' – it should be noted that not a single one of his interviewees was female – Peter hoped that he could reveal a narrative of design intention. In his own words, 'What the founders of modern architecture thought and said is essential to a real understanding of what they did' (Peter 1994: 8). Such beliefs have since been discredited. In a paper published in 2006, British architectural historian Robert Proctor points to the fallacy of the belief that the architect's interview is actually able to reveal the intentions of the architect. Proctor suggests that just as 'artistic intention' has long since been attacked in literary criticism, and following that in other disciplines, pursuing it through oral history is theoretically also difficult to sustain in architecture (Proctor 2006).

Surprisingly enough, Peter seemed aware of the heresy of his belief. In the introduction to his book, he wrote, 'There is frequently a wide discrepancy between [the architects'] words and their works'. He goes on, 'Nevertheless, the tapes have recorded what they said or chose to say. In fact, on hearing their actual voices one cannot help but be struck by the sincerity of and dedication to their beliefs. For the most part, it would seem both cynical and cavalier to doubt whether they were telling the truth as they perceived it' (Peter 1994: 10). The emphasis here is not on historical truth, but on the avowedly relative and subjective, albeit 'sincere', beliefs of the architects about the course of events – what we might today call 'alternative facts' (Sinderbrand 2017).

Here, Peter hints at the relative credence that should be given to the architects' words, when interviewed later in life about their work. In a recent paper, British planning historian David Adams aptly explains what Peter was hinting at, writing that

> [A]rchitects, when ... interviewed [later in life], cannot be easily considered as the same people as when they engaged in the act of design conception, but must be viewed as observing themselves in nostalgic autobiographical mode, interpreting their histories through the prism of the contemporary context ... Their memories are articulated through a form of narration and storytelling that tends to obstruct [rather than facilitate] access to design intention.
>
> ADAMS 2012: 3

Adams points out that while architects might be providing information in oral history interviews, they are often also manipulating this information, be it consciously or subconsciously; certain things are remembered and said, others forgotten or left unsaid in an attempt to build a legacy or perpetuate certain (mis)conceptions about their work. Adams thus goes on to argue that the use of oral history in architectural historiography mitigates the importance of the architect's story, as this story might be no more 'truthful' (or even factual) than any of the other narratives that might accumulate around a single catalyst: the architectural structure. The oral history method, it could be argued, strips the architect's story of its authority and makes apparent its status as just one possible narrative among many potential others that contribute to the production and continual remaking or reimagining of a building's history over time: 'Rather than interpreting architects' narratives as a way of reaching the true meaning of a building, we might begin to consider that these reflective testimonies, actively constructed through the prism of the present, provide an important relational perspective on how architecture is reshaped materially and symbolically' (Adams 2012: 3).

Oral history, architectural affections and confections

Early on in his book's introduction, Peter states that 'with an oral history there looms always the large question of whether the people who created the works under discussion are the best judges of what they accomplished', and asks, 'Are the players the best judges of the game?' (Peter 1994: 8). It soon becomes clear that Peter poses this question for the sole purpose of asserting the authority of the architectural historian who conducted the interview, to edit and curate its content. Peter qualifies the architectural historian as an 'outside authority', capable of giving a 'more objective and accurate appraisal ... with both independence and perspective' (Peter 1994: 8).

Here Peter (unwittingly) points to the peculiar position of an architectural historian who engages in oral history. If oral histories lend themselves particularly well to revealing the speaker as a feeling self, and amplifying the personal dimensions of human existence, architecture – as discipline, practice and profession – mitigates *against* such dimensions (Stead 2014). And yet, even if an oral history interview takes place within this purely professional context, with all the tropes and types, patterns and clichés and performances of professional belonging that it entails, the interviewer's persona always becomes part and parcel of the conversation (Stead 2014: 157). The question should then be asked, can an architectural historian who relies on oral history, with all the personal and interpersonal affects that this methodology entails, truly write a detached, objective history about a building – can such a history even exist? Or is it her or his story rather than history?

Oral history is always a type of collaborative performance, in which interviewers and interviewees play particular parts.[9] Many elements of the encounter, however, remain unspoken: the comportment and deportment of those involved, their style of utterance or vocalizing, their facial expressions and tone, their inclination or declination towards the speaker; all the non-verbal gestures that they make, which could be gathered under the frame of 'posture'.[10] These all have a bearing on the exchange, even if within the realm of architecture they are often dismissed as trivial. Celebrating all this *slag* – the 'messiness' that comes along with any interpersonal encounter – oral history, we posit, has the capacity to puncture through architecture's professional mask and bring to the fore unauthorized, polyphonic human and social narratives by not only the architect, but everyone who has in some way been 'affected' by an architectural structure.[11]

If oral history is used to construct such multi-vocal, affective building histories that neither exclude nor prioritize the architect's interview, but frame it as merely one of many possible narratives, this might – indeed almost certainly will – have implications for architectural theory. Rather than producing singular and static accounts, informed by one (or more) authoritative writers, such methods can assist in producing a multi-vocal and evolving appreciation of the life of buildings over time.[12] Georg Simmel, amongst many other social and spatial theorists, argues that space should not be thought of as static. He contends that spatial boundaries and understandings of space, such as the buildings we inhabit and the cities we live in, are formed and reproduced by social action. In accordance with this position, and through its multi-vocality, oral history thus can not only 'complete' existing architectural histories – by offering accounts of events and periods that are otherwise absent from the historic record in architecture – but also disrupt existing architectural historiography and re-examine historical narratives that have become mythological, fixed in place by repetition. Oral history might even have the capacity to destabilize the very theoretical foundations of architectural history: by perpetually recontextualizing the architectural object.

Oral history is a method in tune with the age. It is well known that since the 1960s, and under the influence of feminist theory and activism, there has been a striking rise in interest in the body, subjective experience and the personal in research and academic work. This 'affective turn' encompasses the subjectivity of both researchers and those researched, as well as later textual accounts and interpretations (Ohmann 2001). British psychologist Jeffrey Gray notes that such a valorization of the personal has multiplied throughout almost all scholarly disciplines (Gray 2001: 51). In this context, Gray argues, the re-emergence of the personal may appear to be an anomaly: 'Wasn't the author supposed to be dead?' (Gray 2001: 51). But of course, only the sole author is dead, and indeed even 'he' has proven hard to kill, especially in architecture.

Oral history beyond myth-making

Architecture commonly still uses oral history for its hagiographic potential – one might note the popularity of 'gift books' made up of quotations from famous architects. *The Architect Says: Quotes, Quips, and Words of Wisdom* (2012) is an excellent recent example, which according to its publisher, Princeton Architectural Press, is 'a colorful compendium of quotations from more than one hundred of history's most opinionated design minds … convey[ing] a remarkable depth and diversity of thinking … [a]lternately wise and amusing' (Dushkes 2012). Beyond such overt myth-making, to this day, few other narratives are regularly recorded or systematically included in architectural histories. Furthermore, as architectural historiography moves closer and closer to the present day, it seems that this persistent singular use of oral history has given architects a sense of entitlement, resulting in them breathing (quite heavily) down the necks of historians.

Another recent attempt at constructing an architectural record solely through the use of oral history again profiles only architects. In 2014, Dean Dewhirst compiled twenty transcribed interviews with Australia's most famed architects in a book titled *From the Ground Up: 20 Stories of a Life in Architecture*. This book, in Dewhirst's own words, foregrounds 'individuals who are, right now, in their studios producing designs that will eventually form the fabric of our cities' (2014: 8).

To a critical eye, the book offers little more than a string of platitudes, with one architect stating that 'architecture is a celebration of space'[13] and another duo arguing that '[m]ost buildings have a purpose and it is important that they fulfil that purpose but then give more . . . We try to infuse spirit in the making of the building.'[14] Whilst trying for the ideal of great architects dropping inspirational pearls of wisdom about their work, the book thus quickly descends into banal statements of the obvious, along with bouts of self-aggrandizement – an affliction that at times also plagued Peter's work.

In this sense, it is perhaps not surprising to discover that the author and interviewer Dewhirst is in fact the head of a recruitment company specializing in the fields of architecture and design. The book is thus revealed as, at least in part, a marketing exercise, building on the mythology of 'genius' architects in order to sell the services of a recruiting agent. But in spite of its rather inauspicious context, we would argue that the book does (inadvertently) reveal something more promising about the potential of oral history in architecture.

Its title, *Stories of a Life in Architecture*, can be understood in two ways: first where 'architecture' is seen as a profession, such a book could chronicle the passion and plight of those who pursue it. This would seem to be the intended meaning for the book's title and framing. But the title also encompasses a second possible meaning: where architecture is understood as those buildings in which people dwell. 'A life in architecture' could then refer to the lives of all manner of diverse, ordinary, extraordinary, architectural and non-architectural people, as lived within buildings. This aspect is not explored in the book, but it perhaps offers a way forward, towards understanding another aspect of how oral history can more fully excavate not only the concepts and ideas pursued by those who design buildings, but also the stories of those who actually spend their lives building, living, working and being in buildings. Whilst these people have historically not been a major part of scholarly and disciplinary conversations about 'life in architecture', oral history remains a way in which these voices can be heard. It thus has the capacity to not only change how architectural history is conceived and understood but can also challenge our understanding of what constitutes 'architectural knowledge', and the routes through which such knowledge has been transmitted, up until now.

Notes

1   The authors wish to thank the editors of the book, and also the reviewers of this paper, for their insightful comments and observations, including questions of the 'truthfulness of knowledge' in oral history in architecture.

2   The authors of this chapter have recently edited a book on the theorization of oral history as a method in architecture, *Speaking of Buildings: Oral History Methods in Architecture*, published by Princeton Architectural Press in 2019.

3   'Theory's History, 196x–199x: Challenges in the Historiography of Architectural Knowledge', call for papers, http://architecture.kuleuven.be/theoryshistory/res/CFP.pdf.

4   See, for instance, Rem Koolhaas and Hans Ulrich Obrist's *Project Japan: Metabolism Talks* (Koolhaas and Obrist 2011).

5   An excellent example is Jesse Adams Stein's essay, which describes how – through oral histories with former workers – the atmosphere and experience of the New South Wales Government Printing Office in Australia, which now serves as a 'cloud computing centre', could be reconstructed or 'co-constructed' (Adams Stein 2014).

6   A key work is Robert Perks and Alistair Thomson's *The Oral History Reader* (1998).

7   For a detailed account of the history of oral history, see also Donald A. Ritchie, 'Introduction: The Evolution of Oral History' (2011).

8   The time that had passed between the recording and the publication resulted in several of them having died in the interval – of the ten interviews of which annotated transcriptions had been included in the book, only three were still alive by the time it was published – so the risk of the historic subject breathing down the historian's neck in the compilation of the material was low.

9   This performative aspect – the playing of a part and the construction of a persona – is of course not unique to oral history interviews, but also recurs in other interpersonal exchanges, such as lectures. In *The Rhetoric of Modernism: Le Corbusier as a Lecturer*, Tim Benton, for instance, highlights the importance of the performative aspect by demonstrating how Le Corbusier in his lectures 'simultaneously charms his audience with his modesty and candour, while positioning himself as a disinterested poet and philosopher engaged in "constant and solitary introspection"' (Benton 2009: 61).

10 With thanks again to one of the reviewers of this paper for the concept of 'posture' and for directing us to the work of Jérôme Meizoz's *Postures littéraires: Mises en scène modernes de l'auteur* (2007) and *La fabrique des singularités: Postures littéraires II* (2011).

11 For a classic text on the 'affective turn', see Ticineto Clough and Halley (2007).

12 See, for example, 'A Night in the Jacobi House' event organized by Deborah van der Plaat and Janina Gosseye at the State Library of Queensland, 20 August 2014, when all the residents that ever lived in the Jacobi House, which was designed by Hayes and Scott (1957), were invited to talk about their experiences living in the house. This resulted in a very polyphonic account of the house.

13 Philip Cox, interviewed by Dean Dewhirst (Dewhirst 2014: 34).

14 Lindsay and Kerry Clare, interviewed by Dean Dewhirst (Dewhirst 2014: 17).

References

Abrams, L. (2010), 'Power and Empowerment', in L. Abrams (ed.), *Oral History Theory*, 153–74, London and New York: Routledge.
Adams, D. (2012), 'Shaped by Memory: Oral Histories of Post-war Modernist Architecture', *Working Paper Series* 12, Birmingham, UK: Birmingham City University, Centre for Environment and Society Research.
Adams Stein, J. (2014), 'The Co-construction of Spatial Memory: Enriching Architectural Histories of "Ordinary" Buildings', *Fabrications* 24, no. 2: 178–97.
Benton, T. (2009), *The Rhetoric of Modernism: Le Corbusier as a Lecturer*, Basel, Boston and Berlin: Birkhäuser.
Dewhirst, D. (2014), *From the Ground Up: 20 Stories of a Life in Architecture*, Melbourne: Uro Publications.
Dushkes, L. S. (ed.) (2012), *The Architect Says: Quotes, Quips, and Words of Wisdom*, New York: Princeton Architectural Press.
Friedman, A. T. (1996), 'Not a Muse: The Client's Role at the Rietveld Schröder House', in D. Agrest, P. Conway and L. K. Weisman (eds), *The Sex of Architecture*, 217–32, New York: Harry N. Abrams.
Gosseye, J. (2014), 'Lost in Conversation: Editorial', *Fabrications* 24, no. 2: 147–55.
Gray, J. (2001), 'In the Name of the Subject: Some recent versions of the personal', in D. H. Holdstein and D. Bleich (eds), *Personal Effects: The Social Character of Scholarly Writing*, 51–76, Logan: Utah State University Press.
Halbwachs, M. (1992), *On Collective Memory*, Chicago: University of Chicago Press.
Holder, J. (1995), 'Modernist "Heroes" with Little to Say', *Architects' Journal* (March): 45.
Koolhaas, R. and H. U. Obrist (eds) (2011), *Project Japan: Metabolism Talks*, London and Cologne: Taschen.
Loosen S., E. Couchez, R. Heynickx, H. Heynen and Y. Schoonjans (2017), 'Theory's History, 196x–199x: Challenges in the Historiography of Architectural Knowledge', call for papers, http://architecture.kuleuven.be/theoryshistory/res/CFP.pdf.
Meizoz, J. (2007), *Postures littéraires: Mises en scène modernes de l'auteur*, Geneva: Slatkine Éditions.
Meizoz, J. (2011), *La fabrique des singularités: Postures littéraires II*. Geneva: Slatkine Éditions.
Niedderer, K. (2007), 'Mapping the meaning of knowledge in design research', *Design Research Quarterly* 2, no. 2: 1–13.
Ohmann, R. (2001), 'The Personal as History', in D. Holdstein and D. Bleich (eds), *Personal Effects: The Social Character of Scholarly Writing*, 335–56, Logan: Utah State University Press.
Perks, R. and A. Thomson (1998), *The Oral History Reader*, London and New York: Routledge.
Peter, J. (1994), *The Oral History of Modern Architecture: Interviews with the Greatest Architects of the Twentieth Century*, New York: Harry N. Abrams.
Polanyi, M. (1964), *Personal Knowledge: Towards a Post-Critical Philosophy*, New York: Harper & Row.
Polanyi, M. (1966), *The Tacit Dimension*, Garden City, NY: Doubleday.
Portelli, A. (1998), 'Oral History as Genre', in M. Chamberlain and P. Thompson (eds), *Narrative and Genre*, 23–45, London: Routledge.

Proctor, R. (2006), 'The Architect's Intention: Interpreting Post-war Modernism through the Architect Interview', *Journal of Design History* 19, no. 4: 295–307.
Ricoeur, P. (1991), 'L'Identité narrative', *Revue des Sciences Humaines* 95, no. 22: 35–47.
Ricoeur, P. (2000), 'L'Écriture de l'histoire et la representation du passé', *Annales Histoire Sciences Sociales* 4 (July–August): 731–47.
Ritchie, D. A. (2011), 'Introduction: The Evolution of Oral History', in D. A. Ritchie (ed.), *The Oxford Handbook of Oral History*, 3–19, Oxford: Oxford University Press.
Sinderbrand, R. (2017), 'How Kellyanne Conway ushered in the era of "alternative facts"', *Washington Post*, 22 January, https://www.washingtonpost.com/news/the-fix/wp/2017/01/22/how-kellyanne-conway-ushered-in-the-era-of-alternative-facts/?utm_term=.1b56724860c2.
Stead, N. (2014), 'Architectural Affections: On Some Modes of Conversation in Architecture, Towards a Disciplinary Theorisation of Oral History', *Fabrications* 24, no. 2: 156–77.
Ticineto Clough, P. and J. Halley (eds) (2007), *The Affective Turn: Theorizing the Social*, Durham, NC: Duke University Press.

CHAPTER NINE

Abandoning the Plan

Michael Jasper

Introduction

In his 2014 Royal Academy of Arts lecture, Raphael Moneo surveyed architectural knowledge across the centuries, finding it rendered in buildings, treatises, drawings and encyclopaedias; in histories, construction technologies, and exhibitions (Moneo 2014). In what follows I take an episode alluded to but not elaborated on by Moneo as my point of departure: a moment in the mid-1960s where direct lines to the parallel legacies of Beaux-Arts planning and Neo-Plasticist space concepts are still vital, a moment when a practice of architectural composition and its associated studio languages are sufficiently present such that potential disciplinary loss could be sensed.[1]

The episode is quietly announced by Peter Eisenman in a little cited text from the late 1960s, where he decries that the importance of the plan as conceptual device has been abandoned. The moment is 1969 and Eisenman is reviewing a recent number of *Perspecta*, the journal of the Yale School of Architecture. In the context of commenting on articles by Kenneth Frampton on the *Maison de Verre*, Alan Greenberg on Lutyens, and Antonio Hernandez on J. N. L. Durand among others, the value of the architectural plan and its apparent demise in practice and education is highlighted. 'In the rush to embrace the tenets of "modernism", and to sweep away Beaux Arts academicism,' writes Eisenman, 'the importance of the plan as a conceptual device has been all but overlooked' (Eisenman 1969: 75). Eisenman makes his position toward the plan even more emphatic when discussing approaches to architectural history 'as an analytical and theoretical medium' with priority at least in part to be accorded to the interrogation of drawings and plans as manifestations of architectural ideas (Eisenman 1969: 75).

In the same period, and as further witness to perceived shifts in sensibility, John Hejduk announced another take on the lingering logic and diminishing value of the plan as locus of knowledge in an essay which first appeared in 1965 in a tribute issue of *L'Architecture d'aujourd'hui* following the death of Le Corbusier. This first publication, which he titled 'Hors du temps dans l'espace' (Out of time and into space), coincided with the end of Hejduk's nearly decade-long experiments on certain of the same formal and theoretical issues in his drawings for the so-called *Texas House* series. Partially documented in a catalogue accompanying a 1980s exhibition, Hejduk developed seven *Texas House* projects between 1954 and 1962, the 'Texas' appellation coinciding with Hejduk's entry to teaching which occurred at the University of Texas at Austin in 1954. At the end of the series, and confronted with the death of Le Corbusier, Hejduk sent out his own missive through the 'Out of Time' essay. Hejduk's text, as I will show, announced a different or additional loss to that identified by Eisenman, one characterized by Hejduk as a slip in architectural time, a slip that signals, I argue, another kind of abandonment.

A Beaux-Arts legacy of cross-axial, plaided composition was still present for Hejduk at that moment. However, Cubist and Post-Cubist formal ambitions and their consequent spatial effects equally inhabited and haunted architectural work and thinking at the time. In his essay, for example, Hejduk discerned specific devices and conditions at stake in the plans of Le Corbusier's *Carpenter Center for the Visual Arts* (1959–63) and contrasts them with those at work in the latter's earlier *Villa Stein* at Garches. While perhaps part of the mourning process following the death of Le Corbusier, Hejduk finds that something has been lost in the gap between the two Corbusian projects. Seemingly let go according to Hejduk are elements of a Post-Cubist or Neo-Plasticist knowledge exemplarily rendered in Garches. The essay provided an analysis of Le Corbusier's *Carpenter Center for the Visual Arts* undertaken in the context of a discussion of the differences between two plastic points of view, the Cubist and the Neo-Plasticist. For Hejduk, painting and architecture generally 'are an embodiment of specific plastic points of view' (Hejduk 1968: xxi). These plastic points of view also correspond for Hejduk to ideas of architectural-painterly space and thus Hejduk's essay was also in part about the potential or limits each implies for the history, trajectory and future of architectural space as a problem for the practising architect and an interpretive category for the critic-historian. In an expanded version of the essay that appeared in English some years later, the Cubist viewpoint in painting is rendered in prototypical manner in Juan Gris's *Guitar, Glasses and Bottle* of 1914, the Neo-Plasticist in Mondrian's diamond-shaped paintings, with singular reference to the latter's late unfinished work, *Victory Boogie-Woogie* (1942–3)[2] (Hejduk 1975: 4).

What characteristics are identified by Hejduk as differentiating Cubist and Neo-Plasticist works? From a close reading of Hejduk's writings, four formal-spatial characteristics or composition effects in the Neo-Plastic canvases of Mondrian are identified. The characteristics are peripheral tensions, boundless field extensions, voided centres and spatial warps

TABLE 1 Characteristics of two plastic points of view. Source: the author, 2019

Cubist	Neo-Plasticist
Directional vectors, or a decrease of activity towards the periphery	Agitated periphery or peripheric tensions due to increased activity
Field, or gridding with interlocking planar figures	Boundless extensions beyond the canvas
Compressed centre resulting from a strong centralization of figures	Voided centre
Figure–ground ambiguities in a gridded field producing flat space	Figure–figure combinations producing spatial warps in the form of vertical and horizontal torqueing

realized from right-angle relationships. These effects were contrasted by Hejduk with those at work in Cubist paintings and thus provided a framework for him to differentiate a Cubist space idea from a Neo-Plasticist idea of space. Table 1 summarizes these differences.

According to Hejduk, architectural manifestations of the two viewpoints are realized – though never in a pure state – in Le Corbusier's *Carpenter Center* and *Villa Stein* at Garches (1926–8) respectively. Confronted with the just completed *Carpenter Center*, Hejduk is perplexed, however, at an apparent return to Cubist space concepts. He searches in vain for evidence of other conditions that he claims mark Neo-Plasticist sensibilities. These conditions include, as noted above, peripheral tensions and voided centres; compression and expansion; the blurring of any stable figure–ground dichotomy in favour of simultaneous figure–figure conditions; and spatial warps generated from right-angled systems.

Propositions

Let us take Eisenman at his word and accept that knowledge diverged from the plan, and adopt as our own Hejduk's parallel claim that the formal and conceptual potential of Neo-Plasticist experiments rendered in the plan of Garches and the architectural lessons of certain canvases of Mondrian and Gris have been forgotten or at best not fully exploited in practice. Assuming both architects would deploy the conceptual power of the plan in their own work, in what manner did these architect-theorists engage with theory in their own practice? Which formal and conceptual problems are revealed from a close reading of Eisenman and Hejduk's period projects? In initially responding to these questions, I postulate that there are specific problems characterizing architectural thought in the mid-1960s and rendered by the plan as conceptual device and locus of knowledge specifically. I conjecture, secondly, that unlike a formative force, there is evidence not of theory in the making but of theory in deformation and dissipation. Only indirectly addressed in what follows, this is to suggest that by the mid-1960s the architect, critic and historian start to lose sight of the plan, their attention directed elsewhere.

I begin to address these questions by identifying key lines of formal and conceptual experimentation at work in Eisenman's *House II* (1969) and Hejduk's *Texas House 5* (1960–2). As demonstrated below, these projects foreground small-scale plan manipulations over and above other concerns and thus provide useful case studies for testing the above propositions. Other projects by the two architects examine different concerns and approaches and thus are outside the narrow limits of this study. Other house projects by Eisenman from the period are concerned with questions of volume and frontality, for example. And Hejduk turns in the subsequent *Diagonal* and *Wall House* series toward other issues.

Theoretical object

In order to approach the above two propositions, and before beginning properly, I need to introduce a third figure – French philosopher and art historian Hubert Damisch – and another term, that of 'theoretical object'. Following Damisch, the relation of thinking to the architectural plan requires one to go beyond an interpretation of the plan as generator of surface and volume, beyond what Damisch characterizes as 'the constraint of the plan' in order to take the plan as thinking vehicle in its own right (Damisch 2016a: 220–1). Damisch alluded to the constraint of the plan as an aside in an essay dealing with the reconstruction of Mies van der Rohe's *Barcelona Pavilion*. This is to extend the logic of the plan as device even further, adopting a concept and an approach that Damisch constructs: that of reading certain architectural manifestations as what he designates 'theoretical objects'. Damisch deployed the term theoretical object in relation to works of art as early as 1958 in an essay on Mondrian and included in the former's *Fenêtre jaune cadmium ou les dessous de la peinture* (Damisch 1984: 54–72). In the domain of architecture, the notion and analytic lens of the theoretical object appeared in print as early as Damisch's 1964 article on Viollet-le-Duc, reprinted in a recent collection of the latter's architectural writing (Damisch 2016b).

According to Damisch, the architectural work is in the realm of theoretical object – whether building, drawing or treatise – when that work 'gives pause for thought' or 'opens the way for reflection'. In generating space for thinking, a theoretical object escapes the gaze of the critic and the historian and the techniques of the architect. In other words, according to Damisch, certain architectural works – in this case a plan – create thought or provide a model for thinking. In contrast to other kinds of architectural manifestations, the theoretical object is 'inhabited' or 'haunted' by thought to such a degree that it eludes, escapes and exceeds the discursive reductions of the critic and historian (Damisch 2016: 179).

Perhaps recuperating in part its potential complexities, a close reading of the plan as theoretical object suspends a reading of structure and volume, of use and expression, and at least provisionally prioritizes an interpretation of ideas and formal relationships. For Damisch, in essence, the plan operates so that certain primary concepts interpenetrate without optical, formal or heuristic destruction of each other, such primary concepts existing in a state of simultaneity. These primary concepts constitute the architectural questions or problems the plan can be claimed to be working on. In their simultaneity, these concept-conditions generate tensions so that the plan eludes discursive reduction, always escaping a single reading. In this state of internal ambiguity, the plan as singular architectural manifestation is 'able to function as a model for thought' according to Damisch (2016b: 107). And in that capacity not only does the architectural object escape the expertise of history and theory, it is potentially able – with the help of the analyst – to rework theory (Damisch 2005: 30). According to Damisch, the architectural object is even potentially able to put theory 'to the test,' without however qualifying how that might operate (Damisch 2005: 179). This and other aspects of the broader interpretive framework will be considered in a subsequent paper.

With such a Damischian apparatus provisionally constructed, and taking as material of study the two period projects, I return to my first proposition. This can now be restated: the analysis of the plan as theoretical object renders or reveals a set of formal and conceptual configurations in the guise of architectural conditions. A close reading of the plan can in certain instances also rejuvenate such architectural conditions. What such conditions or figures might be will be briefly outlined below in relation to the plans of Eisenman's *House II* and Hejduk's *House 5*.

Analysis

House II

If we take Eisenman at his word in that late 1960's moment when he claimed that the importance of the plan as a conceptual device had been all but overlooked, then one may hypothesize that his own efforts will attempt to inject the plan as locus of knowledge with value, to fully exploit, that is, the plan's potential as concept apparatus. This will be to interrogate the plan as catalyst and vehicle for experimentation in certain primary architectural concepts in the Damischian sense.

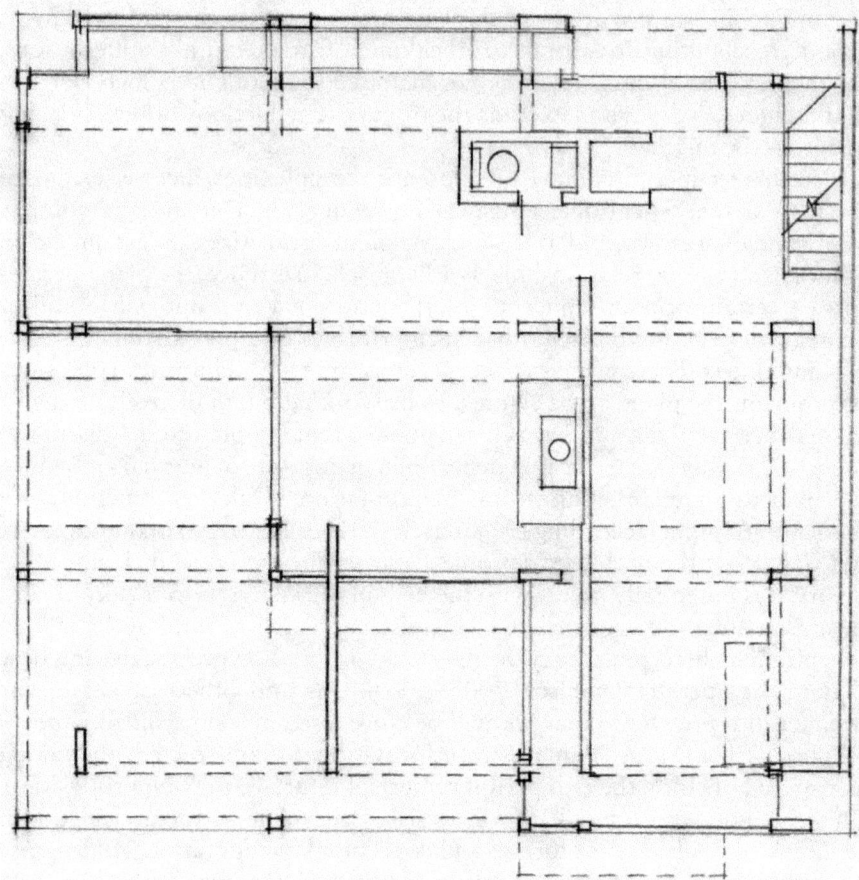

FIG. 9.1 *Peter Eisenman,* House II, *Ground Floor Plan, 1969. Original drawing by the author after a drawing by Peter Eisenman.*

To begin, one observes precise dissonances in the *House II* plan, analysis revealing a uniformly activated field in which a number of architectural figures are tested (see Fig. 9.1). Ambiguity reigns throughout. One enters upper left already on the oblique, such movement never resolving the full-time play between compressions and extensions, horizontal walls potentially constricting, piers perpendicular to those redirecting energy fields outward through openings. It is neither primarily a nine-bay nor a sixteen-column grid structure even though there are instances of both at work. A stable bay reading is blurred as a result of an internal phase shift to the upper left – or lower right depending on the starting point – which in turn creates a constant oscillation between what is fixed and repeatable as regular frame element and what is perhaps without reference or conventional allusion. The plan promotes and at the same time resists a reading of erosion being simultaneously additive (bays or modules being added from the upper left as point of generation) and subtractive (with modules being cut away if starting at the lower right).

The major unbroken wall-line at the top of the plan stands out. It is reinforced by the slightly shorter wall-line just below, setting up a strong if ambiguous horizontal force, ambiguous in that it inverts a more common configuration of bottom-to-top dissolution. Here, rather, things become increasingly dense as one's eye moves to the top of the plan. This occurs at the same time as vertical stratifications are established, in part by the six small vertically oriented fin walls and in part by narrow openings or slots of space contrasted with larger fields or areas. There is moving, left to right, a pattern of alternating A (narrow) and B (wide) that results in an A-B-A-B-B-A rhythm that reinforces this interpretation.

These vertical stratifications start on the left with a slot of space pushed along by the vertical fins; there is equally a tension resulting from the horizontal wall-lines that divert the eye laterally. This system of vertical and horizontal oscillation is further complicated by an animation of the perimeter: there is intensification especially on the upper-right and lower-left corners, contrasted with and contributing to a voiding of the centre. In general, readings of shallow space strata are confronted with potential readings of deep space attributable to an ideal but never fully felt nine-bay or nine-volume figure.

Intimations of formal or visual depth are constantly retracted. There is, for example, a displacement or sidling movement starting with the upper left of the plan, with elements sliding along an echelon toward the bottom right, the eye's movement carried along by the momentum of the larger open spaces themselves and leading to a reading of increased openings to the lower right of the plan. A rift of space is felt opening up, the ratcheted, lateral sliding of the visual field becoming only more determined as the eye travels into the middle of the plan and out again, reinforcing the interpretation of a voided centre. Contrary to a structure of stasis or an architectural model of stability, all is movement. There is, finally, a desire to find an ideal, regular grid in the plan. However, as with Hejduk's *Texas House 5* to be discussed in a moment, this field is set up and then concealed or dissolved so it is both potentially generative and neutral at the same time.

This survey of primary concepts that interpenetrate without dissolution or destruction of each other suggests there is some justification in reading the *House II* plan as a theoretical object following Damisch. The *House II* plan, when examined closely that is, discharges architectural propositions about certain primary conditions. Eluding capture by historical and critical review, the plan works to construct architectural figures and field effects that necessarily remain in a state of ambiguity, suspended in constant tension and thus aligned with the characteristics of the theoretical object proposed by Damisch.

Texas House 5

> ...the seduction of the Spartan, flattened, taut, shallow depth formulation holds its grasp.
>
> HEJDUK 1975: 4

To begin, let's also give Hejduk the first word. In a catalogue entry some twenty years after the drawings were made, reflecting on *Texas House 5*, Hejduk writes, 'In a way it is at once the simplest yet also the most complex investigation' (Hejduk 1980: 76). Wherein lies the complexity that Hejduk finds in the plan for *House 5* some twenty years after its initial formulation? Which architectural conditions are revealed there? Is there evidence that the plan functions as a theoretical object in the sense Damisch proposes? That

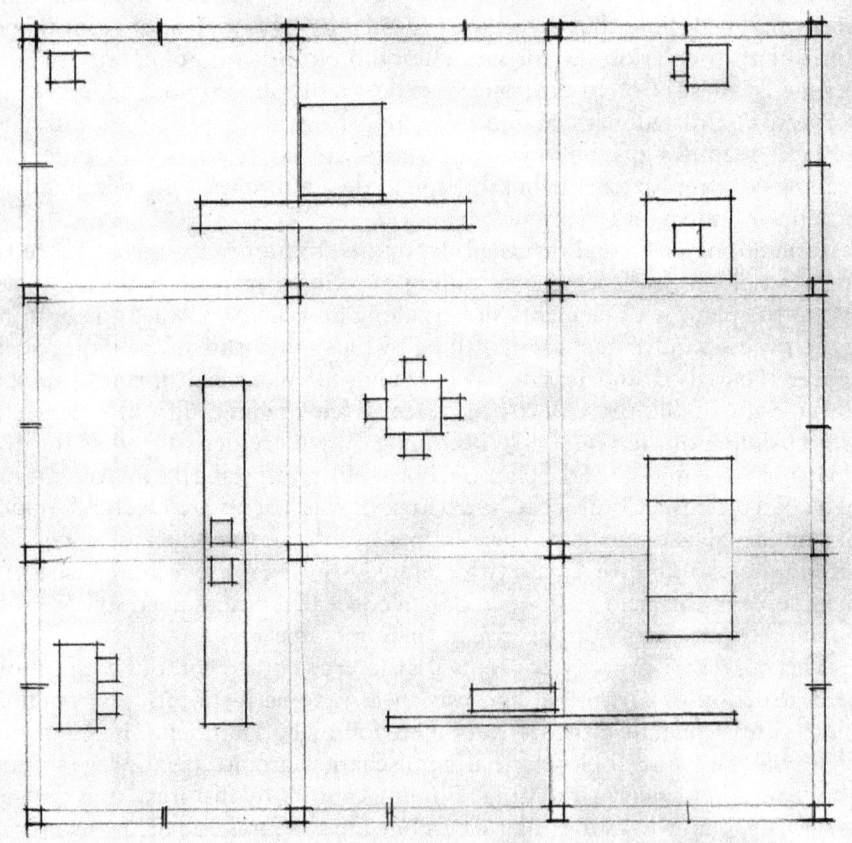

FIG. 9.2 *John Hejduk*, Texas House 5, 1960–2. *Original drawing by the author after a drawing by John Hejduk.*

is, does the plan elude discursive reduction, forcefully operating as a field of speculation, 'putting thought to work' (Damisch 2005: 204) through specific figures and effects? And assuming a positive response to the latter, which architectural propositions and conditions are at stake in *House 5*?

The plan of *House 5* is not characterized by cross-axial plaiting, nor Cubist directionality, nor by those free-plan stratifications and centrifugal forces seen at work in Eisenman's *House II*. Nor is it marked by those forces proposed in Mies van der Rohe's Brick Country House as alluded to by Hejduk, though one could start there to assess differences and in turn reveal *House 5*'s specific qualities. There is an initial desire to read the plan as a regular modulation of space: as a horizontal surface ordered through an apparently regular point grid-structure. The longer one studies the plan, however, the more such assurances slip away. Accepting the challenge of a more complex reading, one starts to discern other effects and certainly Hejduk himself felt more was at stake.

More boldly than *House II*, *House 5* is a nine-bay, sixteen-column plan, the points of the plan field marked by square section posts (see Fig. 9.2). Fins symmetrically intersect fourteen of the outside bay faces, their orientation rotating to follow perpendicularly the glazing line; the two other bay faces have off-centred mullion-fins which introduce a left-to-right twisting or wringing of the plan. There are two major vertical elements overlapping and crossing top to bottom bays three to six and four to seven, counting bays left to right from upper left to lower right of the plan as published. These in turn introduce a top-to-bottom twist or spatial warp if we accept Hejduk's ambitions for the project. Evidence of that warp can also be claimed to be generated in the dining table's eccentric position, drifting to the upper right of its bay. There is an inconsistency between the plan and the axonometric, the former providing a square table with four chairs, one to each of the four faces of the table, while the latter provides a rectangular table with two chairs side by side on each of the long edges, introducing a directionality in a manner that differs from the square table but perhaps has the same effect. With the precision of all other operations, it is clearly not a drawing error, the intended effect being to further build on visual–spatial momentums started elsewhere. For example, visual–spatial dimensions are enlarged through displacement of the entry gallery wall and the figure of the bedroom divider-closet. The position of the seating elements in the living area (lower left), reinforced by the library–toilet–shower block (lower middle), puts in motion a fulcrum-like movement that responds to and continues a momentum set up by the kitchen block (upper right).

A regular bay reading is laid over the plan and then constantly disrupted. The kitchen bench sets up a strong horizontal stratum; the gallery line another, responded to by the bedroom divider-closet element, the dining table pulled slightly to the upper right from an at first assumed central position to create a tension between that area and the bedroom area divider-closet. At the same time, this element contributes to pushing along the implied diagonal created by the shifts in the middle bay vertical fins off-centre to the east and west perimeters.

Texas House 5 is a box with tight, flattened edges. In that sense, it shares some characteristics with Mies' *50 x 50 House* project, another reference for Hejduk. Openings and partitions provide a response to every other condition such that the grid as neutral field or background is never allowed to be read once and for all, leading to that overall ambiguity noted above.

Turning to the columns, one questions whether they can be read as columns with all that implies of a supplement or ornament, or whether it is more accurate to see them as indices of a grid or field condition. The column-post is perhaps better read as an index or mark whose impact is traced by banding, never actually assuming corporeal presence – more like that absent column that Mies van der Rohe sketches for his interior study of the *Barcelona Pavilion* as revealed by Damisch (2016: 129). This is certainly Hejduk's desire, accepting his description of the questions at play in the project: 'I remember playing off singular columnar surfaces [in *Texas House 5*] against the floating elements' (Hejduk 1980: 76). As Hejduk suggests, perhaps they operate as a kind of flat pilaster so that each face or surface somehow animates the adjacent space: each face provided, that is, with the potential to generate effects. It is significant here that Hejduk doesn't refer to the column or post as a vertical element with three-dimensional presence. Rather, it is another surface. Perhaps it has to do with this approach to the plan as a field.

These might be considered conceptual conveniences rather physical ones, but their effect is undeniable as generated from the plan interpreted as a thinking machine. Such an interpretation would situate *House 5*'s square-section posts not as columns with a particular presence but as regular field markers, floor banding contributing to the establishment of a neutral plane or field against which various elements, lines, shapes and surfaces react as suggested above. In this manner they do not constitute a frame, a cage or a three-dimensional bay system other than in a weak sense. Following Damisch, such a reading avoids the constraint of interpreting the plans as generator of volumes. The system of posts creates tensions or vibrations relative to adjacent elements, thus they have impact as singular events and not primarily as part of a larger frame. In his essay, Damisch includes a sketch by Mies that explores internal qualities in the *Barcelona Pavilion*: in the sketch the post is no more than a line with open, non-fixed terminal relations to the floor and ceiling, suggesting one condition Hejduk was aiming to investigate within the potential of the nine-square plan. This is to continue a reading of layer-like stratifications independent of interpretations of three-dimensional volume I started with in relation to *House II*. One never experiences the post as structure, but accepting Hejduk's ambition that each surface is accorded a value, they contribute to constructing that 'Spartan' ideal of shallow space in tension with deep space as suggested in the epilogue to this section of the paper. In this reading, the field event that

Hejduk writes about in relation to the *Carpenter Center* results in figures advancing and receding depending on the relative position taken up. Frontality is not an ambition; or perhaps it is more accurate to say that frontality is not a primary question but rather a minor one, complicated by efforts to accommodate oblique relations realized by tilting on the diagonal orthogonally related elements. Together these might achieve that state of spatial warping Hejduk sought to create (Hejduk 1980: 76).

Conclusion

The plans of *House II* and *House 5* being summarily and very briefly surveyed, and as a form of provisional conclusion, let me return to the opening propositions. The first asked which architectural problems are revealed from a close reading of the plans as objects of plastic experimentation in Eisenman and Hejduk's period projects. In the case of *House II*, analysis revealed a number of conditions, including compression and extension, oblique and diagonal force supplanting any desire or effect of frontality, echelon movement which contributes to the voiding of the centre, and shallow space over deep space. In the case of Hejduk's *House 5*, while certain of these same concepts are being worked on – compression and extension, deep and shallow space in particular – a number of other conditions are in play, resulting in a move towards an overall spatial warping generated from right-angled systems that creates effects different from cross-axial and centrifugal ones. There is a continuous dialectic in *House 5*'s column-post between fact and implication such that a tension between or in concepts exists, reinforcing a state of simultaneity that puts theory 'to the test', following Damisch. As Hejduk suggests following Le Corbusier, the plan 'wants it both ways', demonstrated in his analysis of bay readings in the *Carpenter Center* as both longitudinal and centroidal elements aligned with Cubist and Neo-Plasticist space concepts respectively (Hejduk 1975: 4).

This first proposition was framed as a way to demonstrate that the architectural plan can be the site for a kind of work on architectural knowledge. The plan, in other words, provides one realm in which plastic research can be undertaken. Adopting the terminology of Damisch, certain architectural plans can thus be claimed to operate as theoretical objects, revealing a set of primary concepts as a 'model for thought'. Perhaps more distinctively, such architectural objects do a kind of work 'on' theory as thinking machines and thus can be said to make manifest theory in the making. My second proposition was that the late 1960s is an end point of a period of decline – or at best of transition – with the architect, critic and historian losing sight of the plan, their attentions directed elsewhere: towards the city, towards the symbolic and towards history to name only the most evident concerns.

At least as regards plan-driven theory, the proposition that the plan was in decline in practice would illustrate or provide evidence of theory in dissipation. To address this proposition, however, would require an extended engagement with a number of topics and their associated literatures and manifestations not possible in this initial brief study. As a final, concluding observation, therefore, I offer three topics that seem most immediately at hand as lines for such future research around this proposition. The first concerns the axonometric. I suggest that the appearance and particular use of the axonometric early in the twentieth century started to trigger a decline of the plan's importance in architectural knowledge. The second topic is a more extended development and application of Damisch's concept of the theoretical object, one that would examine more deeply the implications of the architectural object as thinking machine according to Damisch's approach. To formulate this aspect differently, a subsequent project will need to research more rigorously the methodological power in Damisch's idea of the theoretical object and its potential deployment in the reading of architectural works in a more nuanced and deep manner than is possible in this chapter.

To claim that the discipline's passion for the plan lost its vigour is certainly too general as a statement, even if there is some truth to it according to the proposition that architectural knowledge moved at that time, its primary manifestations shifting elsewhere. As a third topic, therefore, I believe we need to call for a reconsideration today of the plan's primacy in architectural education and as an object of deep historical scrutiny and theoretical speculation on projects from that fertile period of the late 1960s and early 1970s considered here through to the contemporary. In other words, and bringing the study towards the present, I believe we need to inaugurate and promulgate in university studio teaching and scholarship that move from a critical stance vis-à-vis the plan to a generative one. A research project testing these will continue the line of questioning opened above into the plan as locus of architectural knowledge.

Notes

1   By Beaux-Arts planning I refer to a compositional approach most closely identified with the nineteenth- and early twentieth-century French tradition of architectural education propounded at the Ecole des Beaux Arts, Paris. I use the term Neo-Plasticist as it is generally understood within art historical spheres when referring to a specific post-Cubist practice and sensibility in painting and sculpture, one most closely aligned with the work and writing of Piet Mondrian. Mondrian's self-characterization of his painterly work as Neo-Plasticist is most fully developed in his essay 'The New Plastic in Painting' (Mondrian 1987: 27–74). For additional development of these ideas, see also Mondrian's 'The Realization of Neo-Plasticism in the Distant Future and in Architecture Today (Architecture Understood as our Total Nonnatural

Environment)' (1987: 164–72). As discussed above, Hejduk relies on Mondrian's term in the latter's analysis of Le Corbusier's work, using interchangeably Post-Cubist and Neo-Plasticist – and I follow this practice.

2   An illustrated catalogue of Mondrian's known sixteen diamond-shaped paintings, with critical essays and select bibliography providing background and further references for those wishing to further research, is found in Carmean (1979).

References

Carmean, Jr, E. A. (1979), *Mondrian: The Diamond Compositions*, Washington, DC: National Gallery of Art.
Damisch, H. (1964), 'L'architecture raisonnée', in E.-E. Viollet-le-Duc, *L'architecture raisonnée: Extraits du Dictionnaire de l'architecture française*, Paris: Hermann.
Damisch, H. (1984), *Fenêtre jaune cadmium ou les dessous de la peinture*, Paris: Seuil.
Damisch, H. (2005), 'Against the Slope: Le Corbusier's La Tourette', *Log* 4 (Winter): 29–48.
Damisch H. (2016a), 'The Slightest Difference: Mies van der Rohe and the Reconstruction of the Barcelona Pavilion', in A. Vidler (ed.), *Noah's Ark: Essays on Architecture*, 212–28, Cambridge, MA: MIT Press.
Damisch, H. (2016b), 'The Space Between: A Structuralist Approach to the Dictionnaire – Viollet-le-Duc as a Forerunner of Structuralism', in A. Vidler (ed.), *Noah's Ark: Essays on Architecture*, 92–109, Cambridge, MA: MIT Press.
Eisenman, P. (1969), 'The Big Little Magazine: *Perspecta* 12 and the Future of the Architectural Past', *Architectural Forum* 131 (October): 74–5.
Hejduk, J. (1965), 'Hors du temps dans l'espace', *L'Architecture d'aujourd'hui* 122 (September–November): xxi–xxiii.
Hejduk, J. (1968), *Three Projects*, New York: Cooper Union School of Art and Architecture.
Hejduk, J. (1975), 'Out of Time and into Space', *A+U* 53 (May): 3–4, 24.
Hejduk, J. (1980), *John Hejduk: 7 Houses*, New York: Institute for Architecture and Urban Studies.
Mondrian, P. (1987), *The New Art – The New Life: The Collected Writings of Piet Mondrian*, ed. and trans. H. Holtzman and M. S. James, London: Thames and Hudson.
Moneo, R. (2014), 'Annual Architecture Lecture 2014', *Royal Academy of Arts*, https://www.royalacademy.org.uk/article/rafael-moneo-annual-architecture.

CHAPTER TEN

Deltiology as History: Informal Communication as Praxis

Nicholas Boyarsky

The collecting and exchange of postcards by architects – known as deltiology[1] – in London around the Architectural Association and in the East Coast of the United States of America during the 1960s and 1970s marked an intense moment of innovation and exchange.[2] Postcards became a means for gossip, for irony, for disseminating shared preoccupations, for advancing architectural positions and, above all, for affirming that ephemera – or, to use Walker Evans's words, 'hack photography' (Evans 1964: 109) – could challenge the narrow constraints and limited ambitions of mainstream architecture and urbanism. Precisely two years after the decisive moment of 1968, the first in a series of influential architectural publications emerged, seeking in various ways to undermine the hegemony of the modernist project and in particular to challenge the paradigm of the modern city. These publications – Alvin Boyarsky's 'Chicago a la Carte: The City as Energy System' of 1970; Robert Venturi, Denise Scott Brown and Stephen Izenour's *Learning from Las Vegas* of 1972; Bernard Tschumi's postcard series *Advertisements for Architecture* of 1978; and Rem Koolhaas's *Delirious New York: A Retroactive Manifesto* of 1978 – represent an insurgent movement that circumvented conventional methodologies of urban design and reconnected to popular myths and narratives of the American city and the individual, anonymous citizen. The weapon of choice within an arsenal of critical references was ephemera, specifically the postcard, both vintage and contemporary. The postcard enabled the perpetrators to build upon an inherent nostalgia and its potential for surrealist interpretations, alongside its documentary potential for social criticism, to fashion multiple narratives and bring to bear unexpected references and content into the discourse on the city that would break with tradition.

Walter Benjamin's argument that photographic reproduction enabled 'the original to meet the beholder halfway' (Benjamin 1970: 223) as its aura withers and the reproduced object becomes detached from the domain of tradition, which leads to 'a tremendous shattering of tradition' (Benjamin 1970: 223), is central to an understanding of this tendency. Yet the second-hand, found nature of much of the ephemera used raises wider questions that are particular to the period. I will argue that Adorno's understanding of how antiquated ephemera can be instrumental in disrupting modernist orthodoxies is a more cogent one. Two deltiological episodes represent these separate strands of discourse latent within ephemera and the notion of obsolescence. The first can be seen in the case of Ferdinand Cheval and his epiphany on a hot and dusty day in 1879, when, in the middle of his rounds, the postman stumbles across a strangely shaped stone. This stone triggers in him a chain of associations that inspire him to construct his *Palais Idéal* near Hautrives over the next thirty-three years (see Fig. 10.1). The structures that Cheval built are all based on his readings and misreadings of images from the rectos of the postcards that he was delivering and it is no coincidence that the first known printed picture postcard, with an image on one side, had been created in France a few years previously. Cheval's motivations and the narratives for his fantastical, naive structures must surely come from his illicit readings of the versos of the postcards, and this form of automatic design inspired by the subconscious was recognized and incorporated into surrealist lineages by Andre Breton, who first visited Hautrives in 1931.³

FIG. 10.1 *Vintage postcard of the Facteur Cheval at his* Palais Idéal *near Hautrives. Source: Courtesy of Alvin Boyarsky Archive.*

The second episode with an emphasis on everyday life – borne of New Deal documentary practices and nurtured by pop art – can be found in a lecture given by Walker Evans in 1964 at Yale, in which he reflected on his lifelong passion for the postcard:

> The very essence of American daily city and town life got itself recorded quite inadvertently on the penny picture postcards of the early twentieth century. The medium was hack photography; but these honest, direct little postcards have a quality today that is more than that of mere social history ... Downtown was a beautiful mess, the tangle of telephone poles and wires attest to that. The architecture is simply indescribable.
>
> in ROSENHEIM 2009: 109

For Evans, an inveterate deltiologist, the postcard's value lay in its ability to represent the actuality of the emerging North American city in a way that was unmediated by academic and professional concerns and preconceptions. As such, the postcard can be seen as found documentation of the raw phenomenon of urban growth (see Fig. 10.2).

This chapter traces how the two strands evoked above – surrealist creation and spontaneous urban growth – resurfaced in the 1970s in radical architectural discourse and how they were adapted and mingled by five protagonists – Alvin Boyarsky, Robert Venturi and Denise Scott Brown, Bernard Tschumi and Rem Koolhaas – to surface in key publications of the period. It will examine the degree to which the different protagonists made

FIG. 10.2 *Vintage postcard of 'Chatham Square showing Doubledeck Elevated', New York City. Source: Courtesy of Alvin Boyarsky Archive.*

use of ephemera and what significance this had in the development of their emerging theoretical positions. It will highlight how these publications established a platform for discussions of architecture beyond the narrow parameters of academic modernism to engage with the political, the banal, eroticism and transgression, and the mythic. While the content and significance of these texts are well known, the role of ephemera is less appreciated. The question as to why the postcard emerged as such a critical tool and how the form and content of the recto and verso became, for a brief period, such a significant medium for postmodern architectural critique is little understood.

The use of illustrative ephemera should be distinguished from McLuhan's celebratory paean *The Medium is the Massage* of 1967, which had argued that society has always been 'shaped more by the nature of the media by which men communicate than by the content of the communication' (McLuhan and Fiore 1967: 8). Vintage ephemera became, rather, the means to adopt a critical position in discussing the contemporary city and, because of its universal resonance with collective memories of the city, its use signalled a rejection of architecture as an autonomous discipline with clearly demarcated aesthetic codes. Venturi, Scott Brown and Izenour were closest to the pop aesthetics of McLuhan's position, whilst Koolhaas has acknowledged the profound influence of Roland Barthes, whose conclusion that 'there is no distinction between significant and insignificant content, and that what we should take note of and decipher are signs' (Barthes 1977: 159) clearly chimed with his own emerging position. The use of ephemera, with its references to the everyday, also had political dimensions that surfaced in the work of Boyarsky and Tschumi as they evolved different but complementary tactics of disruption, which might be traced to Adorno and – in particular – his writings on tradition where, as Andrew Edgar and Peter Sedgwick have written,

> Adorno champions those who throw ephemera, and that which has been neglected, overruled or judged to be "antiquated", against the orthodox demands for immortality, or permanence, within the traditional canon. Adorno thereby questions the inherent meaningfulness of aesthetic tradition, and thus of history itself, as forcibly as the postmodernists, insofar as the rules governing the construction and articulation of historical and practical images are disrupted.
>
> EDGAR and SEDGWICK 1985: 108

Inherent to Adorno's interest in ephemera and the opportunities that the deliberate reuse of the found object might have in disrupting tradition was his recognition of the limited effectiveness of his own philosophical writings, which he likened to the *Flaschenpost*, or 'message in a bottle' that 'nobody wants to have anything to do with . . . it hails unheard, without echoing' (Fruchtl 1985: 1). The potential for the ephemeral to appropriate, for example, the verso and recto of a postcard from 1910 to form a critique of the political power structure in Mayor Daley's Chicago of 1970, or to reveal the subconscious and mythic desires latent within Manhattan, clearly exonerate Adorno's pessimism about the inadequacies of communication.

Against the context of the waning influences of modernism and the emerging hegemony of consumer society and pop culture that Alison and Peter Smithson, amongst others, had highlighted in their article 'But Today We Collect Ads' (1956), the disruptive and anti-establishment possibilities of ephemera, with its proclivities for the random and the contingent, offered an alternative platform from which to launch future narratives and strategies for a critical architecture and architectural theory in itself.[4]

The pages of 'Chicago a la Carte' are assemblages of postcards, maps, texts and photographs which deconstruct Chicago into a multidimensional reading of the city from which Boyarsky elaborates an argument for architecture as 'an urban archaeology of peeling *décollage*' (Boyarsky 1970: 600) in which nineteenth-century 'urban mechanisms of the city and the redundant networks of the tartan field' (Boyarsky 1970: 600) might provide the basis for the city's renewal, despite their decay and omnipresent symptoms of collapse (see Fig. 10.3). Irene Sunwoo has described how this

FIG. 10.3 *'Circling the loop of the screeching overhead railways ... and looking down at the tumultuous, active, mobile and everywhere dynamic centre of a vast distribution centre system, which consisted of broad gridded avenues, commuting railways and expanding electric streetcar networks, on to its re-ordered crust.'* Layout spread from 'Chicago a la Carte' (Boyarsky 1970: 604–5). Source: Courtesy of Alvin Boyarsky Archive.

divergent invocation of *décollage* with 'its implication of "making unstuck" and "taking off" that which has been layered and collaged argues for a broader process of undoing a "mechanistic cycle of growth, redundancy and replacement" unique to America in which the cultural acceptance of technological progress sustains its topographical exfoliation' (Sunwoo 2013: 99).

Boyarsky contrasts the informal processes of urban design that his methodologies suggest to the contemporary preponderance of civic pride and the 'neo-classicising tendencies of the current post-Miesian school, and their preferred disengagement' (Boyarsky 1970: 632) against a background of inequality, civil disturbance and the militarization of a corrupt political establishment. The juxtaposition of postcard, photography and mapping concludes with a more overtly political message as he contrasts the unveiling of an over-scaled Picasso sculpture in August 1968 with images and ephemera that includes a police department shooting target to record the riots of July 1970 in order to underline the failures of conventional architecture (see Fig. 10.4).

In addition to the postcard, a visual tool that serves to unpick the nineteenth-century city of Chicago by referencing its founding myths, symbols and ideologies as the dynamic multilayered immigrant city and contrasting these to actual conditions, further ephemera such as newspaper clippings, snapshots and found objects are then montaged to expose and indict the corrupt political establishment and its Miesian corporate architectural counterpart. Written and assembled against the background of the Chicago Police Riot of 1968 and the ongoing riots, disturbances and sit-ins following the Kent State shootings of April 1970, and alongside the emergence of the Black Panther Party of Chicago, 'Chicago a la Carte' reflects the apocalyptic mood of the time, calling for new approaches to the American city.

Bernard Tschumi's *Advertisements for Architecture* were produced as a series of privately published postcards. Unlike regular postcards, both recto and verso are condensed onto the same plane with the intention that image, caption and message combine to contradict and challenge preconceptions about the very nature of architecture, its representation and its consumption (see Fig. 10.5). In another advertisement from the series, Tschumi presents an image of Le Corbusier's *Villa Savoye* of 1965 in a state of decay and abandonment – in *décollage*, as it were – and in so doing he undermines the villa's iconic status to claim that its embodied ephemeral and ruin-like qualities are now the actual architecture of the building as opposed to its mediated afterlife as an ossified cultural monument. In arguing that 'Architecture only survives where it negates the form that society expects of it. Where it negates itself by transgressing the limits that history has set for itself' (1978a: 6), Tschumi, in a similar vein to Adorno, is denying permanence to the traditional canons of architecture. This tactic is reinforced by his use of the format of the mass-produced postcard instead of the architectural

FIG. 10.4 *Layout spread from 'Chicago a la Carte' (Boyarsky 1970: 640). Source: Courtesy of Alvin Boyarsky Archive.*

book. Tschumi's *Advertisements* suggest a series of inversions of commonly held preconceptions about architecture and also about its means of representation that also clearly reference surrealism.[5] Boyarsky's reading of Chicago had led him to similar conclusions in 1970, when he depicted the city as 'a masterpiece of junk culture whose unexpected lustre, fractures, misalignments and fascinating details invoke an inverted aesthetic acceptance' (Boyarsky 1970: 622). That collecting junk had become a form

FIG. 10.5 *From* Advertisements for Architecture *(Tschumi 1978)*. *Source: Courtesy of Alvin Boyarsky Archive.*

of cultural resistance can also be traced to Walker Evans, photographer and collector of postcards, who in 1971 wrote in a short piece called *Stuff* that a lifetime obsessive collecting had led him to the ultimate aesthetic inversion:

> Yes I'm an incurable and inveterate collector. Right now, I'm collecting trash, literally. I've gotten interested in the forms of trash, and I have bins of it, and also discarded ephemera, particularly in printing. Someday I expect to be infirm and quaking and unable to speak. Rainy days will follow, and I'll sit in my chair, and I'll fool with this stuff.
>
> in ROSENHEIM 2009: 35

The use of junk, detritus, ephemera and obsolescence in performative spatial practices can also be seen in the work of the architect-trained artist Gordon Matta Clark, who in 1971 – before his better-known cutting and splitting projects – produced a work entitled 'Jacks: The auto demolition debris zone rip off imitation neighborhood group action cars abandoned raised propped dismantled and removed 24 hrs service' (Matta Clark 1971: 24–7). In this work, he piled up junk cars under Brooklyn Bridge, often with car jacks and other material, in a continuing performance whereby the detritus of the city was examined and re-examined by the actions of rearrangement.

In 'A Significance for A&P Parking Lots, or, Learning from Las Vegas' (Venturi and Scott Brown 1968), the use of ephemera is subsumed into the presentation of data alongside more conventional devices such as maps, photographs and sketches.[6] The book is closer to a traditional pedagogical architectural publication or treatise than an innovative publication as it flips from manifesto to promotional practice brochure to lecture and back again. Whilst the publication sits outside of the academic canons of architecture of the time, it seeks to engage directly with these traditions as a participant rather than an adversary. An example of this dialectical process can be seen, for example, in the polemical juxtaposition of the postcard 'Arrived Safely. Seeing the "Town"' with an excerpt of Nolli's Map of Rome where the eighteenth-century figure-ground plan is contrasted with an image of the semiotic landscape of Las Vegas to signify, in the manner of Le Corbusier's graphical work for *L'Esprit Nouveau*, the advent of a new spatial paradigm (see Fig. 10.6). There is humour but neither irony nor surrealistic references to the irrational in this extensive documentation of the everyday ugliness of Las Vegas. Opportunities for ambiguity, nuance and the disruption for which Adorno valued ephemera so much are diluted by the authors' attempt to re-engage popular culture with architecture's autonomous discipline and to link the ephemera of daily life to a quirky but eminently consumable classical culture. In their heroic attempt to claim the ordinary by the production of land use maps of casinos and the Strip – in their words, 'How do you *distort* these to draw out a meaning for a designer?' (Venturi, Scott Brown and Izenour 1972: 15) – all modes of representation and references are game, from casino brochures and postcards to Ed Ruscha's self-published photobook *Every Building on the Sunset Strip* of 1966, to Kevin Lynch and Donald Appleyard's work on the aesthetics of highways of 1964, to the classical canons of architecture with the overarching message that everything is ephemera.[7]

Delirious New York marks the apotheosis of the ephemeral in architectural discourse in the 1970s, yet it also signals its abrupt decline. Koolhaas's argument for *Manhattanism*, in which he reinvents the city as a laboratory for the testing of a metropolitan lifestyle and its architecture, is underpinned by his reading of Salvador Dali's paranoiac-critical method which, taken to its ultimate conclusions, leads him to argue for 'the fabrication of evidence

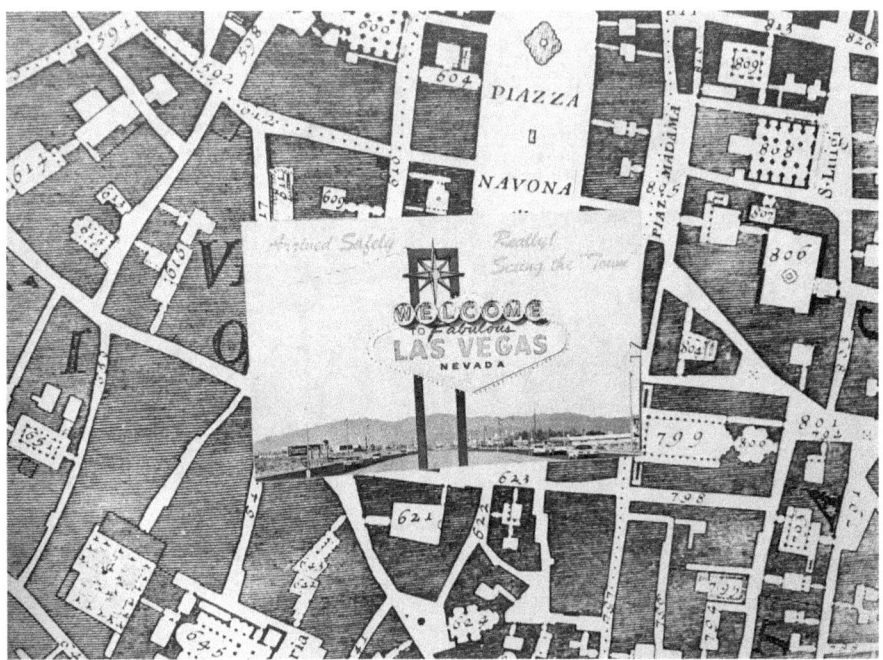

FIG. 10.6 *Arrived Safely. 'Nolli's Map of Rome (detail)'.* Source: Spread from Venturi, Scott Brown and Izenour (1972: 15).

for unprovable speculations and the subsequent grafting of this evidence on the world, so that a "false" fact takes its unlawful place among the "real" facts' (Koolhaas 1978: 202) (see Fig. 10.7). Koolhaas's appropriation of Dali's method is facilitated by the structure of the postcard with its recto image and verso message onto which he collages imaginary narratives of the recto image. Charles Jencks acknowledged the collaborative genesis of *Delirious New York*, describing how Madelon Vriesendorp pushed Koolhaas's narrative into the realm of imagination and desire, 'where it could be relished as a joke that everybody already knew, the sub-Freudian realm of phallic skyscrapers and lighthouses as flashing dick, the world of pop-psychology and postcards' (Jencks 2008: 202). *Delirious New York* had evolved from the obsessive practice of collecting postcards, the 'stuff', as Walker Evans wrote, of the city. In *Savage Mind* (1962), Levi Strauss had first used the word 'bricolage' to describe how mythological narratives are formed by the recombination of found objects and collected tools. The toolkit of ephemera assembled by Koolhaas and Vriesendorp over many years fuelled two parallel delirious trajectories that unravelled and brilliantly exposed the inversions, contradictions and fantasies latent to Manhattan. Yet, as Igor Marjanovic has observed, *Delirious New York* marked a shift to an apolitical stance in contrast to Boyarsky's social criticisms with which he

FIG. 10.7 *Vintage postcard of Coney Island. 'In a laughing mirror-image of the seriousness with which the rest of the world is obsessed with Progress, Coney Island attacks the problem of Pleasure, often with the same technological means' (Koolhaas 1978: 47).*

created 'an architectural history of labor and politics, denying the autonomy of architectural profession and defying the abstraction of labor processes and its separation from the production of urban spaces' (Marjanovic 2004: 575). By contrast, the conclusion to *Delirious New York*, 'The Story of the Pool', describes the ultimate futility of architectural styles in a fable of the arrival in New York of a floating swimming pool from Moscow after a forty-year journey across the oceans powered by constructivist lifeguard/architects. Representing a pure form of modernism, the pool threatened the New Yorkers and the 'limp suspense of their trite complexities' like a thermometer 'that might be inserted in their projects to take the temperature of their decadence' (Marjanovic 2004: 574).

The role of ephemera as a critical medium for architectural discourse was appropriately short-lived. The waning of its polemical and creative influences can be traced to the enigmatic postcard of the Florida Keys that appeared as the front cover of *Europa/America: Architetture urbane alternative suburbane*, the catalogue for the 1976 architectural exhibition and conference at the 37th Venice Biennale, published in 1978 (Raggi 1978) (see Fig. 10.8). Chosen by its editor, Franco Raggi, the book's cover references the influence of the deltiologists but in a very different context, apparently offering a bridge across a divide between the selection of more pragmatic and socially concerned European architects and the more conceptual and poetic American representatives including Raimund Abraham, Emilio Ambasz, Peter Eisenman, John Hejduk and Venturi, Rauch and Scott Brown.[8] Embedded

FIG. 10.8 *Vintage postcard cover from* Europa/America *(Raggi 1978)*.

within the catalogue are a wide range of oppositional strategies to the emergence and short-lived dominance of the postmodern architectural style that the 1980 Venice Biennale was to herald. It can be argued that the ambiguities and references inherent to the Florida Keys postcard seek to disrupt the inevitability of this presumed new canon of orthodoxy.

Ephemera has its own inverted economics. Originally meaning *'that which lasts for one day'*, ephemera accrues value by surviving a generation or more in anonymity. It surfaces as the houses of the dead are cleared and it is then dispersed by scavengers and rag pickers into the lowest levels of the economic chain whether this be street markets, junk shops and more recently car boot sales and eBay. The hitherto forgotten ephemera that does survive assumes a special value, or potency, precisely because of its previous worthlessness. This can be evidenced in the current neoliberal world of high art, where the rarest collectors' items of conceptual art, such as pieces by Alighiero Boetti or Marcel Broodthaers, are those which had no original value because they were intended to be given away. Ephemera had a short-lived currency within architectural discourse of the 1970s, forming a brief interlude before significant content triumphed over the insignificant and led to the formulations of civic pride and political disengagement of postmodernism, which can be seen, for example, in Charles Moore's *Piazza d'Italia* of 1978 and the first architecture biennale, *The Presence of the Past*, of 1980. The postcard had served its purpose as a critical tool that highlighted ambiguity and the unexpected and savoured the nuances of 'messy urbanism' and popular culture to advance alternative theories of architecture. In this process, the postcard mutated into a shared means of communication which deployed irony, humour and deliberate misreadings. It also served, alongside the stamp and the poster, to structure the curricula and pedagogy of Alvin Boyarsky's International Institute of Design Summer Session and ultimately the mediation of architectural discourse at the Architectural Association.[9] Recent research by Irene Sunwoo into the Summer Sessions,

FIG. 10.9 *International Institute of Design, postcard, 1971. Source: Courtesy of Alvin Boyarsky Archive.*

held in London from 1970 to 1972, has revealed how postcards, postage stamps and posters became the media for disseminating and structuring a radically new form for architectural education. Ephemera had now become a device to express and shape the ambitions of the post-1968 generation of students and young architects who were seeking new and alternative forms of education and practice. Sunwoo traces how postcards, stamps and posters were posted out as invitations to an international and nomadic body of architects and thinkers to gather and take part and 'grapple with a host of new challenges and questions in the wake of heroic modernism's demise' (Sunwoo 2017: 14). The selection of postcards illustrated here reveals how ephemera had become part polemic and part curricula for this new prototype for architectural education (see Figs 10.9–10.12).

FIG. 10.10 *'London: Cities like London, Buenos Aires, Tokyo, New York, etc. contain sufficient slack to be used as laboratories and workshops. It is possible to co-opt space from recessed institutions, take over cheap pads from vacationing students and use the abundant resources of information, professional and interdisciplinary back up, co-ordinating agencies and local talent, ranging from those with below-the-surface 'alternative' interests, to the leading guns on the scene to further enrich the learning possibilities for many from all parts of the world.'* International Institute of Design, postcard, 1971. Source: Courtesy of Alvin Boyarsky Archive.

FIG. 10.11 'Caught up in the Byzantine intrigues, labyrinthine curricula, procedures and objectives, as if from some former era. A workshop and a platform. Key Words. A market place and a forum. A well laid table and a banquet for free ranging souls as opposed to your local cafeteria's battery fare. Use the resources of London. Star turns. A cool look at the world scene.' International Institute of Design, postcard, 1971. Source: Courtesy of Alvin Boyarsky Archive.

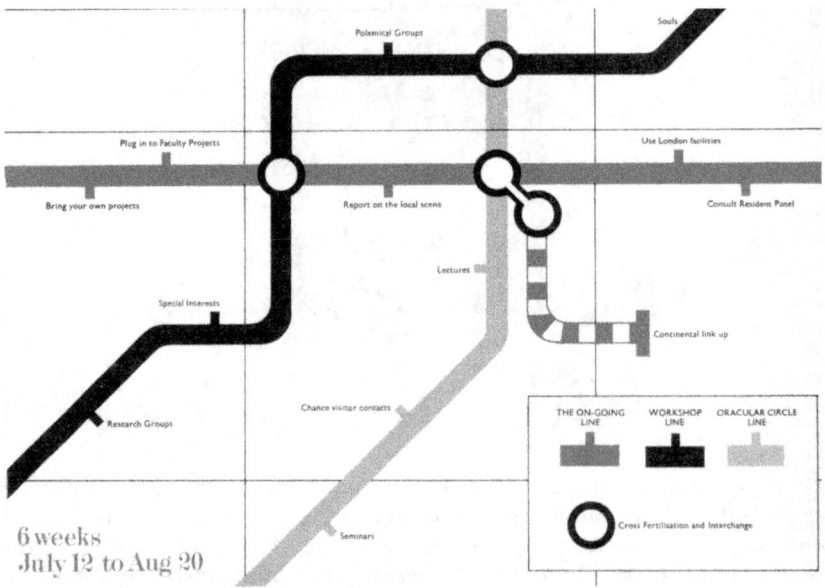

FIG. 10.12 'The On-Going Line: Bring your own projects. Plug in to Faculty projects. Use London facilities. Consult Resident Panel. Workshop Line: Research Groups. Special Interests. Polemical Groups Oracular Circle Line. Seminars. Chance visitor contacts. Lectures. Cross Fertilisation and Interchange. Continental link up.' International Institute of Design, postcard, 1971. Source: Courtesy of Alvin Boyarsky Archive.

Notes

1. Deltiology, from the ancient Greek word for small texts, was coined in 1945 by Professor Randall Rhoades to mean the study and collection of postcards.
2. A discourse centred around the Architectural Association School of Architecture in London and American institutions such as the Chicago Circle, Cooper Union, Princeton University, Yale University and Cornell University.
3. André Breton, who first visited the Ideal Palace in Hautrives in 1931, was deeply influenced by postman Cheval's work (Cardinal 2000: 34).
4. The Smithsons wrote, 'Mass-production advertising is establishing our whole pattern of life – principles, morals, aims, aspirations, and standard of living. We must somehow get the measure of this intervention if we are to match its powerful and exciting impulses with our own' (Smithson and Smithson 1956).
5. There are clear links to surrealist traditions in the *Advertisements for Architecture*, in particular to the dissident surrealist Georges Bataille and the photographer Jacques-Andre Boiffard.
6. The title of Part 1 of the book. The other parts – *Ugly and Ordinary Architecture, or The Decorated Shed* (part 2) and *Essays in the Ugly and Ordinary: Some Decorated Sheds* (part 3) – are increasingly concerned with practice work.
7. In some ways this was a template for Learning from Las Vegas with similarities in graphics and format but without ephemera. Produced under the auspices of the Joint Centre for Urban Studies, the authors write that 'road-watching is a delight, and the highway is – or at least might be – a work of art ... To our way of thinking, the highway is the greatest neglected opportunity in city design' (Appleyard, Lynch and Myer 1964: 3).
8. Raggi knew Alvin Boyarsky and, in 1977, he visited the Architectural Association where he gave Boyarsky a 'scratchy drawing' of two classical temples embedded in mattresses with wheels. It is not inconceivable that postcards were traded on the occasion (Marjanovic and Howard 2014: 114–15).
9. 'The IID was an independent school of architecture without a permanent faculty, a student body, a curriculum or its own premises, save for its director's kitchen, yet in lieu of such conventional academic resources, lines of communication – telephones as well as magazines, postcards and video – supplied an infrastructure that helped launch a new global trajectory in architectural education' (Sunwoo 2017: 11).

References

Appleyard D., K. Lynch and J. R. Myer (1964), *The View from the Road*, Boston: MIT Press.

Barthes, R. (1977), 'From Work to Text', in R. Barthes, *Image–Music–Text*, 155–64, New York: MacMillan.

Benjamin, W. (1970), 'The Work of Art in the Age of Mechanical Reproduction', in W. Benjamin, *Illuminations*, 214–19, London: Fontana.

Boyarsky, A. (1970), 'Chicago a la Carte: The City as an Energy System', *AD magazine* 40.
Cardinal, R. (2000), 'André Breton and the Automatic Message', in R. Fotiade (ed.), *André Breton: The Power of Language*, 23–36, Exeter: Elm Bank Publications.
Edgar, A. and P. Sedgwick (1995), 'Adorno, Oakshott and the Voice of Poetry', in B. Adam and S. Allan (eds), *Theorising Culture: An Interdisciplinary Critique after Postmodernism*, 100–12, New York: NYU Press.
Evans, W. (1964), 'Lyric Documentary: An Illustrated Transcript of a Lecture by Walker Evans presented at Yale University, March 11, 1964', in J. Rosenheim, *Walker Evans and the Picture Postcard*, Gottingen: Steidl.
Fotiade, R. (ed.) (2000), *André Breton: The Power of Language*, London: Intellect Books.
Fruchtl, J. (1985), 'Return of the Bottle Post: Adorno Archive in Frankfurt am Main', *Die Zeit*, 9 August.
Jencks, C. (2008), 'Madelon Seeing through Objects', in S. Basar and S. Truby (eds), *The World of Madelon Vriesendorp: Paintings, Postcards, Objects, Games*, 149–55, London: Architectural Association.
Koolhaas, R. (1978), *Delirious New York: A Retroactive Manifesto for Manhattan*, Oxford: Oxford University Press.
Marjanovic, I. (2004), 'Postcards and the Making of Architectural History: the Cases of Alvin Boyarsky and Rem Koolhaas', in M. Nepomechie and R. Gonzalez (eds), *92nd ACSA Annual Meeting Proceedings – Archipelagos: Outposts of the Americas*, 571–7, Miami: ACSA.
Marjanovic I. and J. Howard (eds) (2014), *Drawing Ambience: Alvin Boyarsky and the Architectural Association*, St Louis: Mildred Lane Kemper Museum & Museum of Art, Rhode Island School of Design.
Matta Clark, G. (1971), 'Jacks', *Avalanche Magazine* 3: 24–27.
McLuhan, M. and Q. Fiore (1967), *The Medium is the Massage: An Inventory of Effects*, New York: Penguin.
Raggi, F. (ed.) (1978), *Europa/America: Architetture urbane alternative suburbane*, Venice: Edizioni La Biennale di Venezia.
Rosenheim, J. (2009), *Walker Evans and the Picture Postcard*, Gottingen: Steidl.
Ruscha, E. (1966), *Every Building on the Sunset Strip. E. Ruscha* (self-published).
Smithson, P. and A. Smithson (1956), 'But Today We Collect Ads', *Ark* 18: 49–50.
Strauss, C. L. (1962), *Savage Mind*, Chicago: University of Chicago Press.
Sunwoo, I. (2012), 'From the "Well-laid Table" to the "Market place": The Architectural Association Unit System', *Journal of Architectural Education* 65, no. 2: 24–41.
Sunwoo, I. (2013), 'Between the "Well-Laid Table" and the "Marketplace": Alvin Boyarsky's Experiments in Architectural Pedagogy', PhD diss., Princeton School of Architecture, Princeton University, Princeton, NJ.
Sunwoo, I. (2017), 'A History in Progress', in I. Sunwoo (ed.), *In Progress: The IID Summer Sessions*, 11–21, London: AA Publications.
Szacka, L. C. (2014), 'Debates on Display at the 1976 Venice Biennale', in T. Arrhenius, M. Lending, W. Miller and J. M. McGowan (eds), *Place and Displacement: Exhibiting Architecture*, 97–112, Zurich: Lars Müller Publishers.
Tschumi, B. (1978a), *Advertisements for Architecture*, Cambridge, MA: MIT Press.

Tschumi, B. (1978b), 'Architecture and its Double', *Architectural Design* 48, no. 2–3: 111–16.
Venturi, R. and D. Scott Bown (1968), 'A Significance for A&P Parking Lots, or, Learning from Las Vegas', *Architectural Forum* (March).
Venturi, R., D. Scott Brown and S. Izenour (1972), *Learning from Las Vegas*, Cambridge, MA: MIT Press.

CHAPTER ELEVEN

Theorizing from the South: The Seminar of Latin American Architecture

Catherine R. Ettinger

Introduction

For the 1987 meeting of the Seminar on Latin American Architecture (SAL), the architect Humberto Eliash drew a caricature: in it, a *chiva*[1] marked with the motto 'Better Late than Never' and loaded with architects, left 'Alienation City' and crossed a wooden bridge towards the 'Valley of Identity'. Below the rickety structure, three crocodiles – named 'demagogy', 'folklore' and '*starchitecture*' – had their mouths open waiting to swallow anyone who might fall from the bus. This image placed Latin American architecture in a precarious situation as it distanced itself from Europe and the United States in its quest for an architecture of identity and thus condenses themes that were central to the SAL meetings. The group of architects themselves, loaded onto the bus with their T squares, plans and models, represented a vehicle for the transformation of regional architecture theory (see Fig. 11.1). The SAL[2] came into being in reaction to a slight. During the first Biennial of Architecture held in Buenos Aires in May of 1985, the European and American architects were invited to speak at the central San Martín Theatre in morning sessions, while Latin American architects were relegated to rooms at the School of Architecture at the University of Buenos Aires in the afternoons and evenings. This organizational lapse ignited irritation and led to a spontaneous meeting and a manifesto signed by a group of South American architects who expressed their concern over the constant focus on Europe or the United States as architectural trend setters. In the manifesto, drafted by Ramón Gutiérrez (the driver of the bus), they called

FIG. 11.1 *Humberto Eliash's caricature illustrates a central theme in the SAL, the search for an architecture of identity. Source: Courtesy of CEDODAL.*

for an Ibero-American[3] proposal for architecture and the development of a regional architecture theory (Gutiérrez 2011: 19).[4]

The early SAL meetings were described by participants as platforms for debate (Marcondes 2011: 11), a space for (often) heated discussions (Esteban and Méndez 2014: 47) and as motivation for permanent dialogue (Ramírez

FIG. 11.2 *A photograph of the second SAL shows the informal character of the round-table discussion. Source: Courtesy of CEDODAL.*

Nieto 2011: 28); they were also characterized as the formation of a family (Deschamps 2011: 51) and the source of deep friendships (Gutiérrez 2011: 19). The effort to construct a shared paradigm came about primarily through informal discussions, and photographs of the first meetings show participants casually gathered around a table, dealing with the problem of defining a Latin American or regional identity and its architecture (see Fig. 11.2). Transcripts of these sessions reveal the way ideas were thrown back and forth and built upon collectively to underpin both academic and professional work in the region. At the early SAL meetings, discussions were the main activity and they led to writing, in contrast to most academic meetings where papers are first written, then delivered. A series of concepts related to region and identity in architecture evolved from the discussions and eventually codified a regional perspective to be disseminated through publications in different Latin American countries.

Forging a new path

After the first meeting in Buenos Aires, the SAL reconvened the following year and subsequent meetings were organized by universities and other organizations in Colombia, Mexico, Chile, Venezuela, Peru, Puerto Rico, Panama, Brazil and the Dominican Republic. The early meetings centred on two activities: first, an informal gathering of colleagues for discussion and debate and, second, the formal presentation of papers and keynote addresses. The first activity was an 'encounter of friends' with no 'a priori rules' or 'formal rigid structure' (Ramírez Nieto 2013: 25) and it was given priority over the presentation of written texts.

From at least the second meeting the group used the motto 'Haciendo camino al andar', which in a literal translation to English means 'forging a path by walking forward'.[5] It is a phrase taken from a popular protest song[6] and is in tune with the well-documented combative nature of the early meetings, reflecting opposition and suggesting political activism. It relates to the end of a period of dictatorships in the region and to postmodernity and the international scene in architecture; explorations of historicism or formal instability were far removed from or irrelevant to Latin American realities. At the SAL there were numerous references to the onslaught of information from the United States and Europe as damaging, and one of the central issues for the group was the defence of local values against the banality and commercial character of postmodern architecture (Segre 2011: 123). The topic remained of interest for over a decade and was clearly formulated at the meeting in Lima that called for the need to 'rethink architecture', considering 'purported cultural movements like postmodernism and deconstructivism' that are 'banally transplanted as a pernicious trend in our cities' (Ramírez Nieto 2013: 56). The relevance of the notion of postmodernity for Latin America was questioned (Zambrano 2015: 46), Marina Waisman writing, 'Since we have never been fully modern, there is not much point in occupying ourselves with postmodernity' (1989: 9).

The SAL gave voice to the concerns of practising architects that pre-dated the meetings. Horacio Torrent (2002) identified some of these concerns in an open letter published by seven Argentinian architects in 1967, while Ramón Gutiérrez had previously reflected on the need to understand Latin American architecture not as a poor copy of European, but as the result of its own creative force and as a response to local conditions. A year before the first SAL, Gutiérrez had called for the development of a theory and practice of architecture for Latin America (Gutiérrez 1984/1997: 713). The most vocal practising architects in the group – Severiano Porto, Rogelio Salmona and Eladio Dieste – had been designing with attention to local culture and materials long before the SAL meetings began (see Fig. 11.3).

Priorities during the early years of the seminar included the rewriting of regional histories of architecture from a Latin American perspective[7] and the establishment of networks that would facilitate the circulation of architecture

FIG. 11.3 *Salmona used traditional brick construction in the Torres del Parque complex in Bogotá. Source: Photograph by the author.*

magazines.[8] The meetings generated agreement among editors for networks for distribution and a shared online platform (ARLA) which continues to be active today (Méndez 2011). The Center for Documentation on Latin American Architecture (CEDODAL), established in Buenos Aires in 1995, became an important repository for information on the architecture of the region.

The ambitious proposal of working towards a shared theory of architecture for Latin America occupied a central place in the group's early meetings. The initial concern centred on questions of identity and region, or, as Zambrano put it, 'the axis of appropriate(d) modernity – Critical Regionalism' (2015: 45). A review of the discussions held at the first meetings illustrates how dialogue supported the creation of shared concepts and how they evolved.

The central themes: region, identity and technology

In his review of the SAL, Ramírez Nieto (2013: 31) mentions a variety of concepts including Adriana Irigoyen's 'coinciding pluralities', Silvia Arango's idea of 'traditions of conscious assimilation' (1990: 43), Fernández Cox's 'appropriate(d) architecture' (1989: 2–5) and Marina Waisman's 'divergent architecture' (1989: 8–10). Although several concepts were posited, I will focus on three parts of the conversation that I consider key to understanding the Latin American perspective – an initial debate on adoption v. adaptation, the idea of 'appropriate(d) modernity' and the proposal for a 'divergent architecture' – and their relationship to the contemporary formulation of a critical regionalism from outside of the region.

Adoption and adaptation were the key words used to open the discussion in 1985. The conversation was structured around the influence of international styles, the relationship between architecture and identity and the problem of local versus imported technologies (Lozano 1991: 10). These topics carried over into the second meeting a year later.

On the first question, there was consensus on the importance of the circulation of architectural ideas; Enrique Browne argued that 'historically, Latin America and its culture have developed on the foundations of these influences, mixing and synthesizing them' (Lozano 1991: 11). He proposed a framework of 'Spirit of Time and of Place': time made modern architecture relevant and place situated the architect in a cultural context. He insisted on being open to 'foreign influence' with a personal (regional) point of view, adducing the richness of hybrids.

During this first debate, there was a strong call for a critical approach to external influences. Juvenal Baracco argued that 'each region, each town and each country defends itself with its identity from the onslaught of foreign influence, and [in the end] what arrives is irrelevant, what matters is what remains' (Lozano 1991: 13). This concern over discerning what was pertinent to Latin America became pivotal in the discussions that followed, with a great deal of attention given to analyzing and critically evaluating foreign influence.

As the debate moved forward on the topic of identity, the difficulty of defining Latin America came to the forefront. Despite a common colonial history, similar cultural background and problems common to the region, important differences were manifest. The indigenous legacy of Mexico and Peru and the African influence in Brazil and the Caribbean contrasted with the impact of European migrations in Argentina, Chile and other Latin American countries, lending cultural as well as geographical specificities to the distinct countries that form the region (Lozano 1991: 12–13); the Colombian Rogelio Salmona argued that there was no such thing as a Latin American identity per se (Lozano 1991: 11). Just as there was no Latin American architecture, neither was there a Brazilian or a Mexican or an Argentinian architecture. In conclusion, the participants moved away from an ontological position on identity in architecture as essence and posited the role of space and time, and particularly history, as defining factors in regional architecture on different scales (Lozano 1991: 11). There was common ground such as historical parallels (colonial history, independence movements, periods of nation building and the end of the century of dictatorships) and language (Spanish and Portuguese) as well as contemporary problems related to development. The contrast between these countries and the English-speaking American countries has contributed to the sense of a shared identity.

The early meetings also dealt with technology, emphasizing tensions between regional space with its traditional materials and building methods and international markets of industrial materials. Practising architects enriched the conversation by relating vernacular traditions to contemporary design; Rogelio Salmona and Eladio Dieste were reworking traditional brick building construction and Severiano Porto was exploring the traditional wooden structures of Brazil for inspiration. At the same time the group was open to foreign influence. As Waisman stated, 'nothing can be tossed out a priori, nothing should be tossed out if it is possible, if High Tech is possible, let there be High Tech'. However, she called for a discriminating attitude and the need to 'think, elaborate, discern and abandon the cult of the model, of the image' when technology wasn't appropriate (Lozano 1991: 26).

These threads – the distinct concerns different participants identified in the discussion – were slowly woven into shared concepts. By 1989 the conversation was much more concentrated and reflected on specific proposals such as that of 'appropriate(d) modernity' proposed by Cristian Fernández.[9] The opening line of his essay, 'Looking at things from here . . .', situates his proposal as coming from the global South and burdened with that perspective. At the start, he noted the difference between a modernity that arose in response to specific conditions (i.e. the Industrial Revolution) and a modernity that came from without, as a pressure to modernize, which was not consistent with the internal situation of Latin American countries. Citing Octavio Paz, he referred to 'importing solutions for problems that did not yet exist' (Fernández Cox 1989: 2) and to the way in which 'the architectural elites were not interested in solving real local problems, but rather in the mimesis of European and American modernities' (1989: 2–3).

He delineated his concept of appropriate(d) modernity as having three meanings: first, as adequate; second as appropriated, or having passed through a process of decantation, analysis and selection; and third, as a modernity of one's own, related to local history and circumstances. This was the most resonating concept that emanated from the SAL meetings. It distanced itself from postmodern ideas about the end of modernity and placed Latin America in a sphere of hope for the future through the redefinition of modernity (Lozano 1991: 10). Fernández Cox rejected the use of the word 'region', which, arguably, shows a sensitivity to contemporary publications on critical regionalism as a way of locating the periphery in a territory of the 'other' or the 'exotic'. Roberto Segre referred to 'the questioning [in the SAL] of categories defined by Charles Jencks, which were interpreted as an intromission of First World critics in the problems of Latin American architecture and an appropriation of the Third World by including it in the critical "recipe"' (Segre 2011: 126).[10]

A few years later, Waisman advanced the discussion, suggesting a 'divergent architecture' in direct opposition to critical regionalism. Rather than refer to 'resistance' according to Frampton, she alluded to the autonomous choice of a distinct path. In an outright criticism of Frampton, whose texts she considered typical of a critic 'alienated from regional reality', she argued that 'His is a passive proposal, of resisting, protecting from behind the front lines, staying in a refuge while the world falls apart', in contrast to how Latin American architects were advancing in the creation of an original architectural culture, 'in an eminently active position that differs profoundly from the attitude of barricading ourselves ... to avoid an invasion' (Waisman 1989: 10).[11] Despite the polemics, Waisman advocated recovering the word 'regional' to eliminate the centre–periphery dichotomy: 'A periphery has an obligatory reference to a centre that provides models as a point of comparison for judging architectural production; a region, on the contrary, is subject to its own rhythms and recognizes no centre to which its production is subordinate or to which it owes models and judgement' (Waisman 1989: 9).

Contested knowledge

The importance of the SAL meetings is widely recognized among scholars of Latin American architecture (Segawa 2005: 128;[12] Carranza and Lara 2014: 308–10) and often considered a movement. Yet, the discourse on regionalism that became manifest in the seminars was more a codification of practice, a putting into words of what Latin American architects had been thinking and doing, than the development of new theory. The meetings were a vehicle for establishing the position of Latin American architects vis-à-vis regionalism; they attempted to give a voice to the region in the midst of the dominance of critical regionalism as the filter for observing Latin American architecture.

At the SAL, critical regionalism was radically interrogated. In contrast to the Latin American movement, critical regionalism was, at least in part, a classificatory action that identified and explained a trend and its characteristics – the attention to light, to tectonics, to regional materials and so on – while the Latin American discussions revolved around principles, the discourse of identity and shared regional conditions. The criticism emanated from practices with a perspective from the South and were not concerned with specific architectural expressions that could identify Latin America, but rather with ideas that could serve as a platform for design. Appropriate(d) modernity or divergent architecture, as concepts, have more to do with an attitude than with architectural characteristics.

Critical regionalism was refuted first as a manifestation of postmodern architecture through Fernández Cox's call for an 'appropriate(d) modernity', which maintained the ideas of progress and hope for the future through modern architecture. It was also seen as relying on traditional dichotomies – developed–underdeveloped, Western–Eastern, civilized–primitive – that placed Latin American architecture in the terrain of 'the other' (Lozano

1991: 93; Eggener 2002). This awareness of the role of outsiders in labelling Latin America's architecture is related to the combative nature of early meetings and helped to unite the group. The sense that architects practising in Latin America were engaged with similar problems and situations encouraged the development of relationships between architects, academics and institutions throughout the region. A greater exchange of information, publications and knowledge ensued and the discussions about identity, region and architecture found their way into publications used in classrooms and became part of formal curricula (e.g. Toca 1990; Waisman 1990). Regionalism was the dominant discourse for a generation caught between the 'heroic' architects of modernity and the younger architects who would be 'free from the discourse of Latin Americanism' (Torrent 2002: 12). This freedom of a new generation is probably related to shifts at the end of the 1990s in the way identity was viewed and to new attitudes toward global flows which changed the nature of the meetings. The period of manifestos was over as the fluidity and multiplicity of identity was posited in cultural theory (Appadurai 1996), and the inevitability of international flows accepted.

Viewing the early years of the SAL from a distance, it is clear that the meetings were a vehicle for the solidification of both concepts and relationships; they gave voice to shared local concerns. The difficulty of making those voices heard beyond the region has become evident as international authority in the discipline continues to reside in Europe and the United States and knowledge is sanctioned through prestigious universities. Despite a surge in publicity in the late 1980s and 1990s (Torre 1994: 16), the position of Latin American architects has often remained peripheral, and their voices, in particular their criticism of 'critical regionalism', were barely heard. This speaks to a broader issue of power and the circulation of architectural knowledge, the idea of centres and peripheries. Marina Waisman recognized the problematic nature of the circulation of architectural trends when she summed up her position on region: 'If we feel that we are a periphery it is because we believe that others are a centre . . . I think that what is beyond consideration, is that we can be the centre of ourselves' (Waisman 1989: 18).

Notes

1 In Colombia, *chiva* refers to a colourful bus used for rural transportation.
2 The first meetings were called 'Encounters'; at the third meeting, held in Manizales, Colombia, the participants – by then a group of twenty-five to thirty – agreed to use the name *Seminario de Arquitectura Latinoamericana* (Gutiérrez 2011: 21). Although the seminars have received the support of different universities, they are self-convened and self-governed and the association is not formally constituted. For clarity, in this text I refer to all meetings as SAL.

3   Later the group would use the denomination of Latin American. The manifesto was written by Ramón Gutiérrez who had recently published a comprehensive history of Latin American architecture using 'Ibero-American' in the title, which probably explains its use here. The appellative 'Ibero-American' refers to a shared colonial past as defining identity. For discussion on the notion of Latin America, see Luis Carranza and Fernando Lara (2014: 2–3) and Del Real and Gyger (2013: 2–3).

4   The manifesto was published in the Argentine architecture journal *Summa* the following month. See Ramírez Nieto (2011: 144).

5   The origin is not clear, but it appears at the end of an unsigned chronicle of the second meeting published by *Summa* (Lozano 1991: 27).

6   Joan Manuel Serrat set Antonio Machado's poetry to music for the song 'Caminante, no hay camino', with the chorus 'Traveler, there is no path. You forge the path as you walk.'

7   Work on the topic had begun in the 1980s, but the SAL meetings provided the opportunity for discussion and exchange of ideas.

8   This was related both to the paucity of publications and to the problems in distribution of magazines, problems compounded by the isolation associated with decades of dictatorships. For a review of the relationship between the SAL and international networks of architecture publications, see Patricia Méndez (2011: 53–8).

9   Fernández had also explored this notion in an article published by *Summa* (200/201) in June of 1983 and reprinted in Lozano 1991: 96–9, initially presented by the author in 1987 in Manizales, Colombia, and in a clearer formulation in 1989 in Tlaxcala, Mexico.

10 Even though he questioned the validity of critical regionalism, Segre recognized the value of LeFaivre, Tzonis and Frampton's work on Latin American architects.

11 These relatively early rejections of critical regionalism can be confronted with more recent critiques. In 2002, Keith Eggener clarified the way in which critical regionalism created opposition between centre and region and placed the so-called regional architectures in a postcolonial space. Exploring the literature on Mexican architect Luis Barragán – often cited as an example of critical regionalism – Eggener identified contradictions in Frampton's discourse. See Eggener (2002).

12 Segawa stressed the role of the SAL as 'articulator of a dialogue not seen in the region since the 1950s'.

References

Appadurai, A. (1996), *Modernity at Large: Cultural Dimensions of Globalization*, Minneapolis: University of Minnesota Press.
Arango, S. (1990), 'La experiencia de la arquitectura colombiana actual frente a la doble crisis del Movimiento Moderno', in A. Toca (ed.), *Nueva Arquitectura en América Latina: presente y futuro*, 42–55, Barcelona: Gustavo Gili.

Carranza, L. E. and F. Luiz Lara (2014), *Modern Architecture in Latin America*, Austin: University of Texas Press.
Del Real, P. and H. Gyger (2013), 'Introduction: Ambiguous Territories', in P. Del Real and H. Gyger (eds), *Latin American Modern Architectures: Ambiguous Territories*, 3–29, New York and London: Routledge.
Deschamps, Y. (2011), 'Reflexiones de un tripulante de los SAL', in P. Méndez (ed.), *Seminarios de Arquitectura Latinoamericana (SAL): Haciendo camino al andar, 1985-2011*, 49–51, Buenos Aires: CEDODAL.
Eggener, K. (2002), 'Placing Resistance: A Critique of Critical Regionalism', *Journal of Architectural Education* 55, no. 4: 228–37.
Esteban Maluenda, A. and P. Méndez (2014), 'Arquitectura y espacio urbano. SAL 2013. Bogotá: 28 años y 15 convocatorias del Seminario de Arquitectura Latinoamericana', *Rita* 1: 44–7.
Fernández Cox, C. (1989), 'Modernidad Apropiada', in *IV Seminario de Arquitectura Latinoamericana*, 2–5, Tlaxcala: Summarios.
Fernández Cox, C. (1990), 'Hacia una modernidad apropiada: obstáculos y tareas internas', in A. Toca (ed.), *Nueva Arquitectura en América Latina: presente y futuro*, 71–93, Barcelona: Gustavo Gili.
Frampton, K. (1983), 'Towards a Critical Regionalism: Six Points for an Architecture of Resistance', in H. Foster (ed.), *The Anti-Aesthetic: Essays on Postmodern Culture*, 16–30, Port Townsend, WA: Bay Press.
Gutiérrez, R. (1984/1997), *Arquitectura y urbanismo en Iberoamérica*, 3rd edition, Barcelona: Gustavo Gili.
Gutiérrez, R. (1990), 'En torno a la dependencia y la identidad en la arquitectura iberoamericana', in A. Toca (ed.), *Nueva Arquitectura en América Latina: presente y futuro*, 141–63, Barcelona: Gustavo Gili.
Gutiérrez, R. (2011), 'Seminarios de Arquitectura Latinoamericana: Una experiencia de reflexión y acción (1985–2009)', in P. Méndez (ed.), *Seminarios de Arquitectura Latinoamericana: Haciendo camino al andar, 1985-2011*, 19–26, Buenos Aires: CEDODAL.
Henrich, J., S. J. Heine and A. Norenzayan (2010), 'The Weirdest People in the World?', *Behavioral and Brain Science* 33, no. 1–2: 61–133.
Lozano, F. (ed.) (1991), *Arquitectura latinoamericana: Pensamiento y propuesta*, Mexico City: Instituto Argentino de Investigaciones de Historia de la Arquitectura y del Urbanismo, Universidad Autónoma Metropolitana-Xochimilco and Ediciones Summa.
Marcondes, M. J. (2011), 'Debates latinoamericanos en arquitectura y urbanismo (1985–2011)', in P. Méndez (ed.), *Seminarios de Arquitectura Latinoamericana. Haciendo camino al andar*, 11–18, Buenos Aires: CEDODAL.
Méndez, P. (2011), 'Los SAL y la convergencia de una dimensión editorial continental', in P. Méndez (ed.), *Seminarios de Arquitectura Latinoamericana (SAL): Haciendo Camino al Andar, 1985-2011*, 53–8, Buenos Aires: CEDODAL.
Méndez, P. (ed.) (2011), *Seminarios de Arquitectura Latinoamericana (SAL): Haciendo camino al andar, 1985-2011*, Buenos Aires: CEDODAL.
Ramírez Nieto, J. (2011), 'Reflexiones en torno de los Seminarios de Arquitectura Latinoamericana', in P. Méndez (ed.), *Seminarios de Arquitectura Latinoamericana (SAL): Haciendo camino al andar, 1985-2011*, 27–44, Buenos Aires: CEDODAL.
Ramírez Nieto, J. (2013), *Las huellas que revela el tiempo*, Bogotá: Universidad Nacional de Colombia.

Segawa, H. (2005), *Arquitectura latinoamericana contemporánea*, Barcelona: Gustavo Gili.
Segre, R. (2011), 'América Latina: la renovación arquitectónica del siglo XXI', in P. Méndez (ed.), *Seminarios de Arquitectura Latinoamericana (SAL): Haciendo camino al andar, 1985–2011*, 123–42, Buenos Aires: CEDODAL.
Toca, A. (ed.) (1990), *Nueva Arquitectura en América Latina: presente y futuro*, Barcelona: Gustavo Gili.
Torre, S. (1994), 'Cultural Identity and Modernity in Latin American Architecture', *Design Book Review* 32/33 (Spring/Summer): 16–21.
Torrent, H. (2002), 'South of America: Then and Now', *ARQ* 51: 10–13.
Waisman, M. (1989), 'Para una caracterización de la arquitectura latinoamericana', in *IV Seminario de Arquitectura Latinoamericana*, 8–10, Tlaxcala: Summarios.
Waisman, M. (1990), *El interior de la historia: Historiografía arquitectónica para uso de latinoamericanos*, Bogotá: Escala.
Zambrano, M. R. (2015), 'Discursos latinoamericanistas en la década de 1980', *Cuadros de Notas* 16: 39–53.

INDEX

A+U 63, 65, 72, 74
Abrams, L. 139, 141
Acropolis 47, 48–9
Adams, David 142
adaptive learning systems 127
adoption v. adaptation 185
Adorno, T. 163, 165–6, 170
Advertisements for Architecture (Tschumi) 167–8, *169*
Agarez, R. 29
agnosticism 112
Allweil, Y. 40
Alofsin, Anthony 44
Alzheimer's disease 31
American Philo 18–19
Anderson, Stanford 6, 86, 87–9, 90
Andreotti, Libero 90
Anglo-American sphere 15–16, 17, 18
Antonakakis, Suzana and Dimitris 5, 44, 45, 51–5
    Archaeological Museum on Chios 46
    exhibition catalogue, Delft *50*
    Greek Festival, Delft *54*
    House at Spata 47
Antoniades, Anthony C. 49, 52
Appandurai, A. 188
appropriated modernity 186, 187
Arango, Silvia 184
Archaeological Museum (Antonakakis) 46
Archaeological Museum (Konstantinidis) 46
Architect Says, The (Dushkes, ed.) 144
Architects' Journal 83, 141
architectural affections 143–4
Architectural Association (AA)
    Cedric Price 120, 125, 127
    Design Research Lab (DRL) 98

International Institute of Design 9, 174–5, *176*, 177n. 1
    Royston Landau 6, 83, 86
    'History and Theory' programme 94–7
Architectural Association Journal 86
architectural authorship 138–40
architectural autonomy 61. *See also* disciplinary autonomy
architectural communication 30–4, 35
Architectural Design 91
Architectural Forum 107
architectural knowledge 105, 140–2, 159, 160
architectural plans 9, 10, 149–60
    House II (Eisenman) 153–5, 159
    Texas House 5 (Hejduk) 156–9
architectural realism 73–4
architectural theory 2
    designers' espoused theroies 4
    Latin American 10, 183–4
        central themes 184–7
        contested knowledge 187–8
    politics 39–40
    travelling nature of 3
'Architecture and Tradition That Isn't "Trad Dad"' (Anderson) 87–9
architecture d'aujourd'hui, L' 63, 150
Architecture in Greece 44
Architecture of Deconstruction: Derrida's Haunt (Wigley) 19, 20–2, 23–4, 25
Architecture of Good Intentions, The (Rowe) 111
Architecture Theory Since 1968 (Hayes) 72
archithese 73–4, 75, 77n. 6
'Arrived Safely' postcard (Venturi and Scott Brown) 170, *171*

INDEX

Art Net 119
Atelier 66 5, 55
authority 139, 141, 142, 143
autonomy. *See* architectural autonomy;
    disciplinary autonomy
axonometry 160

Bachmann, D. 70
Bandini, Micha 94, *95*
Banham, Reyner 87
Baracco, Juvenal 185
Barcelona Pavilion (Mies van der
    Rohe) 152, 158
Baridon, Laurent 124
Baring, Ed 10
Barragan, B. 35
Barthes, Roland 105, 113–14, 165
Bartley, William 86
Bauhaus 84–5
Baumbach, S. 8
Beaux-Arts planning 149, 160–1n. 1
Benjamin, Walter 19, 21, 24, 25, 163
Berman, Antoine 19, 20, 22, 25
Boga, T. 61
Borough Music Hall *130*
Botta, M. 61, 66, 69
Boyarsky, Alvin 9, 162, 164, 165,
    177n. 8
    'Chicago a la Carte' 166–7, *168*
    International Institute of Design
    174–5, *176*, 177n. 2
bricolage 171
Bristol, K.G. 33, 36, 40
Bron, Eleanor 130
Browne, Enrique 185
Building Design 122

Cairns, S. 16, 18, 132
Camenzind, Alberto 63
Campi, Mario 61, 69
capitalism 34, 35, 39
Carpenter Center for the Visual Arts
    (Le Corbusier) 150, 151, 159
Carranza, L.E. 187
Cassin, Barbara 20
'Cedric Price: Aiming to Miss' (Price)
    119–20
'Cedric Price's Non-Plan Diary' (Price)
    119, 131–2

Center for Documentation on Latin
    American Architecture
    (CEDODAL) 10, 184
Chatham Square postcard *164*
chats 121–2, 132
    cybernetics and conversation theory
    125–7
    oral literature 122–5
    popular theatre and improvisation
    127–31
Cheval, F. 163
'Chicago a la Carte' (Boyarsky) 166–7,
    168
Christ-Janer, Albert 109
Cohen, Jean-Louis 52
collaborations 66
Collage City (Rowe) 110–11
Colomina, B. 30, 37
column journalism 122
communicative architecture 30–4, 35
concept-words 24
'Contemporary Protestant
    Architecture' (Tillich) 109
contested knowledge 187–8
'Context for Decision Making in the
    Arts and Sciences' (Landau)
    86–7, 91, 93
contexts 10
contracts 127
conversation. *See* chats
conversation theory 126–7
Cook, Peter 95–6
Couturier, Marie-Alain 112
critical history 137–8
critical regionalism 4–5, 43–56, 186–8
    boomerang effect 51–6
    inward-looking turn 48–51
    origins 44–8
Crysler, C.G. 16, 18, 30, 39, 132
Cubist idea of space *151*
Cubist works 150–1
Cubitt Lecture 110
Cusset, F. 18, 22–3
cybernetics 125–7

Dal Co, Francesco 65–6
Dali, Salvador 170–1
Damisch, Hubert 152–3, 155, 157,
    158, 159, 160

Davidovici, I. 60, 70
deconstruction 17–19, 20–1, 24, 25–6n. 1
deconstructivism 30
Deleuze, Gilles 17, 73
Delirious New York (Koolhaas) 170–2
deltiology 9, 162–76, 177n. 2
    Advertisements for Architecture (Tschumi) 167–8, *169*
    Chatham Square postcard *164*
    'Chicago a la Carte' (Boyarsky) 166–7, *168*
    Delirious New York (Koolhaas) 170–2
    Europa/America (Raggi, ed.) 172–3
    International Institute of Design 174–5, *176*, 177n. 2
    Palais Idéal (Cheval) *163*
    'Significance for A&P Parking Lots, A' (Venturi and Scott Brown) 170
        'Arrived Safely' postcard *171*
Derrida, Jacques 4, 15–16, 17–18, 25–6n. 1
Derrida mystery 23
Derrida's Haunt (Wigley) 19, 20–2, 23–4, 25
Deschamps, Y. 182
design, point of reference for 72
design method 89
design methodology 74
design principles 72
design research 85
Design Studies 90
design theory 39
Detroit Think Grid 130, *131*
Dewhirst, Dean 144–5
dialogue, fictional 122–5
Dickens, Charles 122
Dictionary of the Untranslatable (Cassin) 20
Dieste, Eladio 186
Difference and Repetition (Deleuze) 73
disciplinary autonomy 30, 33, 40. *See also* architectural autonomy
disciplinary premise 40
divergent architecture 186–7
dogmatic knowledge 97, 100n. 14
Double, O. 129

Doumanis, Orestis 44, 48, 52
drive-in theatre 130, *131*
Duffy, Francis 83, 86
Durisch, Giancarlo 69

Edgar, Andrew 165
education 125, 127, 160
Eggener, Keith 43, 188
Eisenman, Peter 9, 15, 37, 38, 39, 149
    House II 153–5, 159
Eliash, Humberto 180
    Latin American architecture *181*
Encyclopédie méthodique 103, 105
Engel, H. 36, 38
English language 16
ephemera 9, 162–76
    Advertisements for Architecture (Tschumi) 167–8, *169*
    Chatham Square postcard *164*
    'Chicago a la Carte' (Boyarsky) 166–7, *168*
    Delirious New York (Koolhaas) 170–2
    Europa/America (Raggi, ed.) 172–3
    International Institute of Design 174–5, *176*, 177n. 2
    Palais Idéal (Cheval) *163*
    'Significance for A&P Parking Lots, A' (Venturi and Scott Brown) 170
        'Arrived Safely' postcard *171*
Esprit 18
Esteban Maluenda, A. 181
'Estranged and Reunited' (Tillich) 108
ETH 60, 61, 63
Ettlin, A. 19
Europa/America (Raggi, ed.) 172–3
Evans, Walter 162, 164, 169, 171
'Exchange, The' (Price) 125, *126*

Fatouros, D. 52
Fernández Cox, Cristian 186, 187
Feyerabend, Paul 6, 86, 93
fictional dialogue 122–5
Finch, Paul 122
Fiore, Q. 165
Flaschenpost 165
Footlight drama club 129–30
foreign influence 185, 186

Formalisme – Realisme 63, 65
Fors Clavigera (Ruskin) 124
Foucault, M. 99n. 9
Frampton, Kenneth
　critical regionalism 5, 45–8, 49, 51, 55, 187
　S. and D. Antonakakis 55, 57n. 8
　Ticinese architecture 63, 66, 70
France 16
Frank, M.C. 3
Frearson, A. 36
French Theory 17, 18–19, 22–3, 25
Friedman, Alice 139
From the Ground Up (Dewhirst) 145
Fruchtl, J. 165
Fumagalli, P. 66
Fun Palace project 125, 129

Galfetti, Aurelio 61, 66, 69
　Casa Rotalinti 67
Gehry, Frank O. 4, 35. *See also* Lou Ruvo Center, Las Vegas
　Oppositions 37
Giamarelos, S. 53
Gilardoni, Virgilio 70
Glanville, R. 127
Gnosticism 113
Goldberger, P. 30, 31, 35, 37
Gombrich, Ernst 86
Goodman, D. 15
Gosseye, J. 139
Graves, Michael 37
Gray, Jeffrey 144
Greece 4–5, 43–56
　boomerang effect 51–6
　inward-looking turn 48–51
　origins of critical regionalism 44–8
Greek Festival, Delft 49, 53, *54*
　exhibition catalogue *50*
'Grid and the Pathway, The' (Tzonis and Lefaivre) 45–51, 52, 53, 57n. 8
Gris, Juan 150, 151
Guardini, Romano 112
Gutiérrez, Ramón 180–1, 182, 183
Gwathmey, Charles 37

Hadid, Zaha 34–5
Hadjikyriakos-Ghika, Nikos 53
Hadjimichali, Angeliki 49, 56n. 4
Halbwachs, Maurice 139–40
Hanisch, R. 63, 70
Hardingham, Samantha 129, 130
Hays, K.M.
　architectural theory 39–40
　Colin Rowe 110
　disciplinary autonomy 30
　Jacques Derrida 15
　Oppositions 39
　Oppositions Reader 37–8
　Tendenzen – Neuere Architektur im Tessin 61, 63, 69, 72
Heathcott, J. 40
Hejduk, John 9, 37, 149–50
　Texas House 5 156–9
heuristics 90, 93, 96, 98
Heynen, H. 16, 18, 132
high architecture 35, 36, 39, 40
Histoire d'une maison (Viollet-le-Duc) 124
history. *See* critical history; oral history
'History and Theory' programme, AA 94–7
Holder, Julian 141
Holdsworth, N. 127
Hopfengärtner, J. 63, 70
'Hors du temps dans l'espace' ('Out of time and into space', Hejduk) 150
House II (Eisenman) 153–5, 159
housing 36–7, 38, 40–1, 41n. 1, 88–9, 91
　Pruitt-Igoe housing estate 31, *34*
housing crisis 34
housing projects 35, 38
Huet, Bernard 63, 65

identity 185–6, 188
improvisation 127–31
induction 89
International Institute of Design 9, 174–5, 176, 177n. 2
Interstate Architect and Builder 125
Irigoyen, Adriana 184
Izenour, Stephen 162, 165, 170

Jencks, Charles 31, 171, 186
Johnson, Philip 107–8

Kahn, L. 66, 90, 140
Kierkegaard, S. 25
Kinder, Anna 3
Kindergarten Chats on Architecture, Democracy and Education (Sullivan) 124–5
Kizis, C. 52
knowledge
    architectural 105, 140–2, 159, 160
    contested 187–8
    dogmatic 97, 100n. 14
    tacit 139
    tree of 103–5
knowledge circulation 1–2, 7
knowledge production 138–9
knowledge transfer 3, 70–2
Koetter, F. 111
Konstantinidis, Aris 45, 48, 49, 52, 53
    Archaeological Museum at Ioannina 46
Koolhaas, Rem 162, 164, 165
    Delirious New York (Koolhaas) 170–2
Krier, Léon 95–6
Kuhn, Thomas 84, 93, 94

Lakatos, Imre 6, 84, 85, 90–1, 93–4, 95, 98
Lamont, M. 16, 17, 18
Landau, Royston 6, 83–4
    'Context for Decision Making in the Arts and Sciences' 86–7, 91, 93
    future of practice 91–3
    'History and Theory' programme 94–7
    Imre Lakatos 90–1, 98
    induction and design method 89
    philosophy of science 85
    Stanford Anderson 86
Latin American architecture theory 10, 183–4
    central themes 184–7
    contested knowledge 187–8
Le Blanc, Guillaume 18–19
Le Corbusier 90, 112, 150, 151, 167, 170
Leach, N. 40

learning 125, 126, 127
lecture notes 119–21
Lefaivre, Liane 5
    'The Grid and the Pathway' 45–51, 52, 53, 57n. 8
    'The Question of Regionalism' 44–5
legacy 139
letters 122, 124
literacy 120
literary criticism 17
literature 122
Littlewood, Joan 125, 127, 129
Lou Ruvo Center, Las Vegas 4, 29–30
    communicative architecture 30–4, 35
    'duck' event space and 'shed' decor 33
    first floor plan and building section 32
    housing 40
Loyer, F. 52
Lozano, F. 185, 186, 187
Lucan, J. 74, 75

Majerowitz, M. 40
Makamura, Toshio 63
Maki, F. 121
Mallgrave, H.F. 15
Manhattanism 170
Marcondes, M.J. 181
Maritain, Jacques 112
Marjanovic, Igor 171–2
Maso, J. 15
McAlpine, Alistair 130
McLaughlin, N. 17
McLeod, M. 30, 33, 36, 37, 39
McLuhan, M. 165
Medium is the Massage, The (McLuhan and Fiore) 165
Meier, Richard 37
Meili, Marcel 75
Méndez, P. 181, 184
mental geography 1–2
message in a bottle 165
Metallinou, Vasilia A. 90
Meyer, Hannes 84
Michaelis, B. 8
Michaud, G. 15

Michelis, Panayotis 53
Mies van der Rohe, Ludwig 52, 66, 112, 140, 152, 157, 158
military junta, Greece 51
Miller, Jonathan 130
miracle of the road 1, 2
mobilities paradigm 1
mobility infrastructures 1–2
modern art 106–7
modern cities 1–2
modernism 110, 111
modernity 111
  appropriated 186, 187
Mondrian, Piet 150, 151, 152
Moneo, Raphael 149
Moravánszky, A. 63, 70
Mota, N. 29
Moyn, S. 3
Müller, K.H. 127
Mumford, Lewis 44
Museum of Modern Art (MoMA) 7, 37, 106, 107, 108
Musicolour 127
myth-making 144–5

Natural History of Selborne (White) 122
Neo-Plasticist idea of space *151*
Neo-Plasticist works 150–1
Neue Sachlichkeit 85
New Brutalism 39
New Directions in British Architecture (Landau) 91, 92
New Harmony, Indiana 107–8
'New York Five' exhibition 37
Niedderer, K. 139
'Non-Plan – A True Mirror of Social Appetites?' (Price) 119
'Non-Plan – An Experiment in Freedom' (Banham et al.) 119
Nünning, A. 8

Ockman, J. 30, 37, 39
Ohmann, R. 137, 144
Olson, D.R. 120
'On the inherent reality of architecture' (Reichlin and Steinmann) 74
Ong, Walter 120, 132
Oppositions 37, 38–9

Oppositions Reader 37–8
oral history 8, 136–7
  and architectural affections 143–4
  and architectural authorship 138–40
  and architectural knowledge 140–2
  beyond myth-making 144–5
Oral History of Modern Architecture, The (Peter) 140–1, 142, 143
orality 8, 120, 126, 132. *See also* chats and oral literature 122–5
'Out of time and into space' ('Hors du temps dans l'espace', Hejduk) 150

painting 150
Palais Idéal (Cheval) *163*
Palmegiano, E.M. 124
Pangaro, P. 127
parametricism 98
Parkinson's disease 31
Parnell, Steve 91
participant observers 126
Pask, Gordon 125–7
Paz, Octavio 186
Perspecta 149
Pessina, F. 66, 69
Peter, John 140–1, 142, 143
Philippidis, Dimitris 52
philosophy of science 84–5, 86. *See also* Lakatos, Imre; Popper, Karl
Piazzoli, N. 69
Pickering, A. 126, 127
Pikionis, Dimitris 45, 48–9, 53
  Antonakakais's interpretation of landscaping project 47
  exhibition catalogue, Delft *50*
  Greek Festival, Delft *54*
Pillet, F. 19
place 185
planning 119
plans. *See* architectural plans
Polanyi, M. 139
politics 39
Popovici-Toma, C. 15
Popper, Karl 84, 85, 86–7, 88, 89
popular theatre 127–31
Portelli, A. 136, 139

Porto, Severiano 186
positional analysis 90
postcards 9–10, 162–76
   Advertisements for Architecture (Tschumi) 167–8, *169*
   Chatham Square postcard *164*
   'Chicago a la Carte' (Boyarsky) 166–7, *168*
   Delirious New York (Koolhaas) 170–2
   Europa/America (Raggi, ed.) 172–3
   International Institute of Design 174–5, *176*, 177n. 2
   Palais Idéal (Cheval) *163*
   'Significance for A&P Parking Lots, A' (Venturi and Scott Brown) 170
      'Arrived Safely' postcard *171*
postcolonial studies 3
postmodernism 31
postmodernity 30, 183, 186
'Present Urban Predicament, The' (Rowe) 110
Price, Cedric 8
   'Cedric Price: Aiming to Miss' 119–20
   'Cedric Price's Non-Plan Diary' 119, 131–2
   chats 121–2, 132
      contracts 127, *128*
      'The Exchange' 125, *126*
      improvisation 129–30
      oral literature 122–4
   lecture notes 119–21
   'Non-Plan – A True Mirror of Social Appetites?' 119
   Royston Landau 91
   'Starting Price' (Price) 122–3
printed text 8, 131–2. *See also* writing
Proctor, Robert 141–2
Pruitt-Igoe housing estate 31, *34*
Pruitt-Igoe myth 36
Psyché 16

'Question of Regionalism, The' (Tzonis, Lefaivre and Alofsin) 44–5
quotes 22, 24

Raggi, Franco 172–3, 177n. 8
Ramírez Nieto, J. 181, 183, 184
Randolph, John 2
realism 56n. 1
'Reality as History' (Steinmann) 72–4
regionalism 185, 186, 187, 188. *See also* critical regionalism
Reichlin, B. 61, 66, 69, 73, 74
   A+U 65
Reinhart, F. 61, 66, 69, 74
   A+U 65
répétition différente 73, 74
   St Alban Tal (Diener & Diener) 76
research programmes 90, 94, 98
residential buildings 35. *See also* housing
Ricœur, Paul 24, 139–40
Risch, G. 66
Risselada, M. 38
Ritchie, D.A. 138
Robin Hood Gardens 38
Rogers, Ernesto 71, 73, 74
Ronner, Heinz 61, 67, 77n. 4
Roofless Church 107–8
Rossi, Aldo 63, 69, 71, 73–4, 77n. 4
Rowe, Colin 7, *107*, 110–12
Ruskin, John 124

SAGE Handbook of Architectural Theory, The 15–16
Said, Edward 3
Salmas, A. 49
Salmona, Rogelio 185, 186
Sartori, A. 3
Savage Mind (Strauss) 171
Schrijver, L. 37
Schröder, Truus 139
Schumacher, Patrick 36, 40, 98
scientific discourse 93
scientific observers 126
Scolari, Massimo 71, 72, 74
Scott Brown, D. 30, 162, 164, 165, 170
secular spirituality 108
Sedgwick, Peter 165
Segawa, H. 187
Segre, R. 183, 186
'Self-Adaptive Keyboard Instructor' 126

Seminar of Latin American
    Architecture (SAL) 10, 180–4
    central themes 184–7
    contested knowledge 187–8
Sex of Architecture, The (Friedman) 139
Shaking of the Foundations, The (Tillich) 108
Sharp, Dennis 83, 86
Sheller, M. 1
'Significance for A&P Parking Lots, A' (Venturi and Scott Brown) 170
    'Arrived Safely' postcard *171*
Simmel, Georg 1–2, 139, 144
Smithson, A. 36
Smithson, A. and P. 38–9, 40, 166, 177n. 4
Smithson, Robert 111
Snozzi, L. 61, 66, 69, 72
    'Die Tessiner' *68*
social realms 139–40
social theory 39
Society of the Arts, Religion, and Contemporary Culture (ARC) 108
space 1, 41n. 2, 144, 150
    Cubist and Neo-Plasticist ideas of *151*
'space between' 38
'Space of Intellect and the Intellect of Space, The' (Randolph) 2
speech 8, 120. *See also* chats
Speyer, A. James 53
Spier, S. 63, 70
St Alban Tal (Diener & Diener) 75, 76
stand-up comedy 129
starchitecture 29, 34–5, 39
'Starting Price' (Price) 122–3
Stead, N. 143
Steinmann, Martin 5, 61, 65, 66, 75, 78n. 11
    exhibition catalogue 67–8
    'Reality as History' 72–4
Stoddart, J. 124
Strauss, C.L. 171
Structure of Scientific Revolutions, The (Kuhn) 93
'Style for the Year 2001, A' 120–1
Sullivan, Louis 124–5

Sunwoo, Irene 166–7, 174–5, 177n. 9
Switzerland 60. *See also Tendenzen – Neuere Architektur im Tessin*
Système figuré des connoissances humaines 103–5, *106*, 113

Ta Nea 52
tacit knowledge 139
Tafuri, Manfredo 37, 39, 111
'Task of the Translator, The' (Benjamin) 19, 21, 24, 25
teaching 125, 127, 160
technology 186
Tendenza 71–2, 73
Tendenzen – Neuere Architektur im Tessin 5, 60–1
    architectural representation 61–5
    exhibition catalogue 61, 63, 67–70, 77n. 3
    exhibition panels 64
    knowledge transfer between practice and theory 70–2
    legacy 74–7
    poster 62
    'Reality as History' (Steinmann) 72–4
    reviews 65–6
Texas House series (Hejduk) 150
    Texas House 5 156–9
theology 105
theology of architecture 7, 105–6
    Colin Rowe 110–12
    gnostic/agnostic 112–14
    Paul Tillich 106–10, 112
theoretical objects 152–3, 159, 160
Theorizing a New Agenda for Architecture (Nesbitt) 15
Thomas, Bronwen 122–3
Thomas, M. 18
Thornley, D.G. 89
Ticinese architecture 5, 63, 64, 66, 70. *See also Tendenzen – Neuere Architektur im Tessin*
Tillich, Paul 7, 106–10, 111
time 185
Torrance, N. 120
Torre, S. 188

Torrent, Horacio 183, 188
Tournikiotis, P. 48
'Towards a Rational Theory of Tradition' (Popper) 88
translation 4, 15–25, 120
   (un-)translation 22–4
   and deconstruction 17–19, 21, 24, 25–6n. 1
   Derrida's Haunt (Wigley) 19, 20–2, 23–4, 25
   as a way of investigation 19–20
'tree of knowledge' 103–5
Tschanz, M. 66
Tschumi, Bernard 15, 129, 162, 164, 165
   Advertisements for Architecture 167–8, *169*
Tzonis, Alexander 5
   'The Grid and the Pathway' 45–51, 52, 53, 57n. 8
   'The Question of Regionalism' 44–5

UIA International Architect 96, 97
'ultimate concern' 107
(un-)translation 22–4
Urry, J. 1

Van den Heuvel, D. 38
Van Gerrewey, C. 37

vehicles 7
Venturi, R. 30, 162, 164, 165, 170
Villa Savoye (Le Corbusier) 167
Villa Stein (Le Corbusier) 150, 151
vintage postcards 9, 162, 165. *See also* postcards
   Chatham Square postcard *164*
   'Chicago a la Carte' (Boyarsky) *166*, *168*
   Coney Island *172*
   Europa/America (Raggi, ed.) *173*
   Palais Idéal (Cheval) *163*
Viollet-le-Duc, E.E. 124, 125, 152
von Moos, S. 60
Vriesendorp, Madelon 171

Waisman, Marina 183, 184, 186–7, 188
Weigel, S. 3
Wiegelmann, Andrea 77
Wiener, N. 125
Wiener Kreis 85
Wohler, G. 111
women 139
Woodman, E. 36
writing 8, 120. *See also* printed text

Zaera-Polo, A. 39
Zambrano, M.R. 183, 184
Zumthor, Peter 75

www.ingramcontent.com/pod-product-compliance
Lightning Source LLC
Chambersburg PA
CBHW072235290426
44111CB00012B/2111